How to Improve Your Personality

BY

ROY NEWTON

Director of Public Relations
Ferris Institute

AND

F. G. NICHOLS

Late Associate Professor Emeritus
Harvard University

DRAWINGS BY ERNIE BARTH

Second Edition

GREGG PUBLISHING DIVISION

MC GRAW-HILL BOOK COMPANY, INC.

New York   Chicago   San Francisco   Dallas   Toronto   London

PUBLISHED BY GREGG PUBLISHING DIVISION

McGraw-Hill Book Company, Inc.

Printed in the United States of America

Preface

THAT PERSONALITY plays a large part in determining the degree of success that may be achieved in all walks of life is acknowledged by all competent authorities on this subject. This book has been written to help people meet this requirement. It is a textbook for use as the basis of instruction in schools, colleges, and classes; but it also is intended for the use of those not attending an educational institution or class who wish to improve their personalities. No one is without the need for self-improvement in some degree. This book shows how self-improvement may be achieved with a minimum of time and effort.

The authors believe that teaching or study *about* personality may result in little or no gain in the right direction; that competently directed *practice in the art of right thinking, talking, acting, and reacting in real life situations* is essential to personality improvement. Accordingly, in addition to a clear presentation of what personality is, how important it is, and what steps to take for its improvement, an abundance of self-testing exercises and helpful self-directed activities are provided.

It is the *habit of acting and reacting properly* in the many life situations common to all of us that really matters, not merely knowing what is right or even having the will to do it. Hence adequate provision is made for the *habit-forming practice* without which the use of the conventional textbook in personality development may result in little real improvement.

The authors believe that much gain will result from the faithful pursuit of an instructional-activity course such as this book makes possible. But the student must be shown how to carry on his self-improvement program after the course or his personal study of the book is ended. What he is to do after finishing the book should be a natural and easy continuation of what he has been doing while studying the book. To this end the authors have clearly shown how self-improvement may go on and on in adult life exactly as it has been going on in this course in student life. In short, this book is one that should have permanent value as a useful and stimulating reference book on self-improvement for all who are conscious of the need for it.

Authors of such a book always are greatly indebted to many other people for contributions of one kind or another to their thinking about the subject with which it deals. The present authors' views are the result of many years' experience as teachers at all levels of education from junior high school to university, as counselors of youth, and as students of personnel problems. Acknowledgment of quoted material is made at appropriate places throughout the book. Acknowledgment is due the Typewriter Educational Research Bureau for permission to use some material written for it by one of the present authors on speech, listening, reading, and similar topics.

Roy Newton

Frederick G. Nichols

Contents

CHAPTER ONE

Importance of Personality to You

You ARE EITHER QUALIFYING for a job or are already in one and looking forward to advancement to a better one. You may be fairly sure that, whatever the job, certain skills will be needed. You either have them or are developing them through study and practice or through work experience. You know that your job, whatever it may be, will call for something with which your education has provided, or will provide, you. Quite true; but there is something else that you yourself must provide, with the help of others, of course. You must be the kind of person who can work with others, not merely one who can work well alone. That is not always easy. There is a necessary give-and-take in daily work situations. You may not like all your associates, but you have to work with them just the same. No matter what kind of people they are, if you are *the kind of person you ought to be*, you will get along with them all right.

The kind of person you are will be shown by the way you get along with other people—your personality. It is this that in your case well may determine just how successful you will be in your first job, and later on as you work for advancement.

Teamwork is what counts most in almost any kind of lifework. You know that to be true of athletic activities where several people compete on a team. It isn't the *star player* alone who wins victories. It is the *team.* So it is in the office, the store, or any other place where several people share responsibility for getting work done. How you play your part as a member of an athletic or office team determines your worth to that team. How you play your part will

1

"Here they are—the papers you need." Being ready and willing to help others is a mark of teamwork.

be determined quite as much by the kind of person you are, your personality, as it will be by what you know and what you are able to do.

It cannot be emphasized too strongly that your prospective first employer will want to know something about your *personality traits* before he spends too much time finding out about your skills and job know-how. He knows that he can improve your skills on the job, but he has learned from experience that if you have undesirable personality traits he may have a hard time overcoming them. This is because it takes determination, time, patience, and much practice to replace a bad habit with a good one. He also knows that, while he can show you what is wrong, you alone can furnish the will to overcome it. So he wants people for his jobs who already have good personality traits and who because of them can be depended on to fit into his work team without causing trouble of any kind.

It is doubtful if there is any one aspect of preparation for a job about which there is less disagreement among employers and teachers alike than that of the importance of good personal traits, and of the necessity for their development during the training or pre-employment period. All agree that personality may be the primary factor in getting, holding, and advancing from a first job to a better one. You want to make good on the job you get. Hence you should do everything in your power to acquire what it takes to make good —including good personality traits.

It should not be necessary here to pile up evidence that good personality plays a most important part in making good in business life. Every survey of employer opinion as to what is essential to success in one's first job and in winning advancement to better jobs reveals almost complete agreement on this point.

In a recent survey this question was asked of employers:[1] "Would you like to secure some recruits who come to you after having had their attention focused on the importance of good personal traits in making a satisfactory adjustment?" Yes, was the verdict. It was the only unanimous one obtained on a long list of questions about training for a job. Answers were most emphatic. "Definitely," "Very, very much," "Certainly would," and "Absence of good traits a glaring deficiency" were among the words and expressions used.

"Give us the right kind of person," say employers, "and we will do the rest." This does not mean that good education and skills are unimportant. Quite the contrary. They are very important. But it is the ability to work well with people that counts most in nearly all walks of life, and employers are looking for such workers.

It should be pointed out here that *personality* and *job competence* rarely are achieved entirely independent of each other. These two all-essentials of real success in business are not entirely separate things, each of which is to be developed apart from the other. The *kind of person* you are right now (your personality) will have a lot to do with your success as a student in getting ready for your first job. You are *working with people*—teachers, students, school officials, and others—every day. How you get along with them will largely determine the benefits you derive from working with them. This is inescapable. In every course you and your instructor and your fellow students are members of a team organized to enable *you* to get the most out of that course. You can play your full part only when your adjustments to your associates are entirely satisfactory every day. Whether or not those adjustments are satisfactory will depend on the kind of person you are.

[1] "General Office Training," *BERA Reports*, Series II, No. 1, McGraw-Hill Book Co., Inc., New York, N. Y.

It has been said that faulty personal traits cause about 90 per cent of the failures of people to make good on their jobs. But it is noteworthy that inability to do one's job is nearly always one of the reasons why a worker is discharged. Often it is hard to say which it is, a personality defect or incompetence, that causes an employer to discharge a worker. Poor transcription. Dictator criticizes the stenographer, whose temper then flares up. "You're fired!" says the employer. Which was it, personality defect or poor workmanship that brought about this unhappy result? Both, of course, operating together. Or an important task is not finished on time. Result, loss to the employer. Cause, lack of dependability or laziness on the part of the worker. Reproof; quick temper; discharge. So it goes. It should be clear to you that good personal traits (personality) and job competence (know-how and skills) are the twin ingredients of sound preparation for success in business life.

Even though an employee is not discharged because of a personal clash with his immediate superior, he may lose his best opportunity for advancement in a job he likes and can handle well because he is transferred to another job in the hope that he and his new superior can hit it off better. In many, if not most, large organizations where enlightened management prevails no employee can be discharged by any foreman or department head. Such a boss may, however, refuse to keep an employee with whom he cannot get along. It is then up to the personnel department to transfer the worker from department to department until a place where he can work well with his associates can be found for him; or, of course, until it is fully determined that no such place can be found for him. This is a great gain over the old practice of hiring and firing at the lower level of management with or without good cause. That the immediate boss may be wholly or partly at fault is recognized.

Even where transfer instead of dismissal is the result of personality trouble, an employee may find his new job less agreeable, and in many cases less desirable from the standpoint of advancement. He has "one strike against him," as the saying goes, because he has failed to make good in another job. He will have to overcome it by extra effort and probably by eliminating whatever bad trait or traits caused his earlier failure. That his first boss may be largely to blame doesn't greatly change the situation. Failure to meet his problem cannot be explained away easily. Management usually has the advantage, and the higher up it is the greater the advantage. Any accomplishment that lessens the hazards of occupational life is worth great effort. The development of good traits may well be your most important achievement from this point of view.

Personality—What Is It?

What is this thing called *personality?* Is it how you look? Or how you dress? Or how you wear your clothes? Or how you use make-up? Or how you smile? Or, in short, how you fix yourself up and how you act to *make a good impression* on someone whose judgment of you at the moment is important to you—one of the opposite sex, a prospective employer, your sweetheart's family, a vocational counselor? By no means! Personality is not something that can be put on and taken off much like one's wearing apparel. It is something much deeper and more abiding than that. It really is the outward evidence of one's character. It is one's automatic or habitual way of appearing and reacting in each and every situation

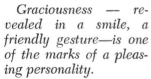

Graciousness — revealed in a smile, a friendly gesture—is one of the marks of a pleasing personality.

Business Etiquette Series,
McGraw-Hill Book Co., Inc.

of daily life in the home, the office, the factory, the professional office, the church, the school, the store, or, in short, wherever one is associated with others in any temporary or permanent activity of mutual interest. What you are in *any given situation* is important, but what you are more or less instinctively in *all situations* is what matters most.

Personality isn't what is called *beauty*. Very plain people may have exceptionally fine personalities. But it often is difficult to dissociate the two since very plain people may so radiate good will, sympathy, interest, co-operativeness, and contagious happiness as to obscure even ugly physical features. You may not be able to do much about your physical features, but you can do much about your personal traits which more than offset what people often think of as lack of beauty.

And it should be noted in passing that no matter how good-looking you are, your need of good personality training still may be very great—indeed even greater than that of your less handsome associates since you may be tempted to place too great reliance on your natural beauty. Yes, good looks may even beget *vanity*, the root of many unfortunate traits. Sure, you beauty-contest winners may have a head start toward good personality; but it isn't the *start* that counts—it is the *goal* you reach that matters most. So even if you are a bit farther out front at the start, don't mistake your *lead* for the *goal* to be sought—a *well-rounded personality,* not merely an *attractive appearance,* however important that may be.

What you really are after is the *habit* of reacting and acting the right way and saying the right thing in every life situation in which you may find yourself. The *habit,* mind you; not merely the *ability,* given time to think the situation through, to do and say the right thing. That may involve too much time. Delays here are dangerous. It is the spontaneous right response to a situation's requirements that reflects what we call *good personality.* This can result only from knowledge of what is desirable and how to acquire it, followed by long continued daily practice to develop and retain right habits of conduct. This is a challenge whose importance cannot be denied and one that you should meet with all the courage and persistence you can muster. Meet it adequately and your success in occupational life, and in all other aspects of good living, is assured. This is not because personality alone will suffice, but because it is your best assurance of the mastery of what it takes in the way of knowledge and skills to succeed in life. You will succeed in school because of good personality, just as surely as you will succeed in later life activities. So here is the place, and right now is the time, to begin work on this problem.

A Universal Need

It may seem to *you* that you don't need to give attention to this matter—that in *your* case there is no problem. You dress well. You are courteous, at least most of the time and toward most people. You have been taught at home to consider others and you usually do. On the whole, you are a quite popular person in the groups to which you belong. All these things may be quite true. Yet there still may be weak spots to strengthen, rough spots to smooth out, and deficiencies never brought to your attention. Then too, your path may have been relatively smooth and easy to follow. Real situations under the strains and stresses of employment conditions may never have been encountered. Your associates may have been largely of your own choosing and, therefore, not the kind that test your personality in any severe way. Less may have been expected of you than will be in occupational life, and thus less notice taken of little deficiencies that may not be equal to the tests of later life without conscious effort to erase them. Tolerances toward young people's conduct may be greater than that usually encountered in employer-employee, or professional worker-client, or buyer-seller, or any one of scores of other occupational life relationships. The short of this whole matter is that you have, and every other person has, personality problems to face, although differing greatly in kind and degree of importance. No one can afford to rest content with achievements, however substantial, in this field of one's development. All must go on and on, recognizing and remedying personality defects as the one best hope for achieving the greatest possible success in all walks of life, but especially in that of occupational life.

Later on, after what good personality traits really are has been established, you will be asked to look about you and observe how successful men and women rate on these traits. Even now, it will be profitable for you to think of the most successful people you know in various business and professional activities, with a view to seeing if you can detect what seem to be their outstanding qualities. Are any of them slovenly dressers? Or usually discourteous? Or lazy and indifferent? Or inconsiderate and thoughtless? Or anything else that you recognize as a quality which makes you think they are people whom you wouldn't care to be associated with in a business way? If the ones you pick are really successful, their personalities are likely to stand close scrutiny, with some exceptions that prove the rule, of course.

The first essential of success in this part of your pre-employment training is a consciousness of need. So for the present, until we get to dealing with specific traits and their cultivation, admit the need even if you think pretty well of yourself.

Desire to Improve Personality

One more thing is necessary for success in this field of training. It is a sincere and deep-seated desire to improve, and a determination to see through, any planned program for achieving this result. This is up to you. No one else can supply this essential ingredient of success in personality development. You want to succeed in a big way in business or professional life. It is doubtful that you can do so without the qualities recognized as essential by all who have studied life-adjustment problems or experienced them in any substantial way. It is safe to assume that all your instructors agree on this point. They know that *their* success in providing you with essential knowledge and skills through *their courses* depends in large measure on how you respond to *this course* in *personality development*. All will co-operate with you in every possible way if they see you want to develop a good personality.

Rewards of Good Personality

Rewards for your effort should be many. Larger earning power, of course. Good initial job, with opportunity for advancement, surely. Quick and smooth occupational adjustment without the floundering among jobs and employers which is the experience of so many novices in the workaday world. These are important rewards, even sufficient ones. But there are others even more worth consideration.

Everyone who lives a normal life is a member of several groups outside his job group—church, social, civic, and recreational. Great satisfaction comes from working well with other members of such groups. It is a great achievement to be able to fit into almost any reasonably congenial group organized for any good purpose. Misfits in any group prevent others from enjoying and profiting from their group membership. They get no personal satisfaction out of their own contact with others in groups to which they voluntarily or involuntarily belong. They are referred to as "fifth wheels" in the organization, or as "monkey wrenches in the machinery"; not particularly flattering distinctions. Only people of good traits and good will can avoid this fate. No stone should be left unturned in your effort to become the *kind of person* who *fits in,* and to avoid the troubles suffered by those who are not that kind of people.

You should know that the real reason for dismissal or transfer is not always, or even often, given for it. Thus the employee does not have the advantage that such knowledge would bring. Halitosis, laziness, discourtesy, tardiness, talkativeness, annoying high-pitched voice, vanity, and scores of other causes of dismissal can be listed. The employer may gruffly say, "You are fired," for this or that specific reason. More likely, he will merely offer some false but less personal reason for his decision—slack business, new office equipment or methods, or some other necessary but impersonal need for staff changes.

Why an applicant for a job is rejected is rarely revealed to him. A young man who excelled in every course of training required for a certain kind of work was turned down a half dozen times, each time because he had not had experience. "But how does one get experience?" he finally asked the last teacher to whom he went for additional training, in the hope that he could overcome his lack. "My friend," said the teacher, "you haven't been turned down for lack of experience, whatever your potential employers may have told you. You were rejected because you are too fat. Don't take more courses. Spend your time dieting and sweating it off." Only thus did the young man learn the truth and what to do to overcome his handicap.

Another young man, the ranking student in his business training group, was rejected for an excellent position. "Why?" his teacher who had recommended him asked. "I don't know," was the reply.

Inquiry at the employer's office revealed that John had "sat on the corner of the office desk and kept his hat on during the interview." Personality defects, of course.

In a Midwestern city it was found that the graduates of a good business training program averaged two years of occupational floundering before making good in any job. Some of these false starts surely were due to failure to meet the job's requirements, but many more were due to personality defects.

Now the point of all this is that "forewarned is forearmed," or at least it should be. Knowing the importance of good personal traits, the fact that the results of poor ones may not be known until too late, and the further fact that only by doing everything possible to ready yourself for the test when it comes, you should resolve to co-operate fully with those whose duty and pleasure it is to work with you in this area of your training.

Do not be fooled by lowered standards prevalent in boom times. They will not last. In times of great industrial expansion in the manufacture of war materials everyone finds employment. Wages are high. Jobs are plenty. Why worry about skills, know-how, or personal traits? Simply because this easy-employment, high-wage situation will not last. Also, because, when the break does come, those who lack the knowledge and the know-how will be the first ones to go. Even those who have what the job requires in the way of competence, but who are personal misfits, will be just as quickly taken off the payroll. It is a further fact that the good will built up during lush periods of employment will stand you in good stead when the time comes to sort out the well-liked people for retention and possible advancement. Never forget that employers like the kind of people who help to create a good atmosphere in which to work and do business; who attract to their businesses new customers and help to keep old ones. They always will. So do not be lulled into an attitude of indifference toward the problem of personality development by temporary employer departure from normal preference for employees and associates who can make quick and satisfactory adjustment as members of a working team.

Personality Development in School and College Programs

Schools and colleges are giving increased attention to this matter of personality in the development of their general education and vocational training programs. An increasing number of leaders in the educational field are tending to emulate the great educator Thomas Arnold, who was more interested in the development of good character than he was in the production of scholars. Alfred E. Stearns, formerly headmaster of Andover Academy, was that kind of educator. Indeed, it may be said of most of the heads of the great private preparatory schools, past and present, that they are primarily concerned with the task of turning out young people of character—possessors of good personality traits. This is easily accounted for. Only such can be expected to succeed in a big way, not only occupationally and financially, but in all good life relationships. Only successful graduates reflect glory on their alma mater.

Too often in the past, even more often in the present, too great dependence has been placed on a *course* in *personality*. What personality is, how important it is, why it is so important, and how it can be developed, are all well taught in such a course. Rating scales, check lists, and other useful devices are furnished and explained. Many references to helpful literature are made. In short, at the end of such a course a student should know a lot about personality and its part in making satisfactory life adjustments. But make no mistake about it—you may rate an A+ in such a course and yet come away from it with about the same personality with which you entered it. *Knowing about personality* is not enough. You must effectively use what you know about it day by day in an honest effort to eradicate bad traits, develop new good ones, and otherwise better your personality wherever it can be improved. Hence, it is *study*, followed by *practice* and eternal *vigilance*, that alone can assure desired permanent improvement in the kind of person you are. Thus, you see, you alone must decide whether you are going to be a mere *course-taker* in this field, or a good *practitioner* of what is learned for the development of abiding good personal traits.

Your school or college will help you, not only in this basic course, but also in your follow-up practice of what is learned. It may not be content to require your teachers to rate you on a personality scale at the end of the year, which is common, if not universal, practice. Memory being the tricky thing it is, too great dependence cannot be placed on year-end judgments based on *memory* of your conduct from day to day. You should prefer a rating based on *spot-judgments* of your conduct from day to day, when your acts and words are fresh in mind. You should welcome criticisms and suggestions from your teachers, school officers, fellow students, and others who are in a position to judge your conduct. You shouldn't resent such well-meant help. You should not be embarrassed by it. You should be stimulated to keep tabs on your own words and conduct and reactions with a view to forestalling criticism by others. Your alertness in this matter should go far toward preventing the outcropping of bad personal traits that you wish to replace, however great may be the provocation in certain situations.

You may have a position already in mind, or you may be able to find one without your school's help. More likely, you will need the assistance of your school's placement office in making a good initial job contact. In that case, be assured that the kind of person you are, as well as the skills and the know-how you possess, will count greatly in your favor. Schools depend on the success of their graduates for their very existence. Their officers know how much more likely young people of good personality are to succeed. They naturally act accordingly at commencement time and give the best openings to those most likely to succeed in them.

There should be no need to dwell further on the importance of this segment of your program of training for life adjustment as a welcome member of many groups—family, church, social, civic, vocational, recreational, and others. The vitally important matter of determining more specifically what are good personal traits and what are bad ones, where you stand in relation to these traits, how personalities are classified especially in relation to occupational life, and how your personality rating may be substantially improved must be given major emphasis in this course. What is even more important, we must devise and put into effective operation a plan for continued practice of the *art of good behavior* toward our associates in an effort to habituate such behavior, the only sure way of making growth in personality really stick.

Suggestions for Study and Discussion

1. After careful study of this chapter, have you any suggestions to make, or questions you would like answered about any aspect of the general topic of personality development?

2. Did you assume that the immediate outcome of such a course as

this might be a well-developed personality? Or did you understand that a course can be nothing more than a point of departure in the development of such a personality?

3. Why is practice in what has been called the "fine art of living" important? What does this expression really mean? What are some of the ways in which it may be practiced by you?

4. What part do criticism and suggestion play in personality development? Do you welcome both? Or do you resent them? Does it make any difference from whom they come? Should it make any difference? Are you likely to discover all your own shortcomings without help?

5. Does personality development go on throughout every day, not merely in the personality course time? Always in the right direction? Or sometimes in the wrong direction? What can be done to insure growth in the right direction if you decide that, in spite of you, this development goes on in some other direction?

6. In what types of work do you think an attractive personality is most important? Can you think of any fields of work in which a person with a very poor personality might have as good a chance for success as a person with an attractive personality?

7. Discuss specific ways in which a pleasing personality is helpful to a physician, a dentist, a salesman, a clerk, a receptionist, a secretary, a druggist, a minister, a nurse, a schoolteacher, a parent, a social worker, a foreman.

8. During World War II, standards for both personality and training were lowered by employers. Why was this done? Discuss the influence of this lowering of requirements on postwar employment policies in business and industry. Should it be taken to mean that you may think less about your personality than was thought necessary before the war?

9. Pick out some profession or vocation with which you are familiar and list some of the traits that you think most important for success in the one you select. Bring your list to class so that it may be considered by other members of the group.

10. What benefits may reasonably be expected to accrue to you as the result of your successfully completing this total personality development activity—not merely this first course segment of it, but the practice to accompany and follow that?

11. Are you sold on the idea that it will be well worth your while to do whatever is necessary to improve your personality, or are you one of those who are satisfied with themselves as they are?

Personality Reminders

1. Have you smiled today?
2. Have you been reasonably pleasant all day, or have you been upset once or twice? Justifiably so? Think carefully.
3. How about your hands and fingernails? Clean?

4. And your general appearance? Good, bad, fair, or what? Shoes especially.

5. Did you brush your teeth this morning? Of course! Let it pass.

6. Is anyone at home, in school, on the playground, or elsewhere being influenced by you? Yes? Well, good or bad influence? No? Why not? Are you the kind of person that influences no one? You shouldn't want to be. "Imitation is the sincerest flattery," you know. Few people influence no one. Make it good influence. Don't be a nobody!

7. Are you able to look back over yesterday's contacts and recall acts or words that suggested good traits? Bad traits?

8. Is something wrong with this question: "In addition to personality, what traits do you think are most essential to success in any profession?"

Personality Development Notebook

From what has been said, it should be clear that in this course we are concerned with the *development of personality,* not merely with the *study of facts about it.* It has been made clear that constant watchfulness over our daily conduct and much practice in thinking, saying, and doing the right thing in each life situation as it arises are essential to the elimination of bad traits and the development of good ones. It should be emphasized that the time to begin the necessary watchfulness and practice is right now—this minute. It also should be noted that a definite plan for keeping at this most important activity must be devised and put into effect. As the old saying goes, "Hell is paved with good intentions." Doing it, not intending to do it, is what counts.

Here is a plan that should work well if carried through. It may be described as follows:

1. Get a notebook of convenient size and shape to carry with you much of the time.

2. As we come to the consideration of specific traits and their manifestations in daily conduct, enter them in your Personality Notebook.

3. Use these notebook lists when checking the items as instructed in each case, making especially conspicuous your traits, habits, or attitudes that need improving.

4. Double underscore those that should be singled out for immediate and drastic attention.

5. Every evening of every day from here on through the course, and beyond as long as is necessary, note any evidences of failure to think, say, or do the right thing in situations occurring during that day.

6. Resolve not to repeat the next day.

7. As a bad trait is superseded by a good one, cross it off, and keep this up until you are reasonably sure that you will not slip back into the old rut.

A lot of work? Perhaps. But the results will be worth it. Besides, it can be such an interesting and rewarding experience as to become more like a game whose scores you are keeping to see how you are progressing. Getting started will not be hard, but keeping at it until the habit is formed of following through each day may be difficult for some. Once the habit is formed, you are safe. So stick to it for a while and see what happens. Even if you slip up occasionally and neglect this activity (we almost said *duty*, for that is what it is), don't give up. Get right back on the job, and resolve to stay on it as long as necessary.

Results may not be very big at first. It takes time to form new habits of thought and action. So be patient. Patience is one of the good traits you should possess. Here's your chance to develop it, or to strengthen it.

From time to time throughout the course, specific instructions will be given as reminders of what you are to do in connection with specific traits as they are discussed and tested. Have your Personality Notebook ready.

Special References[1]

No text can completely round out the case for personality as a must for satisfying life adjustment. None should attempt it. Too little space. More points of view based on more experiences than any author or co-authors can provide are needed. Hence these few very pertinent references to supplement what has been said here about the importance of personality as a possible determinant of the degree or kind of real success that one may hope to achieve in life.

Crane, George Washington. *Psychology Applied*
Dengel, Veronica. *Personality, Unlimited*
Harmon, Francis L. *Understanding Personality*
Bernhardt, K. S. *Practical Psychology*, Second Edition
Bennett, M. E. *College and Life*
Brooke, Esther Eberstadt. *You and Your Personality*
Wheatley, William Alonzo, and Royce R. Mallory. *Building Character and Personality*

[1] For names of publishers of books in special reference lists, see bibliography at end of book. The references in each chapter are arranged according to their relative importance in connection with that chapter.

CHAPTER TWO

Personality Concepts

I<small>N</small> C<small>HAPTER</small> O<small>NE</small> it was pointed out that *personality* is really the *outward expression* of one's real *character;* that it is what one really is all the time, under all conditions, and not something to be put on and taken off as occasion may require.

It may be admitted at the outset that the much-used term *personality* means different things to different people. Perhaps any one of the twenty different definitions found in books on the subject is as good as any other, but for purposes of this course and practice activity some agreement must be reached as to what it is we really are trying to develop.

In one of the questions at the end of the preceding chapter there was one about a quotation in which a distinction between one's *personality* and one's *traits* was implied. It is difficult to see how one's *traits* can be separated from one's *character.* Constantine Panunzio's *Student's Dictionary of Sociological Terms* gives this definition of personality:

The totality of qualities and characteristics of a given person, ordinarily attributed to original nature, expressing themselves in modes of carriage, language, manners, clothes, ways of speaking, interests, attitudes, and other reactions to the social milieu.

While this definition is somewhat involved and obscure, it does carry very clearly the concept that the "totality of qualities and characteristics" (character) express themselves "in modes of carriage, language, manners, and other reactions" in social situations (personality). Thus one might set up the equation, Character = Personality. That is not at all bad. It goes to the heart of the real

16

problem. It endorses the thesis that *what we are will determine our personality*. It goes along with the view that personality must be the outcropping of something deeper than *personal appearance,* or studied conduct in a given situation, or a *behavior pattern* that is followed for temporary gain.

Howard C. Warren, in his *Dictionary of Psychology,* gives numerous definitions, one of which supports the view that character is at the bottom of personality if, indeed, the two terms are not synonymous. It is this: "Those characteristics of an individual most important in determining his social adjustments" are his personality. Here we have the "social adjustment" factor introduced again. It is the way our characteristics (character traits) operate in our relations with other people that really matters. That is what we are concerned with here.

In another definition in the same treatise there is reference to one's "qualities . . . as they synthetically attract or impress others." Leaving out the unnecessary word "synthetically," this concept is acceptable for our purposes.

Carter V. Good's *Dictionary of Education,* a relatively new reference book, gives these two definitions of personality:

1. The characteristic patterns of behavior through which the individual adjusts himself to his environment, especially his social environment.

2. Superficial physical and social attractiveness. . . .

Number 1 is a good statement. Number 2 is, of course, the movie-magazine interpretation of personality. Its most unacceptable word is "superficial," since it tends to nullify the concept of "social attractiveness." It is hard to believe that one can be socially attractive in any permanent sense by means of any "superficial" and presumably temporary traits—attractiveness that is only "skin deep," as the saying goes.

It is unfortunate, but true, that the average young man and woman thinks of personality largely in terms of *physical* characteristics—stature, clothes, complexion, beauty, nice white teeth, a pleasing smile, physical skills, etc. They also usually include the ability to dance well and say the things that are considered clever this season. In other words, younger persons place a disproportionate emphasis on the surface manifestations of personality. The pretty girl may be more popular in high school than her less bountifully endowed classmate, even though the ugly duckling may have a better disposition. The handsome young man may be a more acceptable date than the homely boy, even though the good-looking boy may be more conceited.

This, of course, is one of the many sides of personality, and a more important side today than ever before. But it by no means completes the picture.

A person nearing middle age typically thinks of personality more in terms of good habits, a pleasant disposition, and an even temper. Older persons frequently judge young people of high school and college age by their manners and thoughtfulness much more than by the traits considered so vital by the young people themselves. If you want to make a hit with the old folks, you should be conservative in your deportment, quiet in your manner, and always considerate and thoughtful. They tend to place perhaps a disproportionate emphasis on old-fashioned courtesy. Older people like to have someone listen to their ideas and their reminiscences. Be a good listener and you will get a top-notch rating with almost anyone over fifty years of age.

Dr. Mikesell [1] of the University of Wichita suggests that it is a mistake to think of personality simply as the sum total of a person's traits. He points out that personality is a kind of action—a way of behaving—something progressive and dynamic.

This concept is a good one to keep in mind as we investigate the matter further.

Dr. Louis P. Thorpe, author of two books and many magazine articles on the subject, says, "We can therefore regard personality as an elaborate pattern or combination of all of a person's characteristics." [2]

Dr. Henry C. Link, another outstanding authority on this subject, says, ". . . I define personality as the extent to which the individual has developed habits and skills which interest and serve other people." [3]

This is a particularly good definition because it interprets personality in terms of qualities that some people develop and others neglect to develop. By implication it places the responsibility for

[1] William Henry Mikesell, *Mental Hygiene*, p. 396, Prentice-Hall, Inc., New York, 1939. You will profit by reading this excellent book. It is sufficiently nontechnical so that the layman can understand it.

[2] Louis P. Thorpe, *Personality and Life*, pp. 4–5, Longmans, Green and Company, New York, 1941.

[3] Henry C. Link, *The Rediscovery of Man*, pp. 60–61, The Macmillan Company, New York, 1938.

having a poor personality directly on the individual's shoulders, where it belongs. Personality is not some mysterious, intangible aura that hovers over certain fortunate individuals and capriciously avoids others. It is not some arbitrary gift from the gods. It is rather a pattern of habits of thought and action that can be developed in much the same manner as other habits, such as swimming, walking erect, and playing tennis—that is, by *consistent practice* under *favorable conditions* and *proper guidance*.

Another reason why this is such a good definition is that it interprets personality in terms of social relations. Personality thus is not only something that we *have,* but is also what people *think about us*. It is conceivable that a group of "habits and skills" that would "interest and serve other people" at one place in the world and at one time in history might not be exactly the same habits and skills that would achieve a similar purpose in another time and place. People have attractive personalities in relation to a social environment. One does not and could not develop a good personality in a vacuum.

The only word of caution here is that you should not go too far in the direction of the analogy between the development of physical habits and emotional ones. The worst character in the world might become the world champion swimmer. The swindler can develop the habit of walking erect while planning his next swindle. The tennis player who gambles on his own games may be the world's champion player. These are not people of good *personality,* as we think of that term. Nor would they ever be able to develop habits of thinking and acting in a way that would permanently serve others or make desirable social or occupational adjustments. No, it is not just a matter of acquiring habits by sheer force of repetitive effort and good teaching. Good personality habits must flow from repetitive effort, of course, but effort inspired by an inward urge to interest, serve, and helpfully adjust to the people with whom we live, move, and have our being every day in the year. This should become more obvious as we come to deal with specific personal traits.

Personality Factors

Perhaps a better understanding of personality can be reached by getting away from short definitions and attempting a more comprehensive study of its principal factors.

Important *physical appearance* traits and *ways of behaving* will be considered. Do not mistake the discussion of these factors as an abandonment of the concept that character underlies most, if not all, such factors even though they are easily mistaken for purely physical conduct.

THE WAY YOU LOOK

The way you look includes your stature, features, physique, color and texture of your hair, size of your hands and feet, your teeth, and perhaps a number of other physical traits.

When someone says, "Do you know Harvey Abernathy?" the first thing you do (if you know him) is to call up in your mind a visual image, a mental picture, of Harvey. You think the name "Harvey Abernathy" and you see him in your mind's eye—tall, gangling figure, long arms, big hands, and all. You visualize the lock of red hair that always droops down over his forehead. You "see" his plain, undistinguished features—his nose that is crooked from a football injury, his chin with its inevitable stubble of bristly beard, his big mouth, and his friendly, awkward smile. The name "Harvey Abernathy" brings back in a flash this total picture.

Other mental associations may follow quickly, tumbling over one another for recognition in the center of your consciousness. You may in rapid succession recall where you met Harvey, the spectacular play he made at that football game last winter, the time you went to the hospital to see him when he was recovering from an operation, and a host of other recollections. But the chances are that you will remember first how he looks.

An appealing personality does not depend on possession of any one particular physique, hair color, etc. Most short men want to be six feet tall. Somehow we have come to think of attractiveness in a man as associated with tallness, broad shoulders, narrow hips, and wavy hair. Movies and fiction have idolized and idealized the muscular boys. Illustrations of men's styles picture men who appear to be well over six feet tall. So prevalent is this association of tallness with attractiveness that commercial firms are cashing in on it. In one issue of *Esquire* magazine there were five different advertisements of firms that featured built-up shoes to "add inches to your height."

Over against this current worship of tallness we must place the undeniable fact that some of the world's most attractive masculine personalities are men shorter than the average. As a matter of fact, some of history's most outstanding characters have been little men.

Nor is facial handsomeness indispensable to personality. A man may be positively homely and still acquire a magnetic personality, and we have known several totally bald men who could hold their own in any personality contest.

However, when a man is noticeably deficient in those physical characteristics commonly associated with attractiveness, he should compensate by developing himself along other lines. He can improve himself as a conversationalist, develop poise, brush up on his manners, acquire some new skills, and in general so call attention to his good personality traits that people will overlook his weak ones.

Our observation has been that unusually tall girls wish they were shorter. They think that tallness is a social handicap. They seem to feel that men associate attractiveness with "five feet two, eyes of blue." In contrast with this point of view is the interesting fact that those plaster models on which dresses are displayed in store windows are relatively tall. Tall or short or medium—it doesn't really matter so much to the girl who is willing to work on her total personality development. Similarly, the homely girl, the girl whose face is badly marred by a birthmark or a scar, the girl who "hasn't one single attractive feature," can compensate by developing other aspects of her personality. We know several extremely homely women who have personalities so appealing that one never thinks of their ill-formed features. They have developed graciousness, poise, self-confidence, pleasant voices, and wholesome attitudes to such an extent that no one ever thinks of their being literally homely.

The main point here is that *what you are, how you think, what you say,* and *what you do* are what makes your physical stature important or unimportant as a personality factor. The right kind of person need never worry about the way he looks as to height or any other slight physical abnormality.

THE WAY YOU DRESS

This factor covers the neatness, appropriateness, cleanliness, and style of your clothes, as well as your hats, shoes, and accessories.

Your mental picture of Harvey Abernathy includes not only his physique, face, hair, etc., but also the clothing he usually wears. You see him with that stringy tie, always a little off center, the brown shoes that go poorly with his shiny blue suit. You visualize his long arms projecting too far out of his coat sleeves, and the dandruff on his shoulders looking like a light snowfall on a freshly plowed celery bed.

Chaucer's *Canterbury Tales* describes one lady who was considered overfastidious by the other travelers because she didn't drip gravy down the front of her dress when she was eating. She also kept her fingers clean. When knighthood was in its much-vaunted flower, people were pretty careless about the frequency with which they washed their clothes. An artisan might own one pair of leather pants and wear them regularly for years without benefit of dry cleaners. Underwear hadn't been invented. There were no washing machines, mangles, or cleaning fluids. Soap was almost unknown to the masses of people. Men and women who worked in the kitchen were expected to exude an aura of roast beef and garlic from their clothing, year in and year out. A person's social status was little affected by grooming faults which today would definitely place him beyond the pale.

It is not necessary today to dress in the latest style or to wear expensive clothes in order to be attractive. Nevertheless, we are held to strict accountability in matters of clothing and grooming. The world is style-conscious and neatness-conscious. There is little excuse for the average American to present a slovenly appearance. We are judged today as never before in history by our clothing and appearance.

If you are the right kind of person, one of good character, you will want to look attractive to others, to be considered neat and clean. You will dress right because doing so makes you feel better. "It gives me a lift," as people often say, "to be well groomed within the limits of my financial resources."

THE WAY YOU TALK

Can you talk? This seems like an absurd question at first glance. Almost everyone can talk. Quite true; but how many young people in business know how to talk in such a way as to enhance their chances of winning promotion? Not many. Why? Well, let us see why.

First, too many people mumble their words; force their hearers to listen attentively to catch enough of what is said to understand what they intend to convey. This mumbling habit usually is the result of what may be called "speech laziness." Some people speak without sufficient conscious effort to insure that their words reach the listener as anything more than senseless sounds. A mumbler irritates his employer.

Second, the loud talker may be even more annoying than the mumbler. He makes his listener understand what he is saying, but he has too many listeners. Everyone within earshot hears what he says. Loud talk is a sure barrier to promotion—except in the field of auctioneering.

What is the cause of a loud voice? It may be due to nervous excitement or to intense interest in the subject being presented. In not a few cases, it results from a conscious desire on the part of the speaker to attract the attention of all within range of his voice. Except for incurable physical defects, the loud talker can overcome this handicap to advancement if he will seek and apply the proper remedy.

Business Etiquette Series, McGraw-Hill Book Company, Inc.

Personality is often revealed in the way people conduct themselves in restaurants and other public places.

Third, the "soft spoken" individual carries a decided handicap. People have to strain too hard to catch what he says. Few will do it. Thus what is said is lost on his listeners. Instructions are not followed. Messages are not delivered. Inevitable mistakes follow. The employer is displeased. Why do some workers speak too softly? Some are diffident and shrink from conversation. Others have underdeveloped vocal organs which require regular exercise under wise guidance. A few lack that self-confidence which would enable them to speak so that they can be heard. Once the cause is known, the remedy is plain.

Fourth, the fast talker will wear out almost any but the most rugged listener in any business office or store. He will be too far ahead of his hearers most of the time. Being unable to catch up, they lose interest. Too-fast talk, however good, fails to register. It never inspires confidence. Why do people talk too fast? Nervousness, lack of poise, a quick temper, overeagerness, being in a hurry, fear that all there is to say cannot be said in the time available, or any one of a dozen other reasons may be advanced to account for this defect. Whatever the cause, fast talkers rarely are found in high executive jobs.

Fifth, the slow talker is but little more effective than the fast one. His listeners either are far ahead of him or have lost interest altogether. The employer of a too-deliberate talker easily associates slow speech with dullness or laziness. Barring speech defects, even the slow talker can find the cause and apply a remedy if he is aware of the drag on his career which this trait is likely to be.

Sixth, the incessant talker is a pest. Few, if any, men have enough important things to say to risk talking all or most of the time. One who talks too much irritates his hearers. His employer will not dare trust aim to perform important duties or to meet important people. The only remedy for talking too much is to talk less and think more; to *do* things and let others *talk* about them.

Seventh, the "silent man" may fail to impress his employer with his real ability. He is hard to appraise, except for jobs that call for skill only. Most important positions in business require clear thinking and the ability to tell the results of it. The remedy chosen will depend on the cause of this defect, and the cause is not always easy to find.

So we have seven speech defects, any one of which may bar

advancement in business. Young people who are preparing for a business career should appraise their own speech habits right now. If defects, or even certain tendencies in the wrong direction, are noted, they should set about the task of acquiring the ability to speak *forcefully*—and that means with proper enunciation, with enough force to be impressive, at a speed that can be easily followed, and with no more words than are required to convey the thought.

And remember that it is *speech habit* that really counts, and that good speech habits are the result of persistent, intelligent, purposeful practice.

Many schools and colleges now own wire or tape recorders for use in speech classes. If you will have your speaking voice recorded, you may be surprised to discover voice defects you would never notice ordinarily.

One teacher we know uses the disc-type recorder, making a recording of the student's voice on one side of a six-inch record at the beginning of a speech course, and a recording on the other side at the end of the term. Thus the student has dramatic proof of the improvement in his voice.

In New York City there is a school of speech that undertakes to improve the speech of people who are conscious of voice defects, not speech defects such as stuttering or some other result of physical abnormality. People in high places take this training—principals of schools, business executives, salesmen, association presidents, and others often called upon to speak formally or informally and who desire to speak pleasingly and effectively.

With so much of our personal attractiveness dependent on voice, it is surprising that we don't pay more attention to it. Have you

The ability to make interesting conversation—and the ability to listen—both require training and practice.

ever made any attempt to improve your voice? You need not take courses in speech, though these are helpful. Just listen to the radio and the movies. Notice the voices of William Powell, Claude Rains, Olivia de Havilland, Don Ameche, Clark Gable, Claudette Colbert, Rex Harrison, Laurence Olivier, Ronald Colman, Loretta Young, and Herbert Marshall. Notice the best radio announcers; imitate them. Practice aloud. It is surprising how much you can accomplish, working alone. If you own, or have the use of, a recording machine, so much the better. But you can do a lot for yourself without it.

A too-limited vocabulary and an ignorance of proper grammatical usage are also dangerous barriers to an effective personality. Do you overuse words like "swell," "great," "O.K.," and "fine"? Do you know how good your vocabulary is? There are tests that classify your vocabulary according to grade levels. There are college students whose vocabularies have not been developed beyond the sixth-grade norm!

Do you say "Between you and I," "ain't," "He gave it to she and I," "The data is correct," "The bell has rang," "He laid down," or "Who do you wish to see?" All those expressions are incorrect grammatically. There are tests of grammar on which you can rate yourself according to grade level. Some college students are at the eighth-grade level in knowledge of grammar. The grammar test on pages 131–132 will help you check up on yourself.

It is not hard to learn to speak correctly. Any effort that you may put forth along this line will repay you handsomely.

THE WAY YOU LISTEN

Can you listen? Do you listen? Does it matter? Yes, it does; even quite as much as it does how you talk. All through life you will have to listen to people—your employer, business associates, customers, clients, neighbors, friends, relatives, and many others, depending on what your life adjustments are. How you listen will determine how you respond or react to what is said. This may well determine your success or failure all through life.

To the question, "Can you listen?" you quite naturally say, "Of course I can!" But don't be too sure. Listening, like writing and talking, is an acquired art that reflects a most important character trait. First, let us see how the "fine art of listening" may affect one's vocational life.

How one "listens" is an important index to a pleasing personality.

A. *Devaney, Inc.*

It is admitted that you can hear, but that is not the question. *Hearing* and *listening* are two quite different things. The railroad crossing sign says, "Stop, Look, Listen." And that word *listen* was chosen carefully. One who isn't listening may hear the engine's warning whistle and yet drive on the track and get killed. Let us see why young people should acquire the art of listening.

Without conscious effort we hear many noises every day, almost every minute of every day. But these noises do not affect our conduct or our thought in any way. As you write, without conscious effort, you hear the oil burner, the rustle of a newspaper, or a child shouting out in the yard; but until you think back to see what noises have been heard, you aren't aware of them at all. The crux of the matter is that to listen one must put his mind on the noise he expects to hear. The act of listening requires mental alertness. But people half asleep *hear* noises. Now let us see how this difference is important in office work.

In spite of all the numerous sound-eliminating devices, the average large office is a place of many noises. Even the small office rarely is without its share of distracting sounds. It is important that an office worker shall be able to shut out those noises which tend to distract him and to concentrate on his work regardless of what is going on around him.

But some, indeed many, of these intrusive noises are voices—conversation about many things of no interest to a nearby worker. It is harder to shut out such noises than it is to ignore mechanical noises such as the pounding of a typewriter, especially if the topic of conversation is interesting. But it must be done. Here is where *hearing* may not easily be avoided, but *listening* surely can be.

At times you will be talked to by an associate amidst a babel of voices and other noises. But here you must listen attentively to catch every word and avoid unnecessary and annoying requests for repetitions. Concentration is needed. It can be developed. Get all the practice you can while in school. When your teacher, or principal, or classmate, or counselor addresses you, shut everything else out and give undivided attention to what is said.

Listening implies something more than merely catching the words spoken; more even than being able to repeat them verbatim. It implies understanding to the full limit of one's ability the sense of what is said. This requires thoughtful concentration on what the speaker is saying. It requires an *active state of mind* which registers the thought conveyed and usually reacts to it at the same time.

Some people *hear* lectures while others really *listen* to them. The former often can tell you who lectured and what was the subject of his discourse—both gleaned from the program or previous announcement. The latter can tell you the main points made in the address, or indicate clearly the trend of the discussion, and comment intelligently on it.

In a staff conference about office procedures or the best way to do various jobs, one member will "give ear" to what is said, but fail to make a single constructive suggestion. Another may listen attentively and make suggestions which greatly facilitate office routine. It is not wholly unlikely that the *hearing* member may be quite as capable as the *listening* one; in fact he may come away from the conference saying quite truthfully, "I thought of all those changes long ago, but I didn't really understand that the boss wanted suggestions." It pays to listen.

There are many other things about listening which should be noted. Only a few of the more important ones can be included in this brief statement.

1. When instructions are being given you, listen. Note every detail. Ask for repetition if you don't understand. But do not ask a busy man to repeat if you can avoid doing so—and you can by giving your undivided attention to what he is saying.

2. Look at a speaker while he is delivering an important message. It makes him feel that you are listening. Don't let your eyes wander to other people or things lest your attention be diverted from the listening job then in hand.

3. In noisy offices good listening makes for lower pitched voices, and this tends to lessen the strain on fellow workers. Thus you may help achieve a quieter office.

4. When you have been listening to directions for doing something, give evidence that you have registered them by repeating as much of what has been said as is necessary. Don't leave your employer to wonder whether or not you really know what he wants done and how he wants it done. Reassure him by a few words and thus at the same time impress the matter more firmly on your own mind.

5. Be alert to learn all you can about the business by listening to what goes on about you when it is proper that you should do so. There are lulls in the daily round of work when gems of wisdom are dropped about the work you are doing, or about the business of your employer, which an alert, habitual listener will pick up for future use. Instructions given to your associate, better ways of doing things being discussed, and countless other listening opportunities will come your way. Don't overlook them.

6. But don't eavesdrop. Don't listen to private conversation not intended for your ears. Don't listen to business secrets which you are not expected to know. Don't listen to office gossip about the business, your boss, or your associates. Remember that you can be forgiven for *hearing* such things, but not for *listening* to them.

A proper understanding of the proprieties in office work, a sound character which makes you want to do the right thing, an alert mind that is ready for its work, a desire to master the *art* of listening, and the will to practice this art on every proper occasion, will make you a good listener. And this art will play an important part in determining the degree of success you attain in your business career.

Good listening also is essential to social and family adjustments. Are you one who in friendly conversation lets your mind wander and thus fails to respond properly? Or one who appears bored the moment something just outside the range of your interest comes up? Are you like people we know whose attention to the answer to a question asked by them is easily diverted by someone entering the room—so easily, in fact, that they not only fail to hear the answer but also forget they asked the question?

Are you one of those who *hearing* but not *listening* to things said pass them along to others badly distorted? Do you enter a group already engaged in conversation and start your own line of talk without listening to the topic of conversation and awaiting your turn to change it? Are you one who often wears that "vacant stare" which shows your friend that you are far away and not listening at all?

Many people apologize for their poor memory. Some almost brag about it. In many cases where they forget instructions or news or a good story or a message or an errand or any one of scores of things they wanted to remember and should have, the cause is that they didn't really *listen.*

Remember that a good conversationalist is always a good *listener,* not merely a good *talker.* The latter may be a pest; the former a joy to be with. Also keep in mind the fact that conversational ability is one of the marks of good personality. Cultivate this art through listening as well as talking.

THE WAY YOU ACT PHYSICALLY

Consider here your physical grace and poise, your stride and carriage, the way you sit down and rise to your feet. There is no good reason why everyone should not acquire a certain degree of gracefulness of movement. This by no means implies effeminacy in men or too much masculinity in women.

The most charming young woman in one of our classes in personality improvement had one fault of which she was not aware. As she walked, the amount of "side sway" of her hips reminded one of nothing more than the actions of the trailer of a ten-ton truck. She was much chagrined at the discovery, but willingly undertook to remedy the situation.

When you want to sit down, do you back up to the chair, relax all your muscles, and let gravity do the rest? Do you collapse, rather than sit? Are you a foot twister—do you wrap your legs and feet around the chair legs? Try this rather revealing experiment. Place a chair about twelve feet in front of a full-length mirror and watch yourself approach the chair and sit down. Did you display any more gracefulness of movement than Ferdinand the bull sitting down under the cork tree?

You should "stand tall," "walk tall." Think of something straight and tall—a pine tree, a telephone pole, a skyscraper. Good posture makes you literally feel better, more optimistic, more confident. It is hard to be grouchy and pessimistic when you are throwing out your chest, standing tall, and walking with a firm, springy step.

THE WAY YOU ACT EMOTIONALLY

This factor includes your ability to keep at all times a sane emotional balance, avoiding stolidity on the one hand and hysterical behavior on the other.

This is no reason why we should not express our emotions if the expression is socially acceptable. Indeed, a person with no emotions would not be normal; he would, as a matter of fact, be potentially a most dangerous individual. It is good psychology to give some expression to our feelings. People are intended to laugh, to cry, to be happy or sorrowful, to feel and express righteous indignation, to like some things and dislike others, to experience sympathy, love, revulsion, awe, and reverence. That is the way we are made. To stifle and repress our emotional life is to behave abnormally.

But our emotions should not rule us. They must always, especially in their grosser and more violent expression, be under the control of our will. Uncontrolled rage, fear, hatred, and lust countermand the dictates of reason and reduce us to the level of beasts.

The most helpful emotions, feelings, and moods in personality development are optimism, hopefulness, cheerfulness, happiness, sympathy, and reverence. A sulky, sullen person makes few friends. A cheerful, pleasant person will never lack admirers.

THE WAY YOU ACT INTELLECTUALLY

Here we consider your ability to reason from facts to conclusions without allowing prejudice, tradition, or wishful thinking to influence you unduly. Many persons make the mistake of "thinking with their emotions" instead of their brains.

Intelligence has been defined in many ways. The basic meaning of the word refers to what we usually call brightness, mental alertness, or mental power.

Sometimes intelligence is confused with *education.* This is unnecessary, because education is what you know—the knowledge you have acquired—whereas intelligence is your *capacity* for acquiring more knowledge and education. A person may have much intelligence and little education. It is hard, on the other hand, to imagine a person with a low intelligence level and a lot of education. For example, an imbecile could never finish high school. His brain and nervous system are so defective that he simply couldn't master the usual requirements for high-school graduation.

One of the best explanations of intelligence is that given us by Dr. Peter Sandiford, a Canadian psychologist. Dr. Sandiford defines intelligence in terms of brain and nervous system. If you have one kind of brain and nervous system, you will be bright. If you have another kind of brain and nervous system, you will be stupid and dull. By "kind of brain," we are obviously not referring to its size and shape, or any externally observable indications, but rather to the efficiency with which it works. The way it works seems to depend on the number, complexity, and integration of the tiny neurons, or nerve cells, in our brains and nervous systems. If neural connections are made easily and tenaciously, we are bright. If connections between neurons are slow to integrate and easily disrupted, we are dull.

Basic intelligence is hereditary. It probably cannot be increased or improved through better environment, although placing a child in a better environment will help him to reveal and use the basic general intelligence that he has inherited. Raising him in a bad environment—one that stunts his growth, breeds illness and disease, and offers little mental stimulation—will prevent his potential mental power from asserting itself. There are many cases on record where children who were taken from poor orphan homes and adopted into good private homes have *appeared* to grow more intelligent. There have even been startling increases in the children's recorded I.Q.'s under such circumstances. It is improbable, however, that they have actually been made any brighter. The better living conditions simply uncovered the natural ability that had lain dormant in their previous environments. Also, the effect of repetition of tests may account for higher ratings.

To put it in another way, we are born with a certain *possible* or *potential* intelligence. The way we are raised will determine whether or not we ever utilize our potentialities. There are certain ways of raising children that will permit them to realize most or all of their native abilities. There are other ways of raising children that will almost guarantee that they will utilize only a small fraction of their inborn mental powers. We are convinced that most of us have considerably more mental power or intelligence than we realize or will ever use.

Even though the limits of our basic intelligence are so fixed by heredity that they cannot be pushed up by coaching, education, or better environment, nevertheless our inherited intelligence can be damaged or reduced by birth injuries, by diseases that permanently affect the brain, and by accidents that could destroy portions of the brain.

No *entirely satisfactory* method of measuring basic intelligence has been devised. No *direct* method of measuring it has been devised. Though many measuring devices have been proposed and actually used, the most satisfactory method to date is the "intelligence test." These tests are satisfactory enough to serve the purposes for which they were intended; however, they are not *direct* measures of basic intelligence but are, rather, indirect ones. Much of the confusion current in this whole problem of understanding intelligence is caused by the mistaken assumption that the intelligence tests measure basic intelligence *directly* and *accurately*. Some scholars favor discontinuance of the term "intelligence test" and adoption of the term "scholastic aptitude test."

The temporary adequacy of the intelligence test is attested by its widespread use by schools and colleges all over the country.

Intelligence is usually, though not always, measured in terms of the intelligence quotient, or I.Q.[4] An I.Q. of 100 is considered strictly average. The usual ranking is given in the table.

Intellectual genius	I.Q.	140	or over
Very superior	I.Q.	120	to 140
Superior	I.Q.	110	to 120
Average	I.Q.	90	to 110
Dull	I.Q.	80	to 90
Border line	I.Q.	70	to 80
Moron	I.Q.	50	to 70
Imbecile	I.Q.	25	to 50
Idiot	I.Q.	0	to 25

[4] The American Council on Education tests use percentile ranks; the Army tests use letters, A, B, C, etc.

I.Q. tests measure only intelligence. They do not attempt to measure personality, musical talent, social graces, attitudes, emotional maturity, or acquired knowledge. There *are* tests and surveys which measure these qualities and acquisitions with a fair degree of accuracy. It is interesting to note that some individuals have a high degree of musical talent and only average general intelligence. Similarly, a person may be a "genius" in art, or some other specific area, without a similar degree of superiority in general intelligence.

A pertinent question to bring up at this point is this: Do the brightest people have the best personalities? The answer is No— not necessarily. There appears to be little relationship (or correlation, as it is called in psychology) between a person's I.Q. and his personality integration.

At the extremes of the scale, this may not be true, because an idiot could hardly be said to have an attractive personality, no matter how much coaching he is given. Sometimes geniuses become so preoccupied in intellectual pursuits beyond the comprehension of ordinary men and women that they are thought of as eccentric personalities. Geniuses, however, are not doomed to be eccentric just because they are geniuses. We know a few intellectual geniuses who have superior personalities.

The point we are trying to make here is that for most of us there is no close relationship between I.Q. and personality. For instance, if your I.Q. rating is 110, it certainly does not follow that your personality will be "10 per cent better" than that of your classmate who has an I.Q. of 100. Except for the lowest levels in the scale, people of any intelligence level *can* develop attractive personalities.

Your "intellectual attractiveness" is influenced also by the amount of education[5] that you have. Educated persons rarely consider illiterate persons attractive. On the other hand, a young woman may repel men by an appearance of too much intellectuality. Many an intelligent, clever woman knows the advantage of "playing dumb" at the right time.

We are not implying that attractiveness of personality is in direct proportion to the amount of education, formal or informal, that you may have, for this is not the case. A person with two years of college is not, by virtue of that fact, more attractive than a person with

[5] The term "education" is used here in its broadest sense rather than in the narrower meaning of schooling.

only a high-school education. Regardless of the level of your education, you *can* acquire a pleasing personality.

Before leaving this topic of intelligence, we should note the fact that this term is used by employers and others in a sense far removed from that in which psychologists use it. An employer wants what he calls "*intelligent* workers." We like "intelligent people" for our friends. We shun people who are "not very intelligent." We say, "any intelligent person should know that."

When used by an employer, the word *occupational* usually precedes *intelligence*—occupational intelligence. Since one's personality has much to do with one's occupational adjustment, and something called *general intelligence* is a component of good *personality*, it may be useful to consider *occupational intelligence* as a factor in personality development, as it is in your occupational adjustments that personality will play an important part. We shall use employment by way of illustrating how occupational intelligence may contribute to occupational adjustment in any field of work.

In spite of the best efforts of competent and conscientious teachers, young people often make the mistake of thinking that some simple skill is all that is necessary to meet the requirements of initial positions. There is much more to work situations than this. No employer pays well merely for simple skills. What he really is willing to pay well for is something quite different; something which everyone should strive to achieve before he leaves school or college.

Briefly stated, occupational intelligence is an awareness of the complexities of one's job; an understanding of the personal relationships involved in it; resourcefulness in meeting new and difficult situations; and, in short, a clear understanding of the many exacting demands of almost any desirable position.

Very few things done by any worker can be done without affecting others in one way or another. There is an interdependence among workers which cannot be ignored. A stenographer, for example, must consider office routine which involves the dictator (perhaps several), the file clerk, the supervisor, and often many other co-workers. Only those who are truly co-operative can hope to succeed in life.

There are always certain things that, to be of any value, must be done today. One should think over pending jobs and put the ones that must be done today on top; one must not get caught at the end of the day with urgent work untouched or incomplete. Intelligent planning is essential to efficiency in any position and in most other life situations. The smooth flow of life requires careful, systematic planning of each day's program. But, of course, one must not expect that one's plans for the day will never be upset by circumstances over which one has no control. Something is always "coming up" unexpectedly. One who is adequately intelligent anticipates this, is not disturbed by it, and manages by necessary readjustments to keep it from disrupting the day's work.

The intelligent person knows the value of time. He knows which hours belong to him and which to his employer. He conscientiously tries to be "on time" for his work, and to put aside all personal matters during working hours. But no considerate employer—and who would want to work for any other kind?—expects his employees to work through the day without occasional "breathing spells" or rest periods for relaxation. These respites do not slow up production; but "loafing" does. So does dawdling over work—taking more time than is needed for a task. It is not the possible loss of one's job which makes loafing or dawdling dangerous; it is the risk of undermining one's character which makes these practices most objectionable.

An occupationally intelligent worker knows he must be alert to catch errors that may creep into any piece of work which comes to his desk or for which he is responsible—not his original mistakes, but those made by his superiors or co-workers. One mistake overlooked may cost his employer a tidy sum; one detected may save the equivalent of the worker's month's salary, or more.

An occupationally intelligent worker knows that his employer expects him to be observing; to pick up, as he goes along, information which will increase his efficiency. The employer is willing to teach him those requirements of his job which cannot be learned by keen observation on the job itself. A file clerk comes to a piece of matter which is new to him, but which obviously has been handled frequently in his office. He asks his employer how to file it. Another file clerk in the same situation looks in the file to see how it was filed before. The former lacks occupational intelligence; the latter has it.

YOUR HABITS OF INQUIRY

Few things will help more in making adjustments with new friends, fellow workers, and other associates than will a showing of a desire to learn about their activities and interests. We like to talk about the things we do, the things we like, and the many activities in which we engage. In fact, many of us like that more than we do listening to the information volunteered by our associates. If you really want to make friends of new acquaintances ask them about themselves, their work, their recreational interests, and their views on various subjects. If you want to succeed in your new job, or to advance from your old one, learn all you can from your fellow workers. To do this you must first learn the "fine art of asking questions."

Are you the kind of person who wants to know things? Have you an inquiring mind? Do you add something to your storehouse of knowledge every day? Not just in connection with your school work, but entirely outside your program of studies? The things you learn in your courses will be useful. The important things you learn from the people you meet daily outside your classes will be invaluable.

The amount of useful information you acquire from your daily associates will depend in large part on your answer to this query: Have you mastered the fine art of asking questions?

Do not think that because you are young you have not had time to master this art. Have you ever known a boy who doesn't pester every chance acquaintance with questions? Who doesn't drive his father to cover a dozen times a day with a barrage of questions on all kinds of topics? This goes on until something happens. No one knows just what. But a time seems to come when a boy either ceases to yearn for knowledge or loses the art of asking questions. In school this is bad; but in afterschool years it can be almost fatal to mental growth. Without mental growth and that ever-widening circle of knowledge which is the result of an inquiring mind, one scarcely can hope to advance far in any important occupation.

When you accept your first position, you should be ready and eager to learn from those around you. If you make the most of the educational opportunities which new personal contacts will bring you, it will be because you have developed the art of asking questions and have formed the habit of practicing this art. This habit-forming practice should begin now. Here are a few suggestions which may start you on the road to the achievement of an inquiring mind and the mastery of the art of asking questions.

1. Don't be afraid of "exposing your ignorance" by asking questions. This is the surest way of remaining ignorant. However, you should hesitate to ask for information that you already are expected to possess, if you can and will acquire it promptly in some other way. Don't unnecessarily expose your ignorance when to do so might destroy confidence in your ability—not when the defect can be easily and promptly remedied through your own effort.

2. What to ask about? Above all things don't pry into business secrets. No end of information is given to employees with instructions not to divulge any of it. Be quick to sense such situations and don't ask questions about them. Be just as quick to sense situations which it is your business to know about. Ask about them.

3. Whom to ask? No general rule can be laid down on this point. But you must learn how to judge which of your associates is the best one to ask. Of course it also must be one who is sure to understand why you desire the information; who has the time to answer your questions; and who has shown a disposition to be helpful.

4. When to ask? Never ask questions of one who is intent on some other matter. Don't ask questions in the presence of others when their presence may embarrass the one who is to answer. Don't inject into conversation questions which change the subject entirely. In other words, bide your time and await an opportune moment— but don't forget to ask.

5. How to ask? Don't ask questions until you are perfectly clear as to what you want to know. This is the only way to be sure that your questions will be clear, direct, and to the point. Willingness to answer questions often depends on how they are asked. If the person questioned must ask many questions before he can answer any, he is likely to lose patience and fail to give the information desired. Clear questions beget clear answers.

Success is most likely to come to those who know. Those know who have an inquiring mind. The right questions put to the right people at the right time and in the right way will store the mind with useful information. Resolve now to master the fine art of asking questions.

YOUR PHILOSOPHY OF LIFE

This factor includes your code of personal ethics and morality, your concept of the fundamental values in life, and, in the broader meaning of the term, your spiritual development. It is hard to imagine a really attractive personality without the element of character.

We realize that people attach varying meanings to the word. What you consider an ideal character might be in the estimation of someone else just an ordinary character. We know, too, that we could get into an endless debate over the varying interpretations of good and evil, ethical and unethical, right and wrong. Much time is spent, and we think justifiably spent, in college courses in ethics and philosophy splitting hairs over the problem of good and evil.

But we can agree on at least some of the fundamentals of good character: prudence, basic decency, temperance in everything, physical and moral courage, manliness or womanliness, personal integrity, intellectual honesty, law-abidingness, intelligent unselfishness, and sensible modesty. We can't help liking people with these qualities. These are the qualities we try to develop in our children. These are the virtues the home, school, and church co-operate in stressing. These are the *character traits* toward which every right-minded person, every idealist, strives. They underlie really permanent good personality.

A new acquaintance may meet all your requirements of the ideal personality; but if you later discover that he is a petty thief, an embezzler, or a habitual liar, then your rating of him drops to zero. You want nothing else to do with him. Good character is basic in an attractive personality.

YOUR VERSATILITY

Here is a factor in attractiveness usually overlooked in most analyses. Versatility—the number and variety of socially acceptable activities in which you can engage—is at once an index of potential attractiveness and a means of developing personality.

Barring physical disability, there is no reason why you should not learn to swim, fish, play games like golf and tennis, make a speech, play a musical instrument, and do a host of other things. The more things of this sort you can do, the more acceptable you will find yourself to a wider circle of friends and acquaintances. On pages 121–122 you will find a test by which you can compare your versatility with that of a group of college students.

Hobbies are the finest kind of "mental insurance." One of the best ways of keeping mentally (and physically) healthy is to have a variety of hobbies. Wherever possible, we should pick hobbies that bring us into contact with other people, all types of personalities. Avoid too many lone-wolf hobbies. You'll never develop your personality playing solitaire. *Learn skills that make you do things in the company of other people.* We shall see later that this is probably the most important single rule for developing your personality.

Consider as a case history a certain man. Here is his usual schedule of hobbies and avocational interests for one year.

January through March: badminton, three times a week; winter fishing, occasionally; bridge, usually one evening a week; stamp collecting, at odd moments.

April through August: golf, at least once or twice a week; trout fishing, every possible opportunity; tennis, every week or two; lake fishing, occasionally in midsummer; swimming, several times a week; gardening, mostly puttering around in odd moments with flowers.

September through December: skeet shooting, in the early fall, just before bird-hunting season; small-game hunting, October for birds and squirrels, after snowfall for rabbits; deer hunting, in November; fishing, at odd times throughout the fall; ice skating, around Christmas; bridge or other card games, on occasional evenings; duck hunting, occasionally.

In addition to this schedule, he reads newspapers, magazines, and an occasional book. He attends meetings of two service clubs regularly. Once in a while the whole family goes on a picnic or a wiener roast. His is an ideal program of recreation, hobbies, and sports activities. He is fortunate in being able to do all these things within five miles of his home.

You may well ask, "How does he find time to do anything else?" If you'll check the list again you'll see that all these activities can be done during the hours after work, on week ends, and on holidays. You will also observe that there are not only several things to do each season but there is also a balance between indoor and out-door activities. Actually, there are more outdoor activities in the list, because his profession keeps him in an office during working hours.

His recreation program involves considerably more expense than many of us can afford. But you will be surprised to learn how many of these activities you can engage in at practically no cost.

YOUR WILLINGNESS TO HELP OTHERS

Do you just naturally offer to help others; to be co-operative beyond the requirements of your job or your home life or your social club memberships, or your church connections or your many other associations with people? Willingness to help others is the mark of a good personality. It creates and retains good will. It builds character. It begets the help of others when needed. It gives great personal satisfaction.

This personality trait is important in all walks of life, but no-where is it more important than in occupational life at any level from the lowest menial job to the highest professional one. There-fore we may consider the "fine art of helping others" from the standpoint of one's job. All that is said holds true for all other activities done in association with others.

Very few people have occupations which enable them to work entirely by themselves. Most people work in pairs or in larger groups. Where two or more people have separate, but related, duties in connection with tasks to be performed, it is easy to know what each is expected to do. But when one of a group of workers turns from his own task to help someone else, many mistakes can be made. Hence the following suggestions may not be amiss.

1. Why help others? Because it is good for one to make some sacrifice for others. It builds character, and character is at the base of all really successful careers. Because helping others makes for what is called "morale" among workers; makes for better co-opera-tion in the completion of the whole task assigned to them. Because helping others affords one an opportunity to learn how to do things outside one's own job.

2. When to help others? When they most need it, is a good rule

to follow. Not when you just happen to feel like it. Be quick to sense a need for help and don't be too critical of those who occasionally fail to meet all demands made upon them. At times we all attempt more than we can do in a given time; or we misjudge our ability; or we allow interruptions and get behind. A helping hand is welcome when the need for it arises through no fault of our own, or even when the fault is ours.

3. Whom to help? Those who are willing to accept it, and who appreciate it. But not those whose shirking makes help necessary. Do not be imposed on, and yet, do not be too quick in your judgments of the conduct of associates. It is better to make the mistake of giving help when it is not deserved than it is mistakenly to withhold it from those who merit assistance.

4. Be as ready to help those below you in your organization as you are to relieve those on the same level or above you. While help should not be given for selfish reasons, remember that many boosts from those below you may be as valuable as a pull from those above you. The personnel factor in every business is a vitally important one. Executives choose for positions of leadership those who can get on well with people. A helping hand is an invitation to friendship. The good will of those associated with you counts heavily in your favor when promotions are to be made.

5. How to help others? By all means do not do it grudgingly; nor as a great favor to be returned in kind. Do it in a spirit of friendly co-operation. And as if it were a privilege. Above all things, do what you do as the one you are helping is doing it. Neither criticize nor appear to be dissatisfied with the work of a co-worker. Usually it is not the best time to offer advice when helping out on unfinished work. A mind intent on finishing an overdue task is not receptive to new ideas. A better time to give advice will come. Wait and watch for it.

6. Form the helping habit. It is not enough to know why, when, how, and whom to help. It is important to form habits which will insure that your help will be given automatically and in a way to be most appreciated. Once more, you are reminded that habits are the result of repetition and that practice is essential to the mastery of any art. To be a skillful helper when your first chance for service in business comes, you should practice the art of being helpful now. Do not put this off until you are on your first job.

You must learn to assist your associates in such a way as not to appear to be doing some of their work. So that they will not feel embarrassed by your aid. So that they will not be encouraged to impose on you. So that they will learn better ways of doing things without being resentful of your helpful ideas. So that your offer to help may not be regarded as an intrusion. So that your help will do the most good because it is needed badly. When you have formed the habit of helping in these ways, you will have mastered the fine art of helping your co-workers.

Your Health

We have been considering what are called *personality factors*—dress and general appearance, voice and speech, physical and emotional poise, interest in things, and general philosophy of life. We might wrap up all these things in one package and say that the one most important contribution to their achievement is good *mental and physical health*. Surely, without it, you are not likely to score high on these factors. It may not be amiss therefore to add a few words here on that subject.

In a television program a science teacher gave lessons in elementary science to a little boy or girl. He always began and ended with an equation something like this: Good food + plenty of exercise + fresh air + plenty of sleep = good health. To be sure, he was a booster for a certain breakfast food. But his equation comes close to being one that all should ponder well.

Young people normally are healthy. They too often assume that they always will be. They tend to associate poor health with old age—and to most youth *old age* is any year above thirty-nine. Don't be too sure that the health with which you are born will remain with you throughout life, not even throughout its first thirty-odd years, unless you guard it by every means at your command. On the other hand, don't worry about your health or become a faddist in your conscious effort to keep it.

We have said that your clothes should be appropriate for the occasion. Right; but they also should be such as will help to guard your health. Especially, the dictates of style should not cause you to wear less or more clothing than is needed for comfort and reasonably good appearance. Be clothes-conscious as much because of your need for protection against the weather as you are for the approbation of your friends and other associates. Your clothing needs and theirs may be quite different. Yours come first in planning your wardrobe. Never be governed by what *they are wearing* if in being so influenced you expose yourself to the weather or otherwise endanger your health.

Even one's voice may be improved by good health. No one much under par in health is likely to be well poised physically or emotionally. Your interest in things going on all about you in your job and elsewhere is not going to be what it should be if your mind is distracted by poor health. Nor will your outlook on life be a cheerful one if you are less well than you should be. In short, you will not possess the interest in your job, or the energy to manage it, or the will to succeed in business life if you are physically subnormal. So you should determine to learn how to keep well, and then leave no stone unturned to accomplish that result.

It should be pointed out that your keeping physically fit should not use up your valuable time doing things solely for that purpose. It is largely a matter of *not doing harmful things*. Of course, it is not all a negative matter. Some positive steps must be taken, but even these are likely to follow if negative steps are not taken. Be sure to get enough exercise to keep you physically fit, but avoid overfatigue. At all times you should be the best judge as to when a danger point is reached.

Get the amount of sleep *you* require for the good feeling that indicates good health. It is about as bad to overdo sleep as it is to underdo it. Late hours? Not too late to leave time for the complete rest you need. Occasionally you may lose a little sleep that you cannot make up. That does no harm, so long as losing sleep doesn't become *habitual*.

Eat what is good for you, and like it. No more, no less. Never overeat. Not because occasional overeating will in itself be harmful, but because it takes so little overindulgence in food to establish a craving for more than is good for you. Cultivate a liking for all kinds of good food so that you will never have difficulty eating a "square meal," regardless of the limited or varied nature of the menu. Don't become a food faddist. Just find out what is regarded as a properly balanced diet and stick to it. This should suggest two things: (1) that certain kinds of food are essentials of a healthful diet, and (2) that you should learn what they are. Unless you have some sort of allergy, do not reject any essential food just because you "don't like it." Learn to like it. You can very easily. It will be worth your while to do so.

Fresh air is essential to good health. Get plenty of it. Spend some time *pleasantly* out-of-doors every day. You can learn what out-of-doors activity is best for you. No one else can tell you what you should do to meet this requirement. For some people walking to work every day suffices, while for others this would be a tiresome bore. A game you like may be best for you. But watch out; don't overdo it. Too much golf, for example, may be as bad for you as would be no out-of-doors exercise at all. Try out different things. Try to find several you like to do. Variety helps. Do not become a slave to any one sport or set of physical habits.

Congenial companionship is useful in maintaining good health. Seek it. You may not always find it in your job. Cultivate people outside your job, people who bring out the best that is in you, not those who irritate you.

With the advent of the radio and the more recent distracting television influence in the home, reading is in danger of becoming a lost art. But this need not be so, nor need listening to the radio or watching television always be time-wasting. By the selection of good programs (there are many), you may be quite as much stimulated in the right direction as you possibly can be by good reading. But in most cases, probably in yours, your spare time for this aspect of good, healthful living should be divided between these media for intellectual growth and necessary relaxation.

Some sort of religious experience is essential to mental and physical health. Affiliate yourself with some church or other religious organization and reap the benefits of its sure contribution to your physical and mental well-being.

It will be said many times throughout this course that sound character lies at the bottom of a good personality. It may be added here that good physical and mental health is very close to an absolute essential of good personality. One in whom are combined fine character traits, a sound body, a good mind, and fine spiritual qualities will be the kind of person we think of as a *fine personality*. Everything we have said about personality development in this course indirectly supports the theory that good health is an essential of good personality. Every suggested step for the achievement of good personality, if taken, should contribute to the development and maintenance of good health. In other words, good health is not something wholly apart from good personality. The former may be a result of the latter just as the latter may be a result of the former. What is called a *well-integrated* personality is quite sure to reflect good physical and mental health just as much as it does good personal habits in all the more important life relationships.

Pace yourself from day to day with a view to the development of a clean-cut pattern of living for yourself that will assure you the right kind and the right amount of the essential ingredients of good health in matters of sleep, exercise, food, recreation, fresh air, intellectual advancement, and spiritual growth. Once this pattern of living is established, your present health problems, if any, should vanish and no avoidable future ones should be acquired.

Hereditary or Acquired Personality?

If your personality were something inborn or hereditary, like the color of your eyes, then there would be little likelihood of change or improvement. Certain traits, mostly physical in nature, are largely the results of our heredity.

If you have big feet, you may blame that on heredity; but if you have an evil temper, or if you are afraid of the dark, that is something you have acquired. Hereditary traits, such as skin color, hair texture, stature, resistance or susceptibility to diseases, and the shape of your face, are hard to change radically. True, they may be modified by environment—usually they are, to a certain extent—nevertheless, they are basic in our make-up and are relatively constant. If a man's skin is white, that it will turn black is extremely unlikely. If his eyes are blue, no amount of effort, concentration, exercise, or study will ever make them brown. He is stuck with blue eyes and might as well make the best of it.

But the same thing is not true of personality. It is essentially acquired—built up on the basis of a million experiences, countless impressions from our world.

If there is any one thing that a newborn baby does not possess, it is a personality. Babies are pretty much alike at birth. But follow a group of babies in their maturation and development up to the first grade in school and observe the difference! Here is one boy so shy that he never engages in group play at recess; another, who had the same start as far as personality is concerned, is a little extrovert. Self-consciousness and shyness are unknown to him. He pitches in and helps in all the class activities. One child will be a crybaby, another a little stoic. One co-operates nicely, another is a chronic troublemaker.

As these children grow older their temperaments will be further modified through their environment, and by the time they get through high school their characters as well as their personalities will have crystallized to a great extent.

Personality never becomes so crystallized and fixed, however, that it cannot be changed. A certain student entered college so shy, so easily embarrassed, so timid and fearful that he could not answer a question in class. He would resort to all sorts of subterfuge to keep from being called on to make a report. He would never go to college parties. He could not make friends.

This same boy, less than two years later, walked out on the stage before the entire student body and made an announcement without any outward signs of fear. He also made reports in class, managed introductions at various school gatherings, and assumed a position of leadership in the student body in a way that you would never have thought possible.

It will work. We have seen it work time and again. It *can* work with you. We do not know that it will, because so much depends on you.

We have tried to point out that personality begins to get fixed in the individual long before he starts going to school. Throughout his elementary- and high-school life he is exposed to a larger and larger environment, providing more and more opportunities for personality development whether for adjustment or maladjustment.

The main thing to bear in mind in this connection is that what we ordinarily call personality is acquired.

We must not overlook the fact, however, that some inherited traits exercise a tremendous influence on the personality that we acquire. A high school girl who is over six feet tall, for instance, may become shy and self-conscious on account of her stature. She may feel out of place at the school dances because the boys prefer to dance with shorter girls. She may affect a stoop-shouldered, slouchy posture to minimize her height. She may even grow bitter toward the world and turn out to be a man-hater.

Physical defects may limit a child's sphere of activity and make an introverted bookworm out of a boy, who, if he were normal physically, might have been the most extroverted athlete in school.

Nevertheless, personality is acquired. If you have, through your childhood years, acquired an unattractive personality or a neutral personality, then it is possible, with proper guidance and effort, to bring about the changes that are desirable. Your personality *can* be changed. In countless instances persons have changed themselves so radically as to be hardly recognizable to those who knew them before.

Remaking your personality is not an easy task. It can be done, but it will require patience, perseverance, and guidance. It cannot be done overnight, though remarkable transformations have been effected in a short period of time. *You* must provide the motive, the patience, and the application. The purpose of this course is to provide the information, the guidance, and the opportunity for practice.

Suggestions for Study and Discussion

1. Make up your own definition of personality. How does it differ from the definitions in this chapter?

2. Ask several acquaintances what personality is. Write down their answers and compare them with the definitions given in this book.

3. Look at Dr. Link's definition of personality on page 18. Does it differ greatly from your previous concept of personality?

4. Look again at the section on "Personality Factors" (pages 19 to 46). In which of those areas do you think you need improvement most?

5. Make a recording of your voice and play it back several times. Or ask some friend or relative to criticize your voice as used in ordinary conversation. Is there room for improvement?

6. Discuss the ways in which magazine advertisements have influenced our interpretation of personality.

7. How can a person with a quick temper learn to control it?

8. In the absence of intelligence tests, how do we generally judge a person's intelligence level?

9. Make a list of your hobbies and classify them according to seasons of the year. Do you think you have too many hobbies? Too few? Are your hobbies well balanced?

10. Can you see that one's real *character* has much to do with one's *personality* as it appears to or does affect others? Illustrate your answer by referring to the personality factors discussed in this chapter.

11. Entirely apart from any assistance the personality factors may afford in getting and holding a job, or even in winning advancement to

a higher level of employment, what rewards are likely to be got from the development of these factors to the highest possible point?

12. At the outset in our discussion of personality factors it was said that *physical* ones would be considered first. Which of those considered are *physical* in nature? Why do you classify them thus?

13. Which factors are *mental?* Why so classified?

14. Which are *emotional?* Why so classified?

15. Which involve all three—*physical, mental, emotional?* Explain.

16. "He cannot help it. Just like his dad. Quick tempered." What do you think of that frequently heard statement?

17. "I never can spell. Neither of my parents can." This is sometimes referred to as a *defense mechanism.* What does that mean? What do you think of it?

18. Is it fair to say that, barring serious physical, mental, and emotional defects, all the personality factors discussed are within your control and may be measured up to if you have the vision to see their importance and the will to carry through the program of study and practice begun here and now?

19. Have you in mind people who,

(1) Have attractive physical size, form, and features, or who have distracted attention from physical defects in such a way as to make you forget them?

(2) Dress appropriately and attractively without too great expense?

(3) Talk in well-modulated and easily understood voices?

(4) Who are well poised and never lose their tempers over trifles, or become too exuberant or gushing on slight provocation, or laugh boisterously and out of line with the real humor of the occasion?

(5) Who have the mentality to grasp the meaning of conversation, to take an adequate and interesting part in normal conversation, to think through and reach right conclusions about ordinary problems?

(6) Who seem to have an interest in the welfare of others, assume their just share of civic and social responsibilities, and never are too greatly disturbed by the petty annoyances of life?

(7) Who seem to be able to do well whatever comes to hand to do, and whose skills and know-how are adequate to almost any ordinary task?

20. A baseball club manager recently is quoted as saying that a certain coach of his team "acts like a boy nine years old." What did he mean?

It will be rewarding to note mentally where your associates stand on these qualities. First, of course, you should practice on yourself. In studying the conduct of others do so for your own personal benefit in an effort to understand the factors studied and their importance in making life adjustments. Are those who seem to possess these qualities *well-adjusted* people? Are those lacking these qualities *poorly adjusted* people? Are the former obviously more successful than the latter?

Make it a habit to think of these factors as you deal with people and to learn lessons from your observations. But do not become openly critical of your associates. You, even as they, may be more or less poorly adjusted for lack of these qualities.

Personality Reminders

1. Have you played any game today involving physical exercise?
2. Did you remember to smile and say "Thank you" today?
3. Are your hose fresh and free from odor *now?*
4. Did you keep your temper under control yesterday—*all day?*
5. Are you practicing good posture *now?*
6. Did you speak clearly and distinctly in class?
7. Are you consciously observing personality traits in others? In yourself?
8. Have you a hobby?
9. How do you look?
10. How do you walk?
11. Are you usually mentally alert? Or often mentally lazy?
12. Do you tend to blame others for your shortcomings?

Special References

Carney, Marie L. *Etiquette in Business*

Droke, Maxwell. *People . . . How to Get Them to Do What You Want Them To*

MacGibbon, Elizabeth Gregg. *Manners in Business*

Murray, Elwood. *Speech Personality,* Revised Edition

Osborn, Loraine. *Your Voice Personality,* Third Edition

Baird, A. Craig, and Franklin H. Knower. *General Speech: an Introduction*

Manser, R. B. and L. Finlan. *The Speaking Voice*

Powers, David G. *Fundamentals of Speech*

Sandford, William P. *Speak Well—and Win!*

Sarett, Lew, and W. T. Foster. *Basic Principles of Speech*

CHAPTER THREE

Kinds of Personalities

THERE ARE MANY kinds of real and alleged personalities. Perhaps one of the commonest and the most unconscious groupings is

1. People I like, and
2. People I don't like.

This classification obviously does not get at the heart of the prob lem, because it is entirely personal and subjective. This type of egocentric classification is unscientific and, in general, illogical. Your dislike of an individual, for instance, may be based on some imagined wrong he has done to you, or the association of his name or appearance with someone else whom you dislike.

In this connection it is well to remind you that, no matter what you do to improve your personality, there always will be someone who does not like you. You can't mold a personality that will be uniformly desirable in everybody's eyes.

Nevertheless, as we shall see farther on, there are some kinds of personalities that are almost universally disliked, and some kinds that are admired by the great majority of people.

Introverts and Extroverts

A classification that recently has received much publicity desig-nates everyone as

1. Introvert,
2. Ambivert, or
3. Extrovert.

Characteristic activities of two personality types—extrovert and introvert. Can you identify each picture as to the type of personality represented?

The introvert is typically "the man of thought"; the extrovert "the man of action." The ambivert is half-and-half, a mixture of introvert and extrovert. There are more ambiverts than introverts or extroverts.

Introverts prefer to be alone; extroverts crave lots of company. The introvert stays at home and reads a good book while the extrovert goes to the dance and shows off. Introverts have few acquaintances; extroverts get acquainted with everybody.

The introvert personality should not be thought of as either "inferior" or "superior" to the extrovert. A mistaken notion has been given some circulation that it is just too bad for you if you are an introvert—that you should avoid introversion as you would the smallpox. A few people have confused the word "introvert" with "pervert." There is nothing wrong with being either an introvert or an extrovert, unless, of course, a person reaches such an extreme in one direction or the other that he becomes a freak. The world's work must be done by all sorts of people, tall and short, light and dark, fat and thin, introvert and extrovert.

Take a look at two real case histories, students in college classes, one an introvert and the other an extrovert.

J.B.H., the introvert, is twenty years old, a sophomore in the commerce curriculum. He has a single room in a private home and eats his meals at a downtown restaurant. He plans to major in accounting, receive his degree from college, and work in an accountant's office so as to qualify to write the C.P.A. examination. His ambition is to become a certified public accountant.

He has an I.Q. of 120, which ranks him in the "very superior" group in general intelligence. He has always made good grades in mathematics and other courses that demand concentration and accuracy. He has averaged B+ in all his college courses, and always submits his written work promptly. Because of his high intelligence, his excellent study habits, and his ambition to make good in a specific field, he has always, even in high school, been considered a superior student.

J.B.H. comes from a home in very modest circumstances financially and thus has found it necessary to earn part of his college expenses. For his board he waits on tables at the restaurant. For his room he tends the furnace and does odd jobs at the house where he rooms.

Although he received two bids, he has not joined a fraternity. He doesn't hold too high an opinion of fraternities. He has said that during his freshman year he attended only two of the Friday night all-college dances. He seldom dates; and when he does, he prefers to go to the movies rather than to a party. He has only an incidental interest in sports and athletics but does aspire to make the track team. His specialties are the mile and the cross-country events; and he trains conscientiously, usually alone. He dislikes pep meetings, saying, "I feel like a fool going to those meetings and yelling myself hoarse." He generally stays away from pep rallies and other student gatherings, preferring, as he says, "to do something of more enduring importance."

From 10 to 11 a.m. and 2 to 4 p.m., hours when he has no classes, you will find him in the library studying. He chooses a table where he can have his back to the rest of the reading room and thus not be distracted by other people. He begins studying in his room, alone, at 7:30 every night and generally studies until about 11 o'clock. He follows a time budget and feels uncomfortable if for any reason he has to deviate from his routine.

J.B.H. is a good conversationalist but has relatively few close friends. He has never been elected to any student office. Probably over half of the 475 students in college don't even know who he is.

W.J.M., the extrovert, is a mixer, a joiner, an organizer. A commerce major, twenty years old, in his second year in college, he plans to be a salesman. He isn't sure just what sort of selling he will eventually work into, but he knows he is a "natural" for a career in salesmanship.

In the summer after high-school graduation he sold brushes from house to house and cleared enough for a down payment on his first year's college tuition. Last summer he sold vacuum cleaners from house to house; and, as he put it, had "a rip-roaring good time, met some fine people, and made lots of money." He is now getting lined up with a firm that sells encyclopedias to teachers, college professors, and other professional people. "I want to get as many kinds of selling experiences as possible," he explained when asked why he changed lines.

W.J.M. has an I.Q. of 115, which rates him as "superior" in intelligence. He has never had much trouble with schoolwork, but says, "Sometimes I get interested in so many different things I tend to let my schoolwork slide." He hopes to finish college with what he calls "a gentleman's average—C."

He lives at a fraternity house, is a member of two committees, represents his fraternity on the student council, and has been elected house manager for next year. For this job he will get his board free.

W.J.M. says that he missed only one Friday night dance last year and that was because he was sick in bed with the influenza. He has had dates with some ten or twelve different girls; says, "I like to shop around." He laughs easily, talks a great deal, and likes crowds. Pep meetings and rallies are his dish, and he will make a talk at the drop of the hat.

He is crazy about athletics and may be seen at football games, running up and down the side lines exhorting the team to get in there and fight.

Everybody in school knows him, and everyone seems to like him.

Introverts frequently turn out to be philosophers, poets, thinkers, inventors, research scientists, mathematicians, librarians, and authors. *Extroverts* have a better chance of being explorers, businessmen, salesmen, executives, promoters, personnel directors, foremen, public-relations men, and actors. Extroversion is the basic quality of successful salesmen. Misfits occur when a decided introvert tries to follow a vocation suited to an extrovert. Some of the unhappiest men in the country are salesmen who should have been bookkeepers, or accountants who should have been business executives.

Before leaving this particular classification—Introverts and Extroverts—we must remind you again that there is nothing wrong with either kind of person. We must go further than that and say that one is no better than the other. They simply are *different*. In certain jobs the extrovert has a better chance of success, while in others the introvert may excel. And there are jobs where neither extreme is desirable. This distinction is very real and very important to you. In choosing a lifework you will want to take it into account. Be on the alert to note and mark well tendencies in either direction as you work at this essential task of appraising and improving your personality.

Perhaps a word of caution also should be passed along to you at this point. There can be little doubt that some people are so constituted as to fall naturally and even unavoidably into one or the other of the personality categories under consideration, while others are so classified because of conduct due to environmental or other conditions over which they may or may not have control.

Take the case of J.B.H. for example. He may be the introvert that he seems to be because of home conditions—no brothers or sisters or near playmates, home pressure to "study hard and make good grades," lack of time for extracurricular activities because of work done to pay his way, health defects that make sports unattractive, examples of time-scheduling by parents at home, and innate modesty which keeps him from asserting himself in student associational work. In other words, J.B.H. may not be the natural introvert he seems to be; and in time, under proper conditions and influence, he may escape that category entirely. Note that we say he "may not be" and "may escape" what he "seems to be." We do not say that he clearly is not what he has all the earmarks of being. We do not want you to be fooled by superficial or transient indications of introversion in your own case. Real introversion is something deep-seated and ineradicable. Your tendency in that direction may be due to something quite different, something over which you have control.

W.J.M., the extrovert, doesn't work for his board and thus has time for extracurricular activities. He is not sold on the idea that high marks are desirable. A *C* grade will do. So why study hard? Outside interests cause him to "let schoolwork slide." He likes girls and has many dates. He probably has an abundance of physical energy to run off, so is much on the go. He is "crazy about athletics," but not in the way that most boys are. He belongs to no teams, but runs up and down the sidelines "exhorting the team to get in there and fight"—vanity perhaps, or the wish to impress his girl friends. At home he may have led a happy-go-lucky, carefree life. He may have been told by his dad that the "go-getter is the one who brings home the bacon." In short, he may be what he seems to be by force of circumstances and not by reason of any innate quality over which he has little control. Here again we say "may be," not that he surely will be mistaken for the extrovert that he has all the earmarks of being.

And again we warn you **not** to be too hasty in drawing conclu-

Business Etiquette Series, McGraw-Hill Book Company, Inc.

Each of us has ambitions—as a person and as a worker—and a well-rounded personality is an important key in realizing these ambitions.

sions as to your extroversion on the basis of a cursory study of your preferences and activities. On the other hand, do not ignore these things and their possible implications for your life adjustments.

Nothing that has been said here is intended to question the fact that J.B.H. and W.J.M. are properly described as *introvert* and *extrovert*, respectively. They probably are, as they stand, fine specimens of those kinds of personality. But there may be some question as to the causes and complete permanence of their personalities.

Right here it should be profitable to rate yourself tentatively on the basis of what you know about introversion and extroversion. For this purpose, the following test is supplied. There will be other similar tests. You should have a notebook for use in writing your answers to the questions or entering your check marks against other items included. It also should be pointed out that you should go on beyond this basic course, retesting yourself from time to time, and that the rating forms suggested will be useful for that purpose. So either get a small new notebook for your ratings, or reserve space for this purpose in one you now have.

INTROVERSION-EXTROVERSION TEST

This is a test to determine whether you tend more toward the introvert type of personality or the extrovert. There are no "right" and "wrong" answers to these questions; you should answer them in terms of your own preferences and habits.

DIRECTIONS: Prepare a form like the one on the following page and write TRUE or FALSE after each number according to how that item describes *you*.

1. I daydream a great deal.
2. I frequently rewrite letters before mailing them.
3. Usually I should rather be alone than in a group.
4. I am frequently suspicious of other people's motives.
5. At some time in my life I have kept a diary for several months.
6. In general, I govern my life by reason rather than by emotion or impulse.
7. I have ups and downs in moods without knowing why.
8. I worry considerably about possible misfortunes.
9. I am rather self-conscious and blush frequently.
10. I tend to hesitate in making ordinary decisions.
11. My feelings are easily hurt.
12. I generally speak out what I consider the truth, regardless of how people take it.

13. I can express my thoughts better in writing than in speaking.
14. I am quite persistent in my attitudes and beliefs.
15. I get rattled rather easily.
16. I always avoid speaking before a group when I can.
17. On social occasions I tend to keep in the background.
18. I don't like to give or receive help in doing my work.
19. I prefer a game of cards, checkers, or other intellectual amusements to participation in athletic games.
20. I tend to be quite critical of others.
21. I am sure I should never be a good salesman.
22. I have relatively few acquaintances.
23. When things go wrong, I tend to indulge in self-pity.
24. Most of my acquaintances are members of my own sex.
25. I tend to resent and dislike orders, rules, and discipline.
26. I generally prefer to read a good book or magazine rather than go to a dance or party.

INTROVERSION-EXTROVERSION TEST		
1	10	19
2	11	20
3	12	21
4	13	22
5	14	23
6	15	24
7	16	25
8	17	26
9	18	

Number of items I marked TRUE ....

Number of items I marked FALSE ....

I tend to be *Introvert* ( ) *Ambivert* ( ) *Extrovert* ( )

The items on this test are so worded that an answer of TRUE indicates introversion, and FALSE indicates extroversion. The more you marked TRUE, the more of an introvert you are.

If you answered TRUE to more than thirteen, you tend to be an introvert; if more than thirteen were false for you, you tend to be an extrovert. However, if the division of true and false was almost equal, you are mid-type, the ambivert. The majority of persons are ambiverts, having some of the traits of both introverts and extroverts.

Perhaps you would like to look back now to page 51 and read again the brief descriptions of these three personality types.

For 91 Michigan college men, the average number of items marked TRUE was 10. For 79 women, it was 11. Both groups, therefore, would on the average be slightly extroverted. The highest introvert score was 23, made by a man. The most extroverted score was 2, also made by a man.

There is nothing wrong with being an introvert or an extrovert or an ambivert. No one of them can be considered "good" or "bad," "desirable" or "undesirable," "superior" or "inferior" types of personality.

True, it *is* possible to be too extreme an introvert for your own good; or, on the other hand, too much of an extrovert. If you answered, say 23 TRUE or 23 FALSE, you are probably so extreme a type that you should try to bring about some changes in yourself. It is easier for an introvert to become an extrovert than the reverse, but you can modify your personality in any way you like *if you are truly in earnest about it.*

Your future occupation or profession should be chosen with your personality type in mind.[1]

If they have the other qualifications necessary, introverts may well consider such occupations as accounting, bookkeeping, writing, certain types of teaching, scientific research, portrait photography, classical music, composing, statistics, chemistry, farming, library work, or any occupation that does not demand the ability to manage people, mix easily, and get along with all sorts of personalities. We do not mean to imply here that accountants, bookkeepers, etc., are all extreme introverts who have no social life. On the contrary, some of the best mixers have followed these vocations. Nevertheless, such vocations do not definitely require so much of the "mixing" ability as do, say, salesmanship and personnel management.

[1] Several other factors are also important in your choice of a vocation. Chief among them are intelligence level, health, training and education required, and availability of jobs. There is not room here for an extended discussion of vocational guidance. If you need guidance along this line, some of the books listed in the bibliography on pages 205–212 will be helpful.

Assuming that they have the other job qualifications, extroverts should consider such occupations as salesmanship, news photography, reporting, police work, auctioneering, barbering, business management, personnel work, social work, nursing, banking, beauty culture, medicine, certain types of teaching, public-relations work, certain types of legal work, advertising, directing recreation, or employment as morticians, druggists, cashiers, stenographers—in general, work that brings them in contact with people much of the time.

Ambiverts can generally adapt themselves to almost any type of occupation, because they have the combined temperamental qualities of both introverts and extroverts.

REMEDIAL MEASURES IF YOU ARE TOO MUCH OF AN EXTROVERT

It may be that addressing a section of the book to the extreme extrovert comes under the heading of wasted effort. Extreme extroverts do not read books on personality improvement. They do not voluntarily enroll in classes in personality improvement. They just go on being extreme extroverts and enjoying life in a way that only they can.

Still if you are an extreme extrovert this section is for you.

In spite of all the verbal pats on the back that extroverts are getting in the psychology and personality books, nevertheless it is possible to be too much of an extrovert for your own good.

The suggestions here are addressed, not to the moderate extrovert, but to the person who is in, say, the most extroverted 10 per cent of the population. One personality survey refers to them as "dangerously extroverted." Such persons are likely to miss certain important values in life—values that have to do with introspection, philosophical reflection, and the great world of books and literature. This should not be taken to mean that you, who do not belong to this extreme 10 per cent but who are at least moderately extroverted, may pass up these suggestions. Study them carefully to see which ones and to what extent they are in line with your need.

1. Spend one evening a week in the library browsing around. Get acquainted with the types of magazines on display and the new books. Don't talk to anyone; just look around.

2. Try to read one good nonfiction book a month and one out-

standing novel. This procedure may prove tiresome at first, but stick it out. The extreme extrovert reads too little. He finds reading a tiresome chore. If you hate to read books, start in with something easy, something with an interesting plot to it. Stay away from the heavy classics until your appetite for reading is developed.

3. Once in a while go for a long walk alone, preferably in the woods or a park. Avoid talking to people. Notice the trees, plants, and flowers about you. Observe the cloud formations and other natural phenomena. Allow yourself occasionally to ask the questions, "Why is all this?" "Who put it here?" "What plan, purpose, or meaning is in it?" This may seem silly at first; but if you persevere, you may arrive at some startling conclusions.

4. Spend at least one or two evenings a month in complete solitude, seeing no one, calling no one on the telephone, communicating with no one. Just sit and think. If you can't do that, just sit. This discipline may be so unpleasant as to be actually painful; but it is good discipline for you. It will help you to build up inner resources that will strengthen you in the future.

5. Make the acquaintance of someone who is extremely introverted and shy. Try to talk to him and get his slant on life. Draw him out—it may be difficult—and get him to talk about his ideas. You have much to learn from him. You will find it hard to understand his psychology and appreciate his point of view. His set of values is so different from yours that you and he live in different worlds.

Not only should you get to know some introverts, but you should also make the acquaintance of any other personality types that differ markedly from your own.

REMEDIAL MEASURES IF YOU ARE TOO MUCH OF AN INTROVERT

If the description of the introvert on page 52 fits you perfectly, and if you rated as an extreme introvert in the test on pages 57–58, you might profitably try these suggestions.

1. Every time you go to the movies, go with someone, or better still, go with a party. Never go alone. It may be best for you to go to the movies only rarely. You might better engage in pastimes that require active participation on your part. Going to the movies is passive, solitary recreation; you need active, social recreation, rec-

reation in which you must use your muscles and mix with other people. When you have the choice of going to a movie or playing tennis, choose the tennis.

2. Accept the next invitation you receive to a dance or a party and be with someone throughout the party. Overcome your natural inclination to gravitate to the fringe of the crowd; force yourself to mix with the others. Look pleasant, talk to people, dance, do something! Don't be alone for one minute during the entire evening.

3. Introduce yourself to two complete strangers this week. Draw them into conversation. You can do this without appearing unduly bold or nervy. If you are afraid that the conversation might lag, plan in advance what you are going to say. Do you know any good stories? If not, learn five or six that haven't been worn out by frequent retelling, and have them on tap for instant use. Get a good book of stories.

4. When you go for a walk or a hike, always get one or more people to go with you. Don't walk alone. Your inclination is to do everything alone. You must resist this inclination. We know that it is sometimes difficult to find people who want to walk just when you do, but you can manage it. You *must* manage it if you want to get out of your shell of introversion.

5. Become more versatile, and you will have more opportunities to mix with different types of people. Learn several new skills listed in the versatility test on pages 121–122. Extreme introverts usually make a very low score on this test.

The hardest thing about learning new skills is getting started and moving past the awkward stage. You will have a tendency to avoid new skills like tennis, golf, swimming, and badminton, because beginners in these sports generally look so ridiculous. There are few things more awkward looking than a person just starting to play tennis. Even those who are graceful in other sports look ungainly when they begin tennis; but any normal person can overcome that gawky period and develop into a smooth player. In one season you can make amazing progress if you are coached properly and practice conscientiously. Everybody is awkward when he first tries to coordinate a new set of muscular actions, but you should forget yourself—or think in terms of the future when you will have overcome your initial lack of grace.

Business Etiquette Series, McGraw-Hill Book Company, Inc.

Some people try to find "privacy" even in an informal get-together. What kind of personality does this reveal?

In your program of increasing your versatility do not overlook the nonathletic activities, such as bridge, instrumental music, and singing. In these, as in the strenuous activities, you will appear awkward at first. But remember that the experts had to learn, too; once they may have looked as inept as you.

6. The next time you are asked to make a speech or give a report before a group, say "Yes" before you have time to think about it. Give the speech if it kills you. The mortality rate is fairly low among speechmakers, and you will feel much more self-confident after it is over.

You will have few experiences of greater exaltation and triumph than those following your first successful speech. To know that you are the focal point of attention of a group of people, to sense that your words are in some way influencing your audience, to finally walk to your seat through a stimulating shower of applause —here is a value in life, a joy, a happiness, a pleasure, a thrill, a satisfaction that you cannot afford to miss.

7. Join two or three organizations. It doesn't matter which ones you join, as long as they have lots of people in them. Attend the meetings and force yourself to participate in the group discussions.

You can start out by seconding motions—it is not necessary to stand up to do that. Then, some day, forget yourself and make a motion. The first thing you know, you can be speaking from the floor or the platform without too much difficulty.

8. Attend a convention of some sort. Conventions are usually informal, and everybody is supposed to know everybody else. It will be an easy matter there for you to introduce yourself to strangers. When you get to the convention, circulate. If it is held in a hotel, move around in the lobby and get acquainted. Don't be standoffish. Imagine yourself a fearless extrovert and try to act the part.

9. Try to get acquainted with the people who come into your immediate environment regularly: the garbage man, the newsboy, the mailman, the scrubwoman, the elevator operator, the policeman, and the taxi driver. They probably will not even notice that you are an extreme introvert.

10. Engage regularly in some vigorous sport or game: badminton, tennis, handball, swimming, basketball, hockey, etc. Do not be content to fool around with these activities. Play hard. Work up a sweat. Play until your muscles are fatigued. Vigorous games are among the finest personality developers and are guaranteed to draw the introvert out of his shell of reserve and shyness.

11. Engage in any other activity you can think of that will bring you into contact with other people. All this sort of performance will go against the grain. It is contrary to your years of conditioning and habit formation. There will be times when you will wonder if it is worth while. All the time you will have to buck your natural inclination and force yourself to meet people, to mix socially, to think in terms of other people rather than yourself.

If you persist, however, you will ultimately agree that these suggestions have been extremely worth while. You will find that life has more meaning for you and that knowing other people is, after all, pretty important.

Cycloid and Schizoid Personalities

Another classification of personalities uses the terms

1. Cycloid, and
2. Schizoid,

Cycloid persons are supposed to have cycles of moods. They experience periods of alternate elation and depression, regardless of circumstances. One week they are on top of the world, the next they are in the dumps. Schizoid people are the "withdrawn" type. They tend to live within themselves. They are frequently shy, silent, egotistical, and sensitive. You will notice that this classification resembles the introvert-extrovert classification somewhat.

Cycloid and schizoid types are sometimes broken down into four subtypes, which can be best described by means of diagrams *a, b, c,* and *d,* which follow.

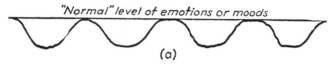

(a)

a. The people illustrated by diagram *a* impress you as being rather withdrawn, melancholy, depressed, pessimistic, and unhappy, although they periodically come up to the so-called "normal" emotional or mood level.

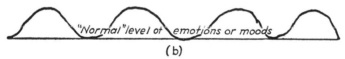

(b)

b. The people illustrated by diagram *b* are the perpetual optimists. They are hopeful, elated, excited, sometimes "hysterically happy," but drop down to the average level at times.

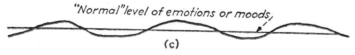

(c)

c. The type of person illustrated by diagram *c* has the reputation of being even tempered. His "emotional swing" is quite narrow. He is thought of as being "dependable" in his moods and poised in his personality.

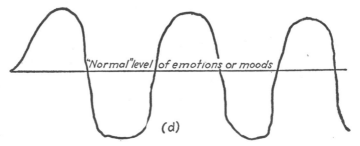

(d)

d. They type of person illustrated by diagram *d* has a wide "emotional swing." He gains the reputation of being unpredictable; you never know how he will react to things. At one time he is highly elated; at another, deeply depressed and gloomy. Psychologists call him the "manic-depressive type."

No one of these four types is the "best type" for everybody. Nothing duller can be imagined than a world in which everybody is precisely like everybody else in personality. Of course, some types are easier to get along with than others; but history shows us that all types have been able to accomplish much in the world.

Dominant and Submissive Personalities

Still another method of classification is to call people

1. Dominant, or
2. Submissive.

These terms mean just what they say. Dominant personalities lead; submissive personalities do not. The latter may, however, make their influence felt in indirect ways. Many of history's most influential personalities were by nature and habit submissive. Schoolteachers, for example, frequently rate as submissive in tests designed to measure these two factors in personality, yet teachers are extremely influential in molding the lives of children.

Dominant individuals rather naturally gravitate to positions of leadership. When an open meeting is called for the purpose of organizing a group to work toward civic improvement or what not, these are the ones who soon stand out as chairmen, officers, committee leaders, etc. The dominant man makes the motion; the submissive one seconds it, or simply votes "Yes" with the uplifted hand.

Some writers on this subject think women are more submissive than men, but we are unable to verify this from our own experience. Sometimes the facts suggest an opposite conclusion, but we should beware of sweeping generalizations in matters of this sort—for reasons of tactfulness, if nothing else.

A person's choice of his lifework should be made with his degree of dominance-submissiveness in mind. A submissive person probably will be unhappy in a vocation demanding a high degree of dominance, and vice versa.

Where do you think you stand as to *submissiveness* and *dominance?* The following test will help you decide.

SUBMISSIVENESS-DOMINANCE TEST

DIRECTIONS: Rule a form like the following one and write YES or No at the right of each number as that numbered item applies to you. Try to "feel yourself into" any of these situations that you have not experienced and answer as you think you would have reacted in the real situation.

SUBMISSIVENESS-DOMINANCE TEST			
1	6	11	16
2	7	12	17
3	8	13	18
4	9	14	19
5	10	15	20

Number of items I marked YES ....

Number of items I marked No ....

I tend to be *Submissive* ( ) *Dominant* ( ) Neither *Submissive* nor *Dominant* ( )

1. In walking down a hall or corridor where other people are present, do you usually walk close to the right-hand wall?
2. When you sound the car horn to pass or warn someone, do you tap the horn button lightly once or twice, "beep, beep"?
3. Do you ever go into a doorway or cross a street to avoid meeting someone?
4. Do you take a back seat or other unsatisfactory seat in a theater or at a meeting rather than walk down the aisle before everyone for a better seat?

5. Do you generally avoid or refuse being chairman or leader of a group?

6. Do you usually "give in" to your superiors in a discussion or an argument?

7. Do you mind very much asking a friend to lend you his tennis racket, golf clubs, skates, etc.?

8. Do you find it difficult to get rid of unwelcome salesmen who come to your house?

9. Do you feel emotionally upset if you have to ask them to leave?

10. When someone pushes ahead of you in line at a ticket window, or in some similar situation, do you "let it pass" rather than object?

11. Do you hate to sell tickets for school performances or other worthy activities?

12. When you accidentally bump into someone in the hall or on the sidewalk, are you usually the first one to say, "Excuse me"?

13. When there is an accident and other people are present, do you let someone else take the initiative in doing things?

14. Do you usually keep quiet in class or other meetings and let the others volunteer to answer questions and carry on discussion?

15. Do you get embarrassed and flustered when you speak to someone you thought you knew, only to discover that it was a total stranger?

16. When you get a serving of unsatisfactory food in a café, do you make the best of it rather than complain to the waiter or manager?

17. Do you feel that you are lacking in "sales resistance" and frequently buy things you later regret having bought?

18. Do you dread introducing yourself to strangers even when it is quite proper for you to do so?

19. Do you find it unpleasant and difficult to further your own interests and push yourself forward in your job or profession?

20. In general, do you believe you give in to people too much—that you are too submissive for your own good?

As you have probably noticed, each of the questions on this test is so worded that the answer YES indicates a tendency toward submissiveness and No, a tendency toward dominance.

Turn back to page 66 and look at the brief discussion of dominant and submissive persons.

If your answers were about evenly divided between YES and No, you are a mixed type—neither very dominant nor very submissive. Most people would make this kind of score, because most people are "average" in everything, including submissiveness-dominance. If you answered YES as many as fifteen times, you are decidedly of the submissive type; if as many as fifteen answers were No, you are dominant.

In a college in Michigan the average number of questions answered YES by 78 women students was 10.7. A group of 77 men students answered YES to an average of 9.2 items. Both groups were, on the average, neither dominant nor submissive, although some individuals answered YES to all. At the other extreme, one exceptionally dominant man answered YES to only one item!

Please keep in mind that, aside from extremes in temperament, there is nothing good or bad, superior or inferior, right or wrong about being submissive. Some of history's greatest characters were extremely submissive. One of the twentieth century's most powerful and influential men, Mahatma Gandhi, would have rated as decidedly submissive.

Being submissive, however, *can* be "bad" for you if you are engaged in a job that demands dominance. Conversely, an extremely dominant person would be maladjusted in a vocation that involved being submissive to a superior.

As we have intimated before, you should not choose a vocation on the basis of any one test. A number of different factors must be taken into consideration before an intelligent choice can be made.

But if you have the other necessary qualifications and are of the submissive type, you might consider such occupations as secretarial work, clerical work, certain types of newspaper work, library work, teaching, dentistry, millinery, dress designing, statistics, certain types of research, most of the types of artistic and literary work, bookkeeping, architecture, etc.

If you are of the dominant type and have the other qualifications necessary, you could profitably consider salesmanship, business management, politics, law, promotional work, social work, newspaper reporting, personnel work, executive positions in schools and colleges, etc.

In spite of what has been said about the value of submissiveness in certain occupations, it is possible that you may be too submissive for your own best interests. If so, you can do something about it.

If you are so extremely dominant that you offend people and give the impression of being too "bossy," something can be done about that, too. In fact, something must be done about this defect because it may be much more serious in one's occupational life, where one's work status is most important, than a little too much submissiveness is likely to be.

REMEDIAL MEASURES IF YOU ARE TOO SUBMISSIVE

If you made a high submissiveness score in the test on page 67, you should try some of the suggestions listed here. But first, turn back to the section just preceding this one and read the suggestions to the extreme introvert. Several of them apply to you. Notice especially items 5, 6, and 10. Then give attention to these additional points:

1. Walk near the middle of the hall instead of near the wall. In hallways and on the sidewalk, walk with your head up. Try to assume an air of self-assurance even though you do not feel it. Don't always be the first to give way when you meet someone.

2. The next time you accidentally bump into someone in the hall, or on the sidewalk, keep your mouth shut, and let the other fellow say, "Excuse me," first. You might even try glaring at him.

3. Practice sounding your car horn for five seconds. People will stare at you or even swear at you, but keep your finger on that button for five whole seconds. Stop being a "beepbeeper" when you drive.

4. The next time you go to church or the movies, keep walking down the aisle until you get at least five rows nearer to the front than you usually sit. Pick a seat in the middle of a row so that you will have to ask people to rise to let you through.

5. The next time an unwelcome salesman comes to your house, say politely but firmly that you don't want any of his products or his sales talk, and then close the door. No, slam it.

6. Pick out an old cracked dish that you don't want any longer and heave it against the wall so it will shatter into a hundred pieces. This will do wonders for your morale, but don't let the habit grow on you.

7. Get the job of selling tickets to some worthy benefit performance. Force yourself to approach people you don't know and ask them how many tickets they want.

8. Force yourself to speak up in class or in some other meeting when the teacher or the chairman asks for suggestions or questions.

9. The next time you are given an unsatisfactory serving of food in a café, call the waiter and insist that he bring you something better. Don't do it apologetically; act mad and insist on your rights.

10. The next time someone starts to argue with you, don't follow your natural inclination to agree with him or remain noncommittal. Argue right back at him. Stick to your guns. Stay in there and fight.

11. Seek for other ways in which you can become more aggressive, more self-assertive. Such a course of action, violating as it does your lifelong habits of giving in, will be difficult and embarrassing at times. But the discipline will be good for you. And you may find that you have gained the wholesome respect of lots of people who used to think of you as a human doormat.

REMEDIAL MEASURES IF YOU ARE TOO DOMINANT

On the *Submissiveness-Dominance Test* on page 67, did you answer No to as many as sixteen of the items? Have you ever observed that your tendency to be "bossy" and to try to run things was resented by your acquaintances? If so, it is possible that you are so dominant that people may dislike your personality.

Before you read further, turn back to page 60 and read the suggestions to the overextroverted person. Notice items 1 and 3 especially. The following suggestions may also be helpful.

1. Don't argue with people. You can never win an argument anyway. When you feel yourself being drawn into a dispute with someone, instead of fighting back at him verbally, ask him questions. What is his definition of the term you disagree on? Just what is his opinion? Will he please restate his ideas on the subject? It is surprising how little excuse there really is for arguments. Get the habit of shifting away from argument into discussion.

2. Give in once in a while, even though you are positive you are right.

3. Never, under any circumstances, allow yourself to be drawn into an *argument* with your boss or employer. Discussion, yes; but argument, never! Even if you win such an argument, you still lose. The boss will hold it against you. If you can't get along with your boss, quit him, and get another job. But don't argue with him!

4. Apologize quickly and sincerely when you bump into people, cause them inconvenience, or hurt their feelings.

5. Instead of insisting on the best seats, the best portions of food, the favored place at the convention or the banquet, force yourself occasionally to defer to the desires and wishes of others.

6. Try to be more unselfish, in general. Think oftener in terms of the other fellow, his rights, his ideas, his desires, rather than your own.

7. Look for ways in which you can agree with people. Go out of your way to be agreeable.

8. Let the others run the meeting for a change. Sit back and give the submissive boys and the introverts an opportunity to develop their personalities.

9. Remember that in the cosmic scheme of things you as an individual are pretty insignificant and unimportant after all.

Normal and Abnormal Personalities

Still another way of classifying personalities is to label them

1. Normal, and
2. Abnormal.

The difficulty here lies in agreeing on a definition of "normal." A raving maniac is certainly abnormal; a person under the influence of alcohol or marijuana is temporarily abnormal. The great German philosopher Nietzsche was insane at the time of his death; who knows precisely at what moment he ceased being "normal" and became "abnormal"? Indeed, the problem of who is normal and who is abnormal frequently puzzles even the psychiatrist.

Sometimes people who have been considered normal all their lives become abnormal under the continued strain of worry, overwork, loss of sleep, grief, illness, or anxiety. There are many persons confined to institutions for the insane who appear to be perfectly normal a great part of the time.

There is certainly a wide range of "normalcy." Sometimes people are considered eccentric, crazy, or in some way abnormal simply because their contemporaries don't understand or appreciate them. Benjamin Franklin was considered by some of his respectable acquaintances to be crazy because of his trying to get electricity out of the sky. The Wright brothers' ambition to fly in a machine was considered more than a little insane at one time. And everybody knows the reputation that settled on Columbus on account of his weird theory that the world is round.

Don't you think we ought to be careful how we arbitrarily brand people as eccentric, crazy, or abnormal?

Other Classifications

KRETSCHMER'S SYSTEM

An Austrian named Kretschmer[2] and others have found some evidence of a close relationship between body build and personality type. Tall, thin people tend to be introvert and schizoid (withdrawn). Heavy-set, roundish people tend to be extrovert and cycloid in personality.

Kretschmer sets up four types, classified as to body build:

1. *Leptosome type.* Relatively tall and thin with little body volume in relation to height. Long, narrow chests, long hands and feet. Examples—Abraham Lincoln, Woodrow Wilson, Gary Cooper. Such persons are supposed to be naturally inclined toward introversion.

2. *Athletic type.* Broad shoulders, narrow hips, well-developed muscles. Examples—most wrestlers and prize fighters.

3. *Pyknic type.* Relatively short and thickset, though not necessarily fat. Great body volume in proportion to height. Big chests. Examples—Charles Laughton, Theodore Roosevelt, Fiorello H. La Guardia. Such persons are supposed to be inclined toward extroversion.

4. *Dysplastic type.* This includes giants, dwarfs, midgets, and any others who do not fit into one or more of the first three types.

It should be pointed out that Kretschmer's theory is now being severely criticized by psychologists. Some think that it has little scientific validity. Nevertheless, it would be interesting to study your own friends and acquaintances to see whether they illustrate Kretschmer's theory.

Kretschmer, however, was not the first person to notice the connection between physique and personality. Far from it. This dialogue occurs in Shakespeare's *Julius Caesar*, Act I, Scene II.

> CAESAR: Let me have men about me that are fat,
> Sleek-headed men and such as sleep o' nights·
> Yond Cassius has a lean and hungry look;
> He thinks too much: such men are dangerous.
> ANTONY: Fear him not, Caesar; he's not dangerous;
> He is a noble Roman, and well given.
> CAESAR: Would he were fatter! . . .
> Such men as he be never at heart's ease
> Whiles they behold a greater than themselves,
> And therefore are they very dangerous.

[2] If you want to follow this up, see Ernst Kretschmer, *Physique and Character*, Harcourt, Brace and Company, New York, 1925.

This relationship between body build and temperament was observed by some of the ancient Greek writers. Very probably it was
one of man's earliest observations on his fellow man.

Do not let this body-build theory bother you too much. Above
all else, do not excuse your shortcomings by using it to prove that
you cannot do anything to overcome them. Since Shakespeare's day
many eminently successful men and women of the wrong body type,
according to Kretschmer, have lived to refute his classification.

An Older Threefold Classification

Kretschmer's system reminds us of an older classification of physique and temperament, the origin of which goes back—at least in
part—to Hippocrates, the Greek physician who is known as the
"Father of Medicine." We do not know what to call this system of
classification or who should get the major credit (or blame!) for it.
For 2,000 years, in one guise or another, it has attracted the interest
of men, probably because it sounds logical and because it is simple.
It should, however, be taken with a grain of salt!

This system sets up three main classes of physique and personality: the mental type, the motor type, and the vital type. Some
writers used different terminology and condensed the last two types
into one. For example, Hippocrates described the *habitus phthisicus*
(long-narrow build) and *habitus apoplecticus* (short-thick build).
In the nineteenth and the early twentieth centuries, however, writers and traveling lecturers generally stuck to the threefold classification.

Mental type. The mental type (according to the proponents of
the system) have the following physical characteristics: slender or
smaller than average physique, long hands and fingers, long and
narrow chest, high forehead; large frontal lobes of the brain, "fine"
features. In temperament they are supposed to be thinkers, idealists,
and dreamers. They tend to be withdrawn and live more to themselves—are poor mixers socially. They have relatively little interest
in food, bodily comfort, and luxuries.

Motor type. The motor type is described thus: big bones and
body frame, big muscles, broad shoulders, large chests, narrow hips,
big hands and feet. In personality they are supposed to be aggressive, constructive, dynamic, energetic, athletic. They are the build-
ers, the hustlers, the go-getters.

Vital type. The vital type has this kind of build: relatively small bones, large bodies, inclined toward obesity, small hands with chubby fingers, small feet, great body volume in proportion to height. In temperament they are jolly, easy to get along with. They are excellent mixers and make good salesmen. They enjoy good food, comfortable living quarters, and all manner of luxury.

Now, the thing you want to know is this: Does this system amount to anything? Is it accurate? Can you depend on it in sizing up people?

In answering these questions we should say that the psychologists haven't a very high opinion of the system. Yet, less than fifteen years ago it was used in many places as the basis of training courses for salesmen. For all we know, it may still be the basic part of a training course somewhere.

Certainly there are many fat people who are jolly and easy to get along with, who love comfort, etc. The problem is, are *all* fat people like that? Or are enough fat people like that so that you could judge them on sight and be right in, say, 95 per cent of the cases? We cannot answer these last questions. We are, however, generally suspicious of most systems that classify people arbitrarily.

Caution. A few words of caution are appropriate here in regard to all these attempts to classify human beings. You can't make one single, simple classification into which all persons will fit neatly. Human nature is almost infinite in its variety, and any attempt to force everybody into two or three pigeonholes of classification is absurd. There are too many exceptions. In some classification systems there appear to be more exceptions than cases that apply. Beware of the man, then, who assures you that everybody fits into his system.

These systems of classifying personality are simply convenient starting points in our study. A few people that you know will fit perfectly the description, for example, of extrovert or of introvert. But be prepared to find many more mixed types than pure types. While these methods of classification are not dependable in their entirety as systems, the traits on which they are based are basic to one's personality. You probably do not fit neatly into the *cycloid* or *schizoid* classification, but in some degree you probably do have moods. At times you may be a bit downhearted, pessimistic, and unhappy, while at other times you are cheerful, excited, happy, and optimistic. Or you may be a person of poise whose moods are not extreme in any direction. These moods, whether they are all one-sided or not, are important to check up on even though they are not such as to classify you as Cycloid or Schizoid. So do not brush them off too lightly.

You may not be sufficiently *dominant* or *submissive* to be classified as a dominant or submissive person. You should determine where you stand on these qualities and avoid becoming one-sided in either direction.

Some Unscientific Methods of Judging Personality

This chapter would not be complete without a description of some of the better known unscientific methods of judging human personality. We want to make it perfectly clear at the outset that these systems are misleading, inaccurate, incorrect, and entirely without scientific validity. They are described here because you will read about them elsewhere, hear lectures about them, and possibly be victimized by one or more of them.

We refer to phrenology, astrology, palmistry, graphology, and physiognomy.

Phrenology. Phrenology is a system of judging people by the contour of the head. It is based on two assumptions: (1) that each small area on the surface of the brain has a unique and separate function, such as "generosity," "self-respect," "caution," etc., and that prominence of a given area indicates prominence of the particular trait governed by the area; (2) that the exact contour of the brain, and hence the prominence of the various traits, can be accurately determined by feeling the outside of the head.

Both these assumptions are false.

Phrenologists tell us that the person with a "bump," or well-developed place, in the back of the head has a powerful love of home and of children. Scientists know that this area is concerned with vision. Phrenologists say that a certain area at the top of the head is the center for religion, and that people with high-crowned heads are religious. Scientists know that this section of the brain is a motor area which controls wiggling of the toes! There isn't a single phrenological brain center that has ever been verified by physicians, neurologists, psychologists, or brain specialists.

Phrenology should be considered as an interesting chapter in the history of psychology in much the way that the concoction of witches' broth is treated as a quaint episode in the early history of pharmacy. It's lots of fun as a parlor game, but don't take it seriously!

Astrology. Astrology is a page, and an early page at that, from the history of astronomy. Astronomy is a science; astrology is hokum.

Astrology claims to reveal the influence of the planets on the personalities and destinies of men. An amazing thing about this system is that it has fooled so many intelligent men and women in recent years, men and women who readily recognize the unscientific nature of phrenology, graphology, etc.

According to one practitioner of this modern hocus-pocus, people born under the sign of Taurus, the Bull (April 19 to May 20), are idealistic, enthusiastic, kind, charitable, and fond of money. They make good salesmen but are pretty good with machinery, too. They will be happy in a congenial occupation.

One secret of the current financial success of this system is that its practitioners (1) say so many different things about you in their "readings" that you get mentally confused and remember the ones which by chance do apply to you, and (2) say lots of favorable things about you, which you want to believe and consequently *do* believe. After all, who would dispute a man who tells him he has a tremendous intellect, a magnetic personality, and a great soul!

Palmistry. Palmistry doesn't fool so many people as does astrology. Yet at least two reputable national magazines in recent years have run feature articles on this system. While in each case the magazine refrained from endorsing the system, nevertheless, numerous readers assumed that, if magazines of that caliber featured palmistry, there must be something to it.

Of course you can learn many things about a person by studying his hands. If they are tanned, he has been in the sun. If he has calluses on his palms, he is a worker. If his fingers are yellowed, he smokes cigarettes. If grease and dirt are imbedded in his fingers, you may reasonably assume that he has been working with motors. If he has calluses on the tips of the fingers of his right hand, you can shrewdly guess that he is a left-handed banjo player.

There are many things that a doctor can tell you about your age and physical condition by studying your hands. Anthropologists can make a few deductions about your racial and family background from your hands. To a certain extent, nervousness, fear, and other emotions are expressed by the hands.

But this is not palmistry. Palmists calmly tell you that a stiff thumb indicates a proud personality. A long index finger proves you to be a most ambitious person. Square hands are a sign of a square and upright character. Long fingers reveal the artist and the musician. One even claims he can predict the number of children you will have by studying the lines at the base of your fingers!

Like phrenology, palmistry is an interesting parlor game, but it is useless in judging and classifying personalities. The only practical value it has is to furnish an excuse for holding the hand of a pretty girl. Perhaps it is worth perpetuating for this reason alone.

Graphology. Graphology is a system of telling all manner of amazing things about people by the way they write—not by *what* they write, but by the way they shape their letters, dot their *i*'s, etc. If your writing slants to the right, you are supposed to have a friendly personality. If it slants to the left, you are cautious and standoffish. Medium-sized letters indicate a kindly, likable personality. If your writing dwindles and gets smaller and smaller, you are diplomatic and tactful. Cross your *t*'s with an upward slant, and you are optimistic; a downward slant means pessimism. Make tiny *o*'s instead of dots over your *i*'s, and it's a dead give-away that your conscience is bothering you!

This is enough to give you an idea about the matter. You shouldn't take it very seriously. It hasn't much scientific respectability.

You should not confuse graphology with scientific handwriting analysis. There is a science of handwriting analysis. Men in this profession, however, are concerned with the detection of forgeries and not with the sort of thing just described.

Physiognomy. Finally we come to a system that people have used, consciously or unconsciously, for thousands of years—the judgment of character and personality by the shape of the face. Physiognomy, as it is called, was widely "practiced" in Europe and America in the middle and latter part of the nineteenth century; and a number of books were written on the subject. One of those books was published in London in 1892. Here are some of the things it taught.

"Most great men have had big noses. A man with a medium-sized brain and a large nose can do more than a man with a very large brain and a very small nose. Large nostrils denote courage; small nostrils denote fear. Nostrils which dilate and curl upwards show great pride." Incidentally, the proof of this last statement is given thus: "Horses are very proud animals, and their nostrils dilate and curl."

A big, jutting jaw is supposed to reveal an uncouth, even a criminal, personality. People with eyes set close together are cunning and sly, like foxes. People with eyes far apart, like cows, are philosophical and deliberate! This is sheer nonsense. But, if a man has whiskers, he hasn't shaved; if he has a black eye, he has walked into a door, or a reasonably accurate facsimile; if he is tanned, he has been exposed to either the sun or a sun lamp. This is, of course, common sense. There is much you can learn by studying a man's face.

Anthropologists can tell something about your racial background from your face. Physicians can tell something about your health by studying your face. Many emotional states are reflected in such reactions as pupil dilation, lip trembling, and blanching.

But the so-called "science" of physiognomy will be of no use to you.

It is a sad commentary on human intelligence that we continue to fall for these unscientific systems and annually spend fortunes on them. If you want some information about your personality, you should go to a person who is qualified to use the best means available to measure your personality. He may not tell you so many flattering things as the old phrenologist, but at least what he does tell you will be dependable.

Suggestions for Study and Discussion

1. Make a *secret* list of people you know personally but dislike. Try to analyze *why* you dislike them. Is it because of their speech and voice? Their appearance? Their manners? Their attitudes? Something they did to you or said to you? Or the kind of work they do?

2. Go over your analysis of the people you dislike and ask yourself this question: Do I have any of the traits that I dislike in others?

3. Make a list of five of your acquaintances and friends that you like best. Try to analyze *why* you like them.

4. Go over your analysis of the five that you like best and ask yourself: How many of their good qualities do I have?

5. Make a list of five of your friends and acquaintances that you

think are introverts; five that you think are extroverts; five that you think are ambiverts. Be sure you have not picked a personality type on the basis of a *single* act that suggests introversion, extroversion, or ambiversion.

6. Where do you stand as to emotional balance or "moods"? Be honest with yourself. It is the only way to improve your personality. Which of the four line graphs best describes you?

7. Are you *dominant* or *submissive?* Which of these traits may be due to an *inferiority complex* or, if not corrected, may lead to that state? Look up the expression *inferiority complex* to see just what it means.

8. Consider some of your friends and acquaintances in the light of Kretschmer's body-build theory of personality. You will not have evidence enough to prove or disprove this theory, but you may get a little evidence that will tend to support or deny it.

9. What do you think of the belief of a personnel director who says, "I can tell all I want to know about an applicant for a job by just sizing him up in a five-minute interview?"

10. Why do people spend millions of dollars a year for the quackery of *phrenologists, astrologers, palmists,* and other fakers?

11. Why do reputable newspapers carry a column or page on *graphology* and thus give credence to this racket?

12. Is an all-round, well-adjusted person likely to be classifiable as *introvert, extrovert,* or *ambivert?*

13. Would your answer be the same as to *cycloid, schizoid* types?

14. Is a *dominant* or *submissive* person likely to be a well-adjusted person in any community?

15. We hear much about the *motor* type person. Sometimes he is described as being the *manual* type. His counterpart is the *mental* or *intellectual* type. How are the two distinguished? In these types are there implications for the selection of a career? Are they always mutually exclusive? Or do some people classify in both categories?

16. Is it possible to worry too much about one's *type of personality* and too little about one's *characteristics* or *traits* regardless of their overlappings as to *type* significance?

17. Finally, how does this whole matter of personality types concern you?

Personality Reminders

1. Are you quick to judge people by their appearance?

2. Have you really tried to like people who on first acquaintance did not appear attractive to you?

3. Do you like a lot of people, or are you very "choosy" in your likes and dislikes?

4. Do you have to make intimate friends of all the people you like?

5. Have you lately noted a preference for being alone much of the time, or even on certain occasions?

6. Have you studied with other students by preference fairly often, or do you prefer to study alone?

7. Have you lost your temper lately? Seldom? Often? Under slight provocation? Only under severe provocation?

8. Have you tried to influence others recently concerning some school or other activity, or have you had a tendency to go along with proposals made by others?

9. Have you excused yourself for some shortcoming as being due to your size, or weight, or build?

10. Have you ever consulted a palmist, or an astrologer, or a phrenologist, or a graphologist, or any other similar "seer"? If so, why? Be honest. Did you believe what you were told?

11. Have you been tactful, courteous, and considerate in your dealings with others?

Special References

Link, Henry C. *Rediscovery of Man*

Cattell, Raymond Bernard. *Description and Measurement of Personality*

Fry, Clement Collard, and Howard Wilcox Haggard. *The Anatomy of Personality*

Sherman, Mandel. *Mental Conflicts and Personality*

CHAPTER FOUR

A Personality That People Admire

WE HAVE CONSIDERED certain major types of people who are properly labeled *introvert, extrovert, ambivert, cycloid, schizoid, dominant, submissive, normal,* and *abnormal.* But we have yet to consider in more detail the outward manifestations of one's personality—the specific things that cause people to like or dislike you.

What Women Admire in Men

"I should like a combination of Fred MacMurray for looks and Clark Gable for personality."

"Physical appearance counts a lot with the opposite sex. A man may not be handsome, but he can dress neatly and in good taste. Little details such as clean fingernails, white teeth, shined shoes, creased trousers, and clean linen give a man a well-groomed appearance."

"I admire a man who keeps his word. In this hectic world of to-day it is hard to tell whom to trust and whom not to. A man should show himself dependable in every way."

"When a man forgets his manners and walks out ahead of me in a public place, I don't give him a chance to do it again."

"It is embarrassing for a woman to be with a man who can't take a joke and isn't a good sport."

"I most admire a fellow who is a man's man; in other words, he must be liked by other men."

"Without ambition, in my opinion, a man just isn't a man."

"I like a man who possesses initiative but will co-operate when someone else is giving the orders."

82

"Respect ranks highest on my list of traits I admire in men—not only self-respect, but respect for the opposite sex as well."

In some such ways does the young woman of today unburden her mind when asked what traits she likes best in men.

For several years students in psychology classes have turned in reports on the subject, "Traits I Most Admire in the Opposite Sex." The reports are so much alike that one can almost predict in advance what a given group will say.

These traits, reported sincerely and in a spirit of co-operation, should furnish a pretty good picture of the specific characteristics young people of today most appreciate in one another.

Summarizing reports submitted over a period of years, one finds that young women most admire in men the following traits. They are tabulated in order of the frequency with which they were mentioned, the most frequently mentioned traits being placed earliest in the list. After each trait is given a typical student comment.

1. *Neatness and cleanliness.* "Girls like a fellow to look as though he had had a recent bath."

2. *Good manners and courtesy.* "Lots of men think good manners are out of style, but they are wrong."

3. *Cheerfulness and pleasantness.* "I had a date once with the original Gloomy Gus. Never again!"

4. *Ambition to succeed in life.* "I like the fellow who knows where he is going in life."

Thoughtfulness for the comfort of others—a mark of the good manners that will always be in style.

5. *Intelligence.* "Girls don't like a steady diet of two-dollar words in their conversation, but they like to know the fellow they're with has a lot of brain power in reserve."

6. *Honesty and uprightness.* "I can't stand dishonest and tricky people. If a fellow is dishonest in little things, I always am afraid he will be dishonest in big things."

7. *Good sportsmanship.* "I've never known a girl who didn't admire a good sport."

8. *Attractive clothes.* "We know all the fellows can't dress like the fashion plates in *Esquire,* but we like them to wear their clothes with a certain natural grace."

9. *A sense of humor.* "A good sense of humor is indispensable. It gets you over lots of rough spots in life."

10. *Use of good English.* "I am proud to be with a fellow who naturally and unconsciously uses good English."

11. *Thoughtfulness and consideration of others.* "One good way to judge a man's character is by the way he treats his mother and father."

12. *Good health.* "I like fellows who are full of pep and energy."

13. *Good posture and carriage.* "The fellow who stands up straight and walks with a springy step makes a good impression."

14. *Conversational ability.* "I like a fellow who is a clever talker, even if I suspect that some of it is just a 'line.'"

15. *Ability to dance well.* "Every man ought to be a smooth dancer. I can't see any excuse for poor, awkward dancing. The man who can't dance just doesn't count with me."

16. *Dependability.* "Give me a man that can be depended on. Most of them can't."

17. *Seriousness of purpose.* "The girls I know like a fellow to have a serious side to his personality. Life is pretty grim sometimes and all our problems can't be solved with wisecracks and light conversation."

18. *Generosity.* "Nobody likes a tightwad. Even though a girl isn't a gold digger, she likes a fellow to take the padlock off his pocketbook once in a while."

19. *Good morals.* "Regardless of all the vulgar jokes and stories that get around, girls *do* admire a man who has a high standard of personal morality."

20. *Ability to mix socially.* "I feel at ease when I have a date with a fellow who is a good mixer in society."

21. *Clean-mindedness.* "Believe it or not, girls (at least the ones I know) don't like dirty jokes. We laugh at them because we don't want to be considered too dumb or naïve to catch on, but we still prefer the fellows who are clean-minded."

22. *Broad-mindedness.* "Women like a fellow who isn't too narrow-minded and prudish."

23. *Adaptability.* "Personally, I like a fellow who can fit in with all sorts of crowds."

24. *Handsome features.* "To me, good looks aren't everything, but you can't blame a girl (other things being equal) for preferring the nice-looking fellow."

25. *Good physique.* "We still like broad shoulders and big muscles."

26. *Culture and refinement.* "You can generally tell what sort of home a fellow comes from by the way he acts. We don't use the word *culture* very much among ourselves, but I know that women like a certain amount of it in men."

27. *Good education.* "A certain amount of general knowledge is important in personality. I don't care whether a man gets it from college or from his own reading, but I admire a man who knows something."

28. *Ability to hold a job.* "Girls are pretty practical and they like to know that a man can earn a living."

29. *Poise.* "I like the kind of poise that William Powell has in the movies."

30. *A liking for sports and athletics.* "It's taken for granted that men today should show an interest in things like baseball, football, etc."

31. *High ideals.* "There is a quality in men I like that I find it hard to express. I think the term 'high ideal' is as near as I can come to it. It is the opposite of vulgarity and cheapness and selfishness. To some people this may sound corny, but nevertheless that's the way I feel about the matter."

32. *Truthfulness.* "I hate a liar. You like to feel that a man's word can be depended on."

33. *Frankness.* "A certain amount of frankness is desirable."

34. *Attractive voice.* "I like a man with a deep, rich voice. So many men sound effeminate when they talk."

35. *Reverence for sacred things.* "If a fellow makes some slighting remark or cheap wisecrack about religion, I don't like him. Even though he doesn't agree with you, he at least should respect the things you consider important."

36. *Attractive teeth.* "Attractive, clean teeth are just as important to a man as to a woman."

One young woman reflected the unexpressed wish of many women, "Let him be superior to me in all respects."

Surprisingly, one girl didn't place a great deal of emphasis on neatness. She reported, "Since sloppiness in this age is the vogue for young people, it is really best to dress as the crowd does."

Quite an array of likes and dislikes that should make men sit up and take notice.

What Men Admire in Women

Here are some sample reactions from the men's reports on desirable qualities in women.

"Neatness is necessary in order to secure attention in the beginning."

"The impression given by a girl without a trim figure is that she probably is careless as to eating or exercise. This impression is many times wrong, but nevertheless exists."

"I admire a girl's understanding of a man's financial status that might prevent his taking her to expensive places."

"A woman should have a certain amount of pride and she should be careful about the company she keeps and the places she goes."

"Rowdy girls are generally resented by men."

"Among the foremost traits I admire in women is honesty. I like a woman who will not be underhanded with a fellow."

"A girl should be agreeable and not always looking for arguments."

"I like a girl without an excess dosage of make-up."

"Beauty and a good figure are not all-important but are not to be overlooked."

Summarizing, we find the most admirable qualities in women are the following, again in order of the frequency with which they were mentioned. In each case a typical masculine comment is quoted.

1. *Neatness and cleanliness.* "A girl must be neat and clean all the time. Nothing discourages romantic ideas more than the discovery that the object of your affections has dirty ears!"

2. *Intelligence.* "I like a girl with some gray matter in her skull."

3. *Courtesy and good manners.* "Girls ought to learn how to act in public. It embarrasses a man if the girl doesn't know which fork or spoon to use in a café, or if she has bad manners in any situation."

4. *Cheerfulness.* "Nobody loves a sourpuss."

5. *Co-operativeness.* "I like a woman who co-operates cheerfully in whatever is going on. Whether it's the problem of getting up decorations for a party, or collecting the stuff for a steak roast, we men admire women who pitch in and help."

6. *A good figure.* "There's no getting away from the fact that masculine attention is attracted by a good figure. I should think that all women would know this, but some of them are pretty careless about appearances."

7. *Smartness in clothing.* "Most of the girls I know have some clothes sense. The ones that don't have two strikes on them before the game starts. With all the ads and magazines and such stuff that are available to women, they should all be able to dress nicely."

8. *Sociability—the ability to mix.* "I like a girl who knows how to manage introductions smoothly and how to mix easily with people."

9. *Beauty.* "A man likes to be seen with a pretty girl though he knows beauty is only skin deep, as the saying goes, and there are other more important personality traits."

10. *Nice complexion.* "So many girls fail to take proper care of their complexions."

11. *Fairly good education.* "We like a girl who isn't completely dumb about what's going on in the world."

12. *Honesty.* "A girl who is dishonest is simply a minus quantity with me. As far as I am concerned, she is the square root of zero!"

13. *An even temper.* "Give me a girl with a dependable disposition."

14. *Trustworthiness and dependability.* "To me the most important trait in a person of the opposite sex is trustworthiness."

15. *Attractive, clean teeth.* "I saw a girl the other day with lipstick on her teeth! It was terrific. Why don't women think about those things?"

16. *Conversational ability.* "We like a girl who can carry her end of the conversation, and I don't mean just a 'line.'"

17. *Unselfishness.* "We dislike girls who have the 'gimmes.' A girl should think of others part of the time."

18. *Good posture and carriage.* "Girls should stand up straight and learn to walk gracefully."

19. *Restrained use of cosmetics.* "Deliver me from gooey lipstick."

20. *Thrift.* "You like to think a girl knows how to manage her own finances and not be wasteful of her parents' or her own money."

21. *Loyalty.* "A woman should show some loyalty to her school, her organizations, and her friends."

22. *Self-reliance.* "Men like to do little things for women, but don't like a woman who is helpless and can't do anything herself."

23. *Health.* "Plenty of sleep and outdoor exercise are good for any woman's personality."

24. *Ability to cook and keep house.* "I like a girl who can be the domestic type if, as, and when the occasion demands it."

25. *Liking for outdoors.* "The girl who can fit in on a fishing trip, hike, etc., is going to have lots of friends."

26. *Good sportsmanship.* "A girl should be a good sport at all times."

27. *Truthfulness.* "Some girls seem to have little regard for the truth in their social lives. We men like a girl whose word can be relied on."

28. *A sense of humor.* "A sense of humor is a lifesaver to a girl lots of times."

29. *Punctuality.* "I'm pretty sick of having to stall around waiting for her to get dressed to go to dances and parties."

30. *Poise.* "Poise comes only through having many different kinds of experiences."

31. *Naturalness—absence of affectation.* "I can't stand a girl who tries to be an imitation of some high-brow movie actress."

32. *Frankness.* "A girl should be open and aboveboard. She can be frank without being crude."

33. *Tact.* "Saying the right thing at the right time is important in personality."

34. *Broad-mindedness.* "The Sweet Alice Ben Bolt type went out of circulation when Dad was a boy."

35. *Good morals.* "A fellow likes to feel that the girl he goes with is morally above reproach."

A word of warning should be sounded in connection with items 2, 11, and 22. College men like women who are intelligent, educated, and self-reliant, but not *too* intelligent, *too* well educated, or *too* self-reliant. Men, even college men, love to play the role of the superior male. Their natural vanity causes them to resent and dislike the woman who proves herself their superior.

Clever girls are well aware of the advantage of being relatively helpless and dependent at the proper time. If a girl is an expert tennis player, she should not defeat her male opponent too badly— that is, if she wants him to play with her again.

Good health—an asset in the development of a pleasing and well-balanced personality—pays off in alertness, cheerfulness, and good posture.

Business Etiquette Series,
McGraw-Hill Book Company, Inc.

The woman golfer may to her advantage dub a few shots when her score threatens to hurt the ego of her male companion. Naturally this sort of thing must be done with finesse. Its purpose would be defeated if the man were to suspect her motives.

It may surprise you that health was twenty-third in the list. In some other surveys, students have placed health first. We suspect that many students consider it much more important than its position in the list suggests, but that they take health for granted. Many students did not mention it at all.

Certainly health is vital in the well-balanced personality. Grouchiness, moodiness, touchiness, and other undesirable traits may frequently be traced to health difficulties. The need for glasses may make you squint and frown and thus distort your features. Loss of sleep not only shows up in your facial expression, but also makes you irritable. Infected teeth or tonsils may sap your energy. Poorly balanced diet may damage your complexion and make you less attractive. Perhaps some of *your* personality weaknesses can be traced to poor health habits.

Look at the two lists again and notice how similar they are. Four of the first five traits in each list are identical: neatness and cleanliness, good manners and courtesy, cheerfulness, intelligence.

Don't these lists give us a pretty good idea of the sort of personality people admire? Of the kind we should want to have?

Inasmuch as most of us are not particularly pretty or handsome, the ranking of these items should be encouraging. The men placed beauty in ninth place, and the women rated handsome features twenty-fourth. Beauty, handsomeness, and perfect physique are clearly not the most important factors in personal attractiveness.

Other Personality Surveys

A few years ago *Good Housekeeping* magazine queried 223 women, "What is the first thing you notice about a man?" Ninety-five per cent of the answers had to do with grooming. Neatness, cleanliness, correct clothes, good figure, good carriage, clear skin, a nice smell, nice-looking hair, and clean fingernails were the items most stressed. Old-fashioned courtesy also received honorable mention. The characteristics exemplified by Ronald Colman, Gary Cooper, and Robert Montgomery were quite satisfactory to the ladies.

Dr. Donald A. Laird reported on a study he made at Colgate University Psychological Laboratory of traits which are of the greatest importance in determining the attitude of other people toward us. According to Dr. Laird, these forty-one are the most important traits that definitely make most people like us:[1]

1. Be depended on to do what you say you will do.
2. Go out of your way to help others.
3. Do not show off your knowledge.
4. Do not let yourself feel superior to your associates, and be careful lest they get the impression that you do.
5. Do not reprimand people who do things that displease you.
6. Do not exaggerate your statements.
7. Do not make fun of others behind their backs.
8. Do not be sarcastic.
9. Do not be domineering.
10. Keep your clothing neat and tidy.
11. Do not be bold and nervy.
12. Do not laugh at the mistakes of others.
13. Do not take a vulgar attitude toward the opposite sex.
14. Do not be inclined to find fault with everyone else.
15. Do not correct the mistakes of others.
16. Do not tell jokes at the expense of those listening.
17. Do not try to have your own way.
18. Do not lose your temper.
19. Do not take the initiative in an argument.
20. Smile pleasantly.
21. Do not talk continuously.
22. Do not pry into other people's business.
23. Do not keep your end of the conversation up by asking questions.
24. Do not ask favors of others.
25. Do not be out of patience with modern ideas.
26. Do not be flattering.
27. Do not talk about your personal troubles.
28. Do not spread gossip.
29. Do not be dignified.
30. Be cheerful.
31. Be enthusiastic.
32. Do not mispronounce words.
33. Do not be suspicious that people are trying to put something over on you.
34. Do not be lazy.
35. Do not borrow things.

[1] Donald A. Laird, *How to Make People Like You*, pp. 18–26, Blue Ribbon Books, Inc., New York, 1933.

36. Do not tell people what their moral duty is.
37. Do not tell people what is right and wrong.
38. Do not try to get people to believe as you believe.
39. Do not be a political radical.
40. Do not talk rapidly.
41. Do not laugh loudly.

This is an imposing list. It is the result of a study by an experienced researcher. It no doubt represents the answers to the researcher's query addressed to an adequate sampling of normal people. But some of the items may not be universally true under all circumstances. You should not immediately resolve never to do or be any one of the things advised against.

Take, for example, No. 19. Arguments are not all bad, and at times you should take the initiative in starting or carrying on one where both desire to clarify some issue. You should not resolve never to argue a point, but you should do it in the right spirit and end it when the other party reacts in the wrong spirit.

Take No. 23. Why not "keep up your end of the conversation by asking questions"? Is there objection to keeping up conversation? What better way to keep someone interested than to ask questions he can answer? Of course, don't "pry into other people's (secret) business," but be assured that most people like to talk about their business or occupation.

What about No. 24? Why not, at the proper time and of the proper person and in the proper way, "ask favors of others"? We all do it. But, of course, don't overdo it. We shouldn't want a friend who couldn't ask a favor occasionally. Would you? You will be lucky indeed if you get through life without asking favors.

Is No. 25 quite sound? Suppose certain "modern ideas" do violence to your sense of right and wrong. Can you avoid being "out of patience" with them? Should you avoid taking issue with people on moral questions at times?

No. 26. Why not "be flattering" at times? Not dishonestly so, of course. But when the truth about someone is very flattering, tell it by all means.

"Do not be dignified," says No. 29. Of all things! What is the matter with that trait? Not overbearing, of course, but truly dignified as the occasion may demand.

No. 37. There surely are times when people have to be told what you regard as "right and wrong." Else how can you or anyone else help to make the right prevail. You shouldn't be intolerant of the views of others, but you should have convictions and stand by them on proper occasions.

What can be more absurd than No. 38, about trying to get people to believe as you believe? No, of course we shouldn't set out to convert everyone to our way of thinking, but we need not wholly abstain from trying to win people over to our side on matters of real concern to them or the community in which they live. In fact, trying to do so may be a good way to clarify our own thinking. In the process we may change our views to the benefit of all concerned.

The point of these comments is that in many of the forty-one statements about traits that make people like us there should have been qualifications.

Anna Steese Richardson reports in the *Woman's Home Companion* the results of a questionnaire sent to a large number of girls in high school and junior college. In describing the replies to questions about the type of men they admire most, Miss Richardson relates:

A girl wants a boy to have good manners. He needn't be rich, handsome, or intensively educated. . . . In the matter of looks most of the girls shy away from the handsome man but they demand neatness and cleanliness. . . . To get one of these girls, you boys have to be honest, ambitious, and moderate in your habits. . . . Practically all of them want a cheerful disposition, a sense of humor, and a sociable nature. . . . Not a single girl who answered the question asked for a rich husband. . . . Thirty-five per cent express a preference for a college graduate husband and most of the girls ask for a good education in high school or business college and the ability to use it intelligently.[2]

In 1936, Dale Carnegie wrote a book which proved to be a best seller in the nonfiction field. The name of it is *How to Win Friends and Influence People*. If you haven't read it, buy a copy for your personal library. Read it through at one sitting, and then reread it slowly over a period of two weeks, carefully noticing the very specific rules that Mr. Carnegie sets forth for making people like you and for getting along with people.

Mr. Carnegie lists these "Six Ways to Make People Like You":[3]

[2] Anna Steese Richardson, "American Girl, 1940," *Woman's Home Companion*, March, 1940, p. 31.
[3] Dale Carnegie, *How to Win Friends and Influence People*, p. 146, Simon and Schuster, Inc., New York, 1936.

1. Become genuinely interested in other people.
2. Smile.
3. Remember that a man's name is to him the sweetest and most important sound in the English language.
4. Be a good listener. Encourage others to talk about themselves.
5. Talk in terms of the other man's interest.
6. Make the other person feel important—and do it sincerely.

If you will do these six things, people will come to think of you as a more delightful person, a person with an extremely attractive personality, unless other traits are too bad.

Note that No. 1 goes contrary to the one in the previous list where you are cautioned against asking questions about other people's interests—their "business." How better can you "become genuinely interested in" anyone than by learning more about what he does and in what he is interested? And how better can you encourage others to talk about themselves (No. 4)? Or "talk in terms of the other man's interests" (No. 5)? Or "make the other person feel important" (No. 6)?

Get the true import of No. 3. In conversation use the name of the one you are talking with, not merely to tickle his ego, but to fix his name in your mind by associating it with his voice and face. But don't overdo it. It can become monotonous. Interviewers on the radio repeat the name of the one addressed more often than is desirable in normal conversation for the purpose of keeping the parties straight in the minds of listeners who do not see the speakers. On television this is not so necessary.

Implied in what has been said about things that people admire in us are many traits that are very much disliked by people whose respect and good will we want. It should be helpful to consider such traits in a more positive way.

Personality Traits Most Disliked

From time to time, over a period of several years, we have asked students in our classes to hand in a list of their "pet peeves," things they consider most irksome and annoying in the people that they know. The papers are always interesting, although there is a certain sameness in the reactions from year to year.

It would appear that certain attitudes, habits, and physical characteristics are very generally disliked. These same attitudes, habits, and physical characteristics are mentioned not only by our students from year to year but also in similar studies made by other teachers and psychologists. Here are some sample student reactions.

"One of my pet peeves is the fellow (or girl) who tells dirty stories—stories in which the dirt far outweighs the humor."

"The people I can't stand are the people who borrow cigarettes, borrow clothes and fail to take care of them, are too sloppy, and too loud."

"I hate to see people smoke just to try to impress others, when they do not enjoy smoking."

"I dislike teachers who keep me waiting while they do something unimportant. This is not to be confused with long waits for teachers who are really busy doing worth-while things."

"I don't like people who make statements about themselves which you are supposed to contradict and turn into a compliment. Usually you feel like a hypocrite for doing so."

"Pet peeves: perspiration odor, halitosis, tobacco breath, dirty shirt collars, food stains on clothes, messy-looking hair, teeth that show food particles when the person talks or smiles."

"I can stand crybabies whose faces are teary, but I hate salesgirls who call me 'dearie.' "

"Things I can't abide: girls with 'gaposis'; boys with sloppy sox; anybody with dirty fingernails; girls with crooked hose seams and run-over heels."

"It seems to me that everyone can develop a pleasing voice. My pet peeves are people with shrill, rasping voices and people who never know when to use the soft pedal."

"I don't like people who start every sentence with I (like this one), and who always drag the conversation back to themselves. Especially when I want to talk about myself!"

"Faultfinders and chronic criticizers are my pet peeves. Some people apparently can't see anything but the wrong thing."

"I dislike a 'wet blanket'—one who never wants to take part, and is afraid to laugh. There are some people who can't even take part in one sport or game fairly well."

Dr. William Moulton Marston made an interesting report in *Good Housekeeping* on men's reactions to certain habits and traits of women.[4] His conclusions were based on reactions from a large number of men, studied over a period of years.

Dr. Marston gives women this "Decalogue of Don'ts":

1. Don't wear styles that men consider queer.

2. Don't neglect the romantic illusion. Men are disillusioned by such things as hair curlers, leaving hairs in the washbasin, awkward position and posture, frequent talk of ailments, unattractive noises in the throat, too much lipstick at kissing time, make-up in public.

3. Don't fail to answer a man when he speaks to you. This inattention seriously offends a man's ego.

4. Don't nag a man. Men flee to office, club, other women—anywhere but where the nagger is.

5. Don't tell off-color stories or use bad language. Some women think these things are smart; most men resent them.

6. Don't show jealousy. Men, married or single, abhor a jealous woman; man's defense is usually deception or concealment.

7. Don't compare your male companion unfavorably with another man. How would *you* like to be told that Mary is smarter, or more ambitious, or better looking, or more successful financially?

8. Don't give the orders—in a restaurant, for example, or a cab. Etiquette gives the man these rights. He is resentful when they are ignored.

9. Don't giggle, shriek, or otherwise be loud in an effort to attract a man's attention; he feels embarrassed and thinks you're silly.

10. Don't spend joint funds or household money for purposes not approved by your husband; men feel cheated, righteously indignant.

Several years ago a group of students were asked to write down the traits that they most disliked in their grade-school and high-school teachers. The traits most frequently mentioned were unfairness, use of ridicule and sarcasm, harshness in discipline, dissatisfaction with the teaching profession, dowdy appearance, lack of sympathy with pupils, quick temper, impatience, nervousness, and peculiar mannerisms of speech and movement.

Harry W. Nock, Office Manager of the Service Department of E. I. du Pont de Nemours & Company, Inc., in an address made this criticism of the personalities of young business-school graduates:

We find lack of confidence or the opposite, too much egotism; unwillingness to co-operate with others; disagreeable disposition; too much talking; malicious gossip; foolishness; neutral personality; untidy or freakish appearance; body odors; gum-chewing; lack of tact; bad manners; in-

[4] William Moulton Marston, "The Reaction of Man to Woman," *Good Housekeeping*, February, 1941, pp. 26–27.

sincerity; disloyalty; unwillingness to accept instruction; untruthfulness; disobedience; intolerance; lack of pliability.[5]

This criticism by Mr. Nock is very much like a number of others in business magazines and books. It also agrees in the main with oral reports received directly from several business executives. Make no mistake about it. You are being watched from the day you go on the job. You are being judged, evaluated, and criticized, and usually in terms of mature people's standards. Your earnestness and application are being judged in terms of the earnestness and hard work that your employer himself gives to his job.

These various lists of do's and don'ts are most imposing. They are very much alike. They deal with *specific acts* rather than with *composite traits*. They may be a bit bewildering at first. While it will not do to say that all can be covered in the single word *character*, it may be said that they can be, and should be, boiled down into a relatively few *composite traits* that can be made the basis of effective trait development. It should be worth our while to attempt such a condensation before going too far in this course. We shall do so a little farther on. In the meantime, keep in mind the fact that the things listed as do's and don'ts are but the *manifestations* of *traits* and in most cases not really *personal traits* as they stand.

Suggestions for Study and Discussion

1. Make a list of the personality traits that you like best in people of your age and sex. Do the same for the opposite sex. Compare your lists with the lists in this chapter.

2. Jot down the qualities and traits you most admire in people about the age of your parents. Are they the same as the traits you listed under No. 1?

3. Ask several older people to name the qualities and traits that they most admire in young people of high-school and college age. Compare them with your own lists and with the lists on pages 83–88 in this chapter.

4. Jot down a list of your own "pet peeves"—things that you most dislike in

    a. People of your own age and sex.

    b. People of your own age but of the opposite sex.

    c. Older men.

    d. Older women.

[5] Harry W. Nock, "As the Employer Sees It," *Eastern Commercial Teachers Association Thirteenth Yearbook*, 1940, p. 36.

Analyze your lists and try to determine honestly whether or not these "pet peeves" are justified. Ask yourself these questions: Am I in any way responsible for any of them? Are any of them due in part at least to my own peculiar likes and dislikes? Are some of them due to the fact that I haven't taken into account the difference in ages between younger and older people? Just try to be sure that the things you dislike in people are things that really are bad before you keep them in your lists.

5. A criticism made by older people regarding high-school and college students is that they have poor manners. Is this a just criticism? Don't simply answer "Yes" or "No." Consider what really are *good manners*, and then think over what you have noticed about the manners of students about you—and your own conduct of course. List the essentials of good manners as you think over this problem.

6. What traits have you observed in office clerks, receptionists, and secretaries that you think hurt the business of their employers?

7. What do you think are the most important personality traits for a secretary? A teacher? A salesman? A student association president? A bank teller?

8. In the *Good Housekeeping* survey referred to women were asked "What is the first thing you notice about a man?" "Grooming," nearly all replied. Does this mean that grooming is the all-important thing from the standpoint of making and holding women friends? Or of getting a wife? Two words in the question asked by *Good Housekeeping* must be noted carefully if you are to appraise the findings accurately. What are those words and their implications?

9. Do you want to consider the implication of the authors' comments on the wisdom of playing a little dumb or unskilled when a woman wants to win and hold the affection of a man? Remember, it is *personality development* we are dealing with. Where do the alleged female arts and wiles come in?

10. Go back over the Laird list of traits that make people like us and see if you can supply qualifications wherever needed before accepting them as guides for your personality development.

Your Personality Notebook

1. In nearly all cases eminently successful people are in general likable people. They have many friends. They inspire confidence. They are the kind that just naturally are turned to by others for needed help of one kind or another. They do not possess the traits listed as those we dislike in others. You want to be that kind of person. You can be. Perhaps you are, right now. At any rate "eternal vigilance" here, as in other aspects of life, must be exercised if you are to become and/or remain the kind of person other good and reasonable people like.

In your notebook write out a brief appraisal of where you stand from the point of view of being liked by your associates in and out of school. Answer honestly these questions: Where do I stand as a likable personality? What are my strong points? My weak points? Am I growing more or less likable? Or remaining stationary?

Single out for immediate attention the characteristics that most obviously prejudice people against you. Do something about them. Leave space for later ratings and comments as from time to time you feel you have made some real progress in the right direction.

This project is a little different from one requiring a checking of specific traits from time to time. Attitudes and actions, as well as traits, are to be taken into account and to be appraised in terms of their effect on your associates.

Your notebook is your work sheet. Don't neglect it. Use it as a stimulus to active personality development and keep in it a record of progress toward your goal.

2. You have been asked about traits you have observed in office workers that may be costly to their employers. It well may be that you can recall few, or even no, such instances of bad conduct. It will be helpful to you to become observant of office, store, and other workers with whom you come in contact with a view to noting good and bad conduct in the performance of their duties. Make a note of these instances in your notebook. Bring them to the attention of your instructor who may want to discuss them in his class. Always ask yourself this question: Would I act like that under similar circumstances? Have I ever done so?

One of the most fruitful aids to personality development is the habit of *observing good and bad conduct in others,* but of course only when the observer is honest in appraising his own conduct in terms of what he observes, and diligent in bettering his own score.

Personality Reminders

1. Did you refrain from passing on that juicy bit of gossip that you picked up today?
2. How do you know you do not have halitosis?
3. Have you said something nice about someone lately?
4. Have you brushed your hair fifty strokes today?
5. Do you have on a clean shirt, blouse, or sweater *now?*

Special References

Carnegie, Dale. *How to Win Friends and Influence People*
Fosdick, Harry Emerson. *On Being a Real Person*
Hepner, Harry Walker. *It's Nice to Know People Like You*
Laird, Donald Anderson. *How to Make People Like You; Why We Don't Like People*
Stratton, Dorothy Constance, and Helen B. Schleman. *Your Best Foot Forward*
Stephenson, Margaret Bennett, and Ruth Millett. *As Others Like You*
Archer, Alma. *Encyclopedia of Beauty and Charm*
Tead, Ordway: *Art of Leadership*

CHAPTER FIVE

Four Steps in Personality Development

THERE ARE FOUR essential steps in the process of personality improvement:

1. *Realization* of the need for improvement.

2. *Motivation,* a strong desire for improvement.

3. *Inventory,* an analysis or stock taking of strong and weak points.

4. *Systematic plan* for improvement.

These four steps are fundamental. They are always the first steps in the right direction when anyone undertakes to improve himself. Often, however, a person may not be aware of having taken all of them. Many who have achieved gratifying self-improvement have not realized that their improvement has been accomplished through these four stages.

Now let's see briefly what each step involves.

Realization of the Need for Improvement

The man who considers himself perfect (and there are too many men and women in this category) never takes even the first step. It never occurs to him. Conceited people are convinced of their own immediate perfection. For them life holds no possibilities or opportunities for modification in the direction of improvement. God made them perfect and then broke the mold.

We dare say you who are pursuing this course are not in the classification just mentioned. It is possible, though not probable, that a perfect creature might treat himself to an intellectual slumming party to see how "other people" can be improved.

You have, consciously or unconsciously, taken the first step. You realize that there is room for some improvement.

There are people, however, who, although they are not at all conceited, have yet never realized any need for improvement. They would try to improve if they suspected their need. Their personality faults have never been called to their attention.

We are, as a rule, the last ones to recognize our own faults. Our friends and acquaintances see them, but hesitate to mention them. Robert Burns certainly stated a universal need when he said,

> O wad some Power the giftie gie us
> To see oursels as ithers see us!
> It wad frae monie a blunder free us,
>   An' foolish notion. . . .

Particularly hard for us to realize are those little mannerisms, habitual gestures, nervous jerks and twitches, pet expressions, and the like, which grow on us gradually and become fixed. One professor in college always used the word "paramount" when he meant tantamount. It was one of his favorite words. By actual count he used "paramount" eleven times in one lecture! Nobody had the nerve to correct him.

One teacher pulls at his necktie, another twirls a watch chain, another gestures continually and pointlessly with both hands. One person may tug at an ear lobe, another may suck air noisily through his front teeth, while another bites his nails.

The safest thing for you to do is to assume that you have some of these annoying habits and then set out to discover what they are.

Instead of saying, "Does my personality need improving?" it might be better to say, "My personality *does* need improving. Now, in how many areas does it need improving? Where should I begin?"

In connection with this subject, it is interesting to note how frequently personnel directors in colleges and universities find cases of serious personality maladjustments among students.

One study of over 1,000 college juniors and seniors revealed that at least half of them were having emotional difficulties serious enough to prevent them from realizing their highest potentialities in life; and approximately 10 per cent had personality maladjustments serious enough to warp their lives and, in a few instances, to cause mental breakdowns unless they were properly treated.

In an Eastern girls' college, over a period of one year, the freshmen students brought to the personnel bureau 200 problems of five different types. All these young women realized the need for improvement.

In a large Midwestern university, out of 104 juniors and seniors, 85 suffered from severe timidity, stage fright, or self-consciousness; 74, from feelings of insecurity and inadequacy; 72, from problems arising from inability to get along with their parents; 55, from problems relating to love affairs; 14, from problems in the field of religion; and 14, from inability to choose their careers.

From a survey of thirty-five Methodist colleges with a total of 3,515 students, it was found that some of the personal problems causing the most trouble were getting acquainted with the opposite sex, fear of failure, inability to get along with instructors, timidity, and worry.

Motivation

You know people who take the same attitude as one student did when he said, "Oh, I realize I need improvement—I know I'm far from perfect—but so is everyone else. I have lots of company. Anyway, it's too much trouble." This attitude of apathy, the point of view that "what you say is all right, but it takes too much effort," has held back thousands from the advancement they should have made in their professional and personal lives.

We know several store clerks who have ample ability to be store managers, but they will not take the necessary steps to develop their personalities.

The world is full of people who drag out their days in work far below their real capacity just because they are too shy, too much convinced that they have an incurable "inferiority complex," too afraid, or too apathetic to try to develop their latent powers.

Self-improvement is not easy. It involves holding to an ideal for a long time. It involves breaking old habits and establishing new ones. It sometimes involves revolutionary changes in established ways of thinking and behaving. We do not condemn a person who prefers to take the easy way. That is his privilege.

There is another objection to the idea of self-improvement and personality development. A good friend recently said, "Your plan of personality improvement, like all the other plans, tends to make people artificial. It takes away their naturalness and substitutes a phony culture no deeper than an application of nail polish. I would rather be myself."

This friend has missed the point entirely. And he is also saying something that he does not believe or live up to at all. Being a college graduate, he must have spent some sixteen years attending educational institutions. For what purpose? To stay the same? To retain his so-called "naturalness"? Hardly! He spent sixteen years improving his knowledge, skills, and attitudes, for such is the avowed purpose of schools and colleges. Yet he balked at the idea of carrying his program of improvement on to a logical conclusion and developing himself in an area that is frequently neglected by educational institutions. His position, from the standpoint of logic and common sense, is untenable.

Anyway, we are not advocating a veneer of good manners or a set smile or a Pollyanna attitude toward the world. If you have read thoughtfully to this point, you have already realized this fact.

Motivation which is strong at first frequently lags with the passing of time. That is why the program of improvement suggested in Chapters Seven, Eight, and Nine sets up immediate, easily attainable goals at first. The achievement of a minor improvement acts as an incentive to spur one on to further changes. It is always better to have a series of minor achievements, which can be attained one at a time, than to set up one big, glorious goal which may appear unattainable in a short while, when enthusiasm has waned.

Human motivation is a complex thing and sometimes a baffling puzzle. We act from many motives, some of them apparently native, or inborn, and some of them acquired, or learned. There are many ways of classifying motives and many different lists of motives. We have never seen a list that was complete.

It is not our intention to try to give anything resembling a complete list of human motives. We shall, however, list a few common motives that can be utilized in your program of self-improvement. You should tie up as many of these motives as possible with your plan of personality development, so as to offset that almost universal motive, the dislike of doing anything that doesn't have to be done.

Here, then, is a list of some motives that you will bring into use to keep you working toward a better personality.

THE DESIRE TO BE ATTRACTIVE TO THE OPPOSITE SEX

This motive appears to be present in most people between the ages of four and one hundred and four. It is present among the young and the old, the married and the unmarried, the pretty and the homely, the serious and the frivolous, the bright and the dull. This motive has been given various names by different writers, but no matter what the name, the motive is the same. We like to have the opposite sex admire, look at, seek, and in general, be attracted to us. This is one of the strongest motives we have. It can be brought to the support of a personality improvement program. Whoever improves his personality will then naturally be more attractive to the opposite sex than before.

We don't mean to imply that you will be besieged by great swarms of ardent admirers if you read a book on personality development. You will not have to hire a secretary to handle your fan mail. But if you get rid of your worst personality weaknesses and develop a more attractive self, you will, in your own sphere, be better liked by persons of the opposite sex.

THE DESIRE FOR PUBLIC APPROBATION

We want to be well thought of. We want people of both sexes and of all ages and walks of life to approve of us. We want people to like us and speak to us and be friendly toward us. One of the worst things that can happen to anyone is to be ostracized.

In English secondary schools the custom used to be to "put in Coventry" any student who incurred the dislike of the others. For one to be "put in Coventry" meant that nobody looked at him, spoke to him, walked with him, sat near him, or had anything to do with him for the duration of his "punishment." It was an extremely effective way of keeping the boys on their good behavior.

We will do almost anything to make people approve of us. Think how many times you have done something, or refrained from doing something, because of "what people might think." Certainly this motive influences us in one way or another every day of our lives.

This is a motive that should strongly bolster your resolution to improve yourself. You will naturally receive more public approval if you rid yourself of traits that the public dislikes and develop traits that the public likes.

THE DESIRE FOR SECURITY

We like to feel safe—safe in our persons and safe financially. One of the commoner worries of Americans is the worry about insecurity. We devise all sorts of ways for making ourselves safer, farther away from possible harm. We have locks on our doors, put money in the bank, join unions, and, as a nation, maintain an army and a navy— all for the sake of feeling more secure.

We have already pointed out how an agreeable disposition helps to make a person more secure in his job. You can help keep up your enthusiasm for the arduous task of personality improvement by remembering that a well-integrated personality does add to your security in a number of ways.

THE DESIRE FOR POWER

Man wants power—any and all sorts of power. His wish for power is expressed in a number of ways. One common way is in accumulating wealth. Another is in seeking positions that are supposed to bring prestige and high standing. We want to feel important. We buy a 100-horsepower car when we could just as well use a 65-horsepower machine. We like to show off our influence, our titles, our college degrees, our various offices, our loving cups and trophies—anything that bolsters our feeling of power and importance.

We wear coats with padded shoulders to suggest physical strength. We mail all our friends copies of the paper with the story of our election or promotion to a higher position. We insinuate that we have a pull with the governor or our senator, even if we have not. If we haven't any power, we daydream about being powerful and influential.

An improved personality will increase your influence (and therefore your power) over people. It will open up avenues of promotion and advancement in your job or profession, and thus bring you more power.

Thus you see that in improving your personality you will be satisfying, at least in part, some of the most powerful urges that

human beings have. An improved personality will make you more
attractive to the opposite sex, will bring you a greater degree of
public approbation, will help you in achieving more security, and
will be a means to greater power.

A Personality Inventory

It is a good idea to find out just where you stand before launching
your program of improvement. What are your strongest points?
Your weakest? Where do you anticipate the greatest difficulty? In
what ways are you already far ahead of your friends and associates
in personality?

These questions are not always easy to answer. We have already
seen how difficult it is to recognize even our glaring personality
defects. There is no magic mirror that will reflect for you the traits
that others see in you and dislike. You will certainly need some
assistance in taking your personality inventory.

The ideal place to answer these questions is in a class in personality improvement and under the guidance of a psychologist or
a teacher trained for this sort of work. Your instructor will supplement the tests in the next chapter. From all these tests and surveys,
you can get as clear-cut a picture as can be had of your own personality.

*Are you systematically try-
ing to improve your personality? An inventory of your
strong and weak points will
help.*

Even if one is not enrolled in a class in personality improvement, it will be useful for him to test himself and compare his scores with scores made by other people. This type of introspective analysis will, of course, be accompanied by a certain margin of error, but on the whole, it can be rather effective; that is, it can be effective if he is honest with himself in writing the tests. Most personality scales and surveys, whether self-administered or given by a psychologist, depend for their accuracy directly on the willingness of the person to play fair with himself.

The next chapter is made up largely of tests and scales on which you can rate yourself. The accuracy of your personality inventory will depend on the accuracy and fairness with which you write these tests and scales.

Do not be satisfied to end your inventory with the tests. Even though they may reveal a number of unsuspected personality faults, do not stop there. Ask yourself, "Are there any other weaknesses that I should remedy, any personality weaknesses not indicated by the tests?"

A Systematic Plan for Improvement

With an outline of your strong and weak points before you, the next question is what to do. The general idea, of course, is to keep up the good work in your points of superiority and to do something constructive about your weaknesses.

Benjamin Franklin, in his *Autobiography*, describes a system of personal improvement that he carried out over a period of years, apparently with considerable profit to himself. Franklin made a list of what he considered the thirteen most important qualities that a man should possess: temperance, cleanliness, industry, order, etc. Instead of trying to improve himself in all thirteen areas at once, he took one trait and concentrated on improving it for one week. At the same time he kept a record of the number of times he exhibited faults in the remaining twelve areas.

After a week's concentration on the first trait, or quality, he would spend a week improving the second trait in the list. Again he would keep a record of the times he showed faults in the other twelve traits.

In this manner he undertook to go through the entire list, trying to perfect himself eventually in all thirteen areas.

You may wish to take a tip from Franklin and concentrate on one particular phase of personality at a time. This may be a sound procedure for you, although some people prefer the tactic of trying to improve every weakness every day.

Perhaps you can strike a happy medium between these points of view. It may be best to devote some time each day to as many different areas of self-improvement as you can, while concentrating on one particular area. For example, you might concentrate on grooming and appearance for a number of days and, at the same time, try to improve your versatility, overcome stage fright, be more tactful, and so on through all the deficiencies you need to work on.

We do not intend to leave the impression here or anywhere else that personality improvement can be neatly rounded out in, say, six weeks, or a semester. Personality improvement is something that should continue indefinitely. None of us will ever be perfect. There always will be something more to accomplish. It is true you may be able virtually to remake yourself in three months of concentrated effort. You may be so much changed and improved that friends who haven't seen you during that time will hardly recognize you. But unfortunately we have a tendency to relapse. Without the strictest self-discipline and continued effort we may slip back into our old ways, especially if those old ways represent habits of many years' standing.

This fourth step in personality improvement is the hardest one. It is the test of motivation and of character. It takes perseverance, tenacity of purpose, and self-discipline. But this is the step you must work on assiduously if you are going to attain the kind of personality that is your goal.

Suggestions for Study and Discussion

1. Is it true that many, if not most, people do not realize their personality defects? On what do you base your answer? How about yourself?

2. Of those who do recognize their personal shortcomings, what proportion go on without doing anything to correct them? This neglect may be due to what? Laziness? Failure to consider defects important? Ignorance as to how to go about correcting defects? Or just plain *inertia?* (Be sure you know the meaning of this word. It plays an important part in life.)

3. Consider the things that may motivate one in trying to improve one's personality—those that should interest you in particular.

4. Where must one begin the task of improving one's personality? By reading about it? By picking out the easiest remedied defects? Or the harder ones?

5. Why adopt a plan for improving oneself and sticking to it? Why not just stop and tackle each single major defect as it crops up occasionally in one's daily conduct?

6. What should be your first steps in this task? Have you taken at least some of them?

Your Personality Notebook

In the preceding chapter we dealt with traits that we *like* and traits we *dislike* in others. Here we are dealing with traits that we believe have *really retarded people* in their careers, and with traits of our own which we regard as *really beneficial* or *harmful*. Traits we like or dislike in others may or may not be really good or bad in themselves as they apply to us individually.

1. On a new page in your notebook write this heading: "Some People Whom I Have Observed."

List a few older people, under fictitious names, who have not succeeded in a big way; people who seem to have worked hard but who still seem to be about where they have been a long time. Of course you are not an expert judge of the reasons for their little or no progress. So don't come to any final conclusions. Just see if you can spot in their conduct, attitudes, or views any of the defects you have previously listed or studied as being responsible for failure or near failure, or at least less than a full measure of success—shyness, inferiority complex, fear, slovenliness, overaggressiveness, egotism, etc. Don't try to analyze fully the character of the people you select. Merely concentrate on one or two outstanding characteristics which may have kept them from realizing their full potentialities in their fields of service.

2. Head another page as follows: "My Own Superiorities As a Personality."

List what you regard as your own outstanding qualities in comparison with others of your age and sex. Be honest. Be conservative. Don't be overmodest. You have some such qualities. Everyone has. Merely trying to single them out will help you. Leave space under each trait for future notations. A few lines will do.

3. From day to day be on the alert for evidences of the rightness of your listing of your outstanding good characteristics. Note such evidences very briefly under the proper trait in your listing. Such observations as a check on your estimate of your strong points will in themselves be vitally important factors in your attempt to better your personal traits.

4. On another page list a few, say not more than four or five, of your weaknesses in comparison with others of your age and sex. Again be honest, but don't be overcritical. You have weak points. We all have; some

of us even after years of conscious effort to weed them out. Leave space for future notations, say a half dozen spaces.

As evidences of the rightness or error of your estimate of your weak points come up in your daily conduct, note them under the proper trait in the space left for that purpose. This watchfulness over your conduct in itself is an excellent personality developer—if you do something about what you observe.

Note carefully: You must *work at* the business of personality development, not merely study and talk about it, if you really mean to improve yourself.

Personality Reminders

1. Have you gone out of your way today to be helpful to someone?
2. Are your fingernails clean and neatly trimmed *now?*
3. When did you last polish or clean the shoes you are now wearing?
4. Have you been tactful today?
5. Is there any dandruff on your shoulders *now?*

Special References

Laird, Donald Anderson. *Increasing Personal Efficiency*
Leeper, Robert. *Psychology of Personality and Social Adjustment*
Marsh, Hattie M. *Building Your Personality,* Second Edition
Ruch, Floyd Leon, and others. *Psychology and Life*
Thorpe, Louis Peter. *Personality and Life*
Vaughn, Gwenyth R., and Charles B. Roth. *Effective Personality Building*

CHAPTER SIX

Appraising Your Own Personality

No DOUBT, AS WE have gone along with our study of personality, you have been mentally noting your own good and bad points. We all have both kinds, you know. You are now far enough along to begin a more complete inventory of your own personality. For this purpose a number of tests and *rating scales* are given to help you to single out traits that need special attention.

In taking these tests you should try to be perfectly frank and honest. Base your answers on *facts* that you know about yourself. It may be all right in certain situations to fool other people, but don't kid yourself.

Check List of Fifty Physical Characteristics That Hurt Your Personality

Frequently we offend others unknowingly. The list of harmful physical characteristics given on pages 112 and 113 was compiled from the results of hundreds of answers to the question, "What physical traits keep people from presenting a good appearance and hence hurt their personalities?"

DIRECTIONS: Rule a sheet in your notebook like the form on page 112. Five or six spaces for checking will do to allow for that many rechecks. Place a check opposite the corresponding number for each item in the list which applies to you.

This checking is for your own use only. So, don't spare yourself. Only an honest facing up to the facts will help you overcome what is wrong.

HARMFUL PHYSICAL CHARACTERISTICS						
Item Number	Dates					
	Sept. 20					
1						
2						
3						
4						
5						
6						
7						
8						
9						
10 to 50						

Number of checks . . . .

1. Dirty fingernails
2. Dirty hands
3. Beard
4. Excessive make-up
5. Powder smears or dabs
6. Unshined shoes
7. Dirty, dusty shoes
8. Body odor
9. Halitosis
10. Too few baths
11. Yellow or unclean teeth
12. Food between teeth
13. Visible blackheads
14. Pimples on face
15. Dirty neck
16. Dirty ears
17. Greasy hair
18. Dirty scalp
19. Dandruff
20. Hair too long
21. Ragged fingernails
22. Dirty shirt
23. Soiled underclothes
24. Dirty collars and cuffs
25. Baggy trousers or skirt
26. Soiled suit or dress
27. Runs visible in hose
28. Hose seams crooked
29. Holes visible in hose
30. Run-over heels
31. Inappropriate clothes
32. Stoop shoulders
33. Slouchy walking
34. Awkward posture
35. Hair not combed
36. Greasy skin
37. Gaudy fingernails
38. Broken shoestring
39. Buttons missing
40. Tie poorly tied
41. Tie crooked
42. Tie wrinkled
43. Collar wrinkled
44. Clothes fitting poorly

45. Dirty handkerchief
46. Too much perfume
47. Wrinkled suit or dress

48. Soiled, dusty purse
49. Torn gloves
50. Dirty gloves

These items are not all of equal importance. Hence, unless each is given a relative value no dependable score can be arrived at. Furthermore there is some overlapping for the sake of emphasis. "Too few baths," for example may be the cause of "body odor," or "halitosis," and not an offensive condition in itself. Surely "ragged fingernails" are not quite so bad as "dirty" ones. The former *may be* due to brittleness of the nail, while the latter *is* due to carelessness. A "crooked tie" may be temporary and even unknown to the wearer, but a "poorly tied" one probably is due to neglect or indifference. Thus it should be seen that it is not a *score* we are after in this checking. It is for the purpose of bringing out into the open the physical characteristics that need attention.

These items are very personal. You, and you alone, can do something about them if you find that you have been careless as to your personal habits to an extent that may offend your associates.

It has been said by one authority that if you check fewer than five items, you are neater and better groomed than the average college student. But if you check between five and ten items you are below average in neatness and should do something about it now.

The same authority goes on to say that if you check between ten and fifteen items, you probably have a reputation for being unkempt, dowdy, and physically unattractive. Also, that if you check more than fifteen, you are in pretty bad shape and should take drastic action to remedy your defects.

It all depends on two things: (1) how the "average college student" really measures up against this yardstick, and (2) which items are checked. We all tend to make some allowance for the defects of dress and general appearance of school and college students. We should consider whether or not the standard with which you should compare your physical-appearance status is that of average business and professional people.

We also should expect that you will have to do your checking more or less in groups, because what causes one of these defects tends also to cause others. For example, if you find it necessary to check dirty fingernails, you probably will agree that this is caused

What negative qualities of personality are represented here? Are you guilty of any of these defects?

by indifference or carelessness which also will force you to check dirty hands, dirty neck, dirty ears, and dirty scalp. If you have to check unshined shoes, you probably also will have to check dirty or dusty shoes, broken shoestring, dirty gloves, and other items due to neglect. If you are content to wear a dirty shirt, you probably will be equally indifferent as to dirty collars and cuffs, baggy trousers or skirt, soiled suit or dress, runs in hose, wrinkled tie, and other similar items.

It all comes down to this: There is no particular *score* that will tell you much more about yourself than will any other score, since nearly all these items reflect carelessness and indifference as to one's personal appearance. Surely, if you check six or eight of the items, each of which is indicative of serious neglect, you should be very much concerned. Remember, every item is a personality defect *in the eyes of other persons. Every one of them can be eliminated. Every one should be. Here's the $64 question:* Are you willing *to try* to eliminate the grooming defects that apply to you? On your answer and determination to act accordingly may well depend your success in those fields of life that matter most—occupational, social, and home.

Determine to make your next checking of this list a more satisfactory one, no matter how good this first one is.

Start now! Pick out some defects that can be eliminated at once—dirty hands, dirty fingernails, dusty shoes, poorly tied tie, crooked tie, etc. Don't wait a minute. Next, attack the ones that can be eliminated as soon as you get a moment at home—unshined shoes, dirty shirt, soiled dress, runs in stockings, dirty gloves, etc. And those that simply require physical effort—stoop shoulders, slovenly walk, awkward posture, etc. Just see how quickly some of these defects can be made to disappear. And what a difference their going will make! Go this far, stick to it, and the rest will be easy. But watch your step! Every hour of every day!

Habits That Handicap and Attitudes That Antagonize

The items listed here are based on the results of hundreds of answers to the question, "What habits and attitudes cause you to dislike people?"

DIRECTIONS: First prepare a form like the following one. Then check each item in the TRUE or the FALSE column as it concerns you. Columns are included for future checkings to determine whether or not you are progressing in your personality development. Be honest! Don't kid yourself. You cannot kid anyone else!

HABITS THAT HANDICAP AND ATTITUDES THAT ANTAGONIZE									
Item Number	First Check —— Date	True	False	Second Check —— Date	True	False	Third Check —— Date	True	False
1									
2									
3									
4									
5									
6 to 50									

Number TRUE ....   Number FALSE ....

1. I talk in a too-loud voice in public.
2. I make audible sounds while eating or drinking.
3. I use profanity when I am angry.
4. I sometimes appear in public under the influence of alcohol.
5. I pick my nose.
6. I belch audibly in public.
7. I put my feet up on tables and seats.
8. I hawk (cough) up phlegm and spit it out publicly.
9. I sneeze and cough in the presence of others without covering my mouth and nose with a handkerchief.
10. I remain seated when talking to an elderly person who is standing.
11. I rush through doors, into elevators, etc., without consideration of the rights and feelings of others.
12. I am egotistic and conceited.
13. I am convinced that my opinions are usually the only correct ones.
14. I am habitually too grouchy.
15. I am the "crybaby" type. I "can't take it."
16. I am too quick tempered.
17. I feel that I am inferior to most people.
18. I am too serious most of the time.
19. I am too frivolous and giddy.
20. I am a typical "smart aleck," a "wise guy."
21. I am narrow-minded and intolerant.
22. I use foul language, "gutter talk."
23. I yawn audibly and visibly at lectures, in class, or in church.
24. I am a habitual and confirmed gossiper.
25. I am a liar. My word frequently cannot be relied on.
26. I have a habit of tardiness.
27. I am careless and frequently fail to speak to friends and acquaintances.
28. I am frequently sarcastic.
29. I am sometimes dishonest in little ways.
30. I am rude and discourteous.
31. I am usually selfish, thinking of myself first.
32. I am a habitual borrower.
33. I am careless of other people's property.
34. I am stingy—a "tightwad."
35. I talk too much.
36. I am a human clam—don't talk enough.
37. I am usually lacking in tact.
38. I think practical jokes are great fun.
39. I am mentally lazy.
40. I habitually put things off.
41. I am no good as a conversationalist.
42. I am deceitful and tricky.
43. I have no sense of humor.
44. I have no ambition to succeed in life.

45. I use tobacco to excess.
46. I am a careless automobile driver.
47. I interrupt other people's conversations.
48. I have little nervous habits and mannerisms that are habitual.
49. I frequently "pass the buck." I am unwilling to assume the responsibility for my own acts.
50. I think religion is a "racket" and use every opportunity to criticize the church.

In this test, every answer of TRUE indicates a personality defect in the eyes of people of culture. Some defects are naturally more serious than others. But each offends.

If you marked fewer than eight items TRUE, you are less likely to offend than the average person. If between nine and fifteen statements are TRUE for you, something should be done about it soon.

If you marked more than fifteen as TRUE, you alienate and antagonize people in large droves. You find it hard to get along with friends and associates. You find it extremely difficult to make new friends.

Look again through the items you marked TRUE. In every case you will find that *the defect can be remedied.* Are you interested enough to try? Pick out the easy ones for attack first. Then those that may take a little more time. And so on through your TRUE list of defects of which you now are conscious.

In the test you have just taken you must have marked some of the items TRUE, meaning that some bad habits must have been recognized. If you didn't, you are either a paragon of all the virtues, a self-deceiver, or a prevaricator. Do the following five things and keep everlastingly at them if you wish to improve yourself where defects are noted.

1. Look at your notebook and see what your score is.

2. On a separate sheet of paper or, better still, in a pocket notebook for easy reference, jot down every item that you marked TRUE.

3. Try to analyze these bad habits and attitudes. Which ones have you been engaging in simply because it never occurred to you that they hurt your personality? Which ones can be most easily remedied? Which ones do you think you will have the most trouble trying to overcome?

4. Take the one item you think can be most easily remedied and try to remedy it *now.*

5. Keep the list in a handy place so that you will be constantly reminded of your personality weaknesses. As you eliminate or master each one, cross it off the list. Keep up the good work until every one is gone. Don't be discouraged when you occasionally relapse into your old ways of thinking and doing. Keep trying. There isn't a personality defect in the list that can't be either completely mastered or greatly modified in the direction of improvement.

Recreational Versatility

Today the world looks for versatility in people, not only as to the jobs they know how to handle, but as to the other things they can and like to do. You are judged by your versatility to a considerable extent. Your personality growth is directly affected by participation in games and other recreational activities. Furthermore, recreation is one of the factors which will play a big part in making successful life, career, and other adjustments. Few people realize this early enough to give it proper attention as they prepare for their lifework. In fact, many are likely to look on recreation as something to be obtained furtively, or as something which is not consistent with their more serious work. This attitude toward recreational activities is a survival of an earlier day when people didn't play regularly because there was so much work to do, so many chores always waiting to be done, such long hours of work, so few opportunities for enjoyment, and a general lack of appreciation of the fact that "all work and no play makes Jack a dull boy" is something more than a copybook motto.

In earlier times, most people lived in the country and tilled the soil for a livelihood; now, the majority of people live in cities and villages. Then, reading, an occasional party, a picnic now and again, fishing, and visiting relatives were about the only diversions which adults indulged in during the few spare hours that were not required for their duties. Now, there are scores of things to do. Movies, television, radio, automobile trips, clubs, golf, and a dozen other adult games all compete for one's leisure time. There are expensive recreational activities and inexpensive ones. No one is beyond the reach of more things to do than there is time to enjoy them. So it has come about that nearly all people play more or less.

Courtesy Great Northern Railway

Personality growth—and health—are directly influenced by wholesome recreational activities.

Hence the importance of giving some thought to this matter early enough to include it as a part of preparation for vocational life.

There are recreational activities which lessen one's vocational efficiency; there are others which increase one's ability to do work. It also is true that what is good for one person may be bad for another. Bowling, for example, may cause Jones too great physical fatigue, while it may "pep up" Baker for the next day's work. Each must find out for himself just what is best.

Then, too, some recreational activities require too much time—far more than can be afforded. Thus time that is needed for work is taken. While recognizing the importance of play, one should remember that for most of us work comes first—at least a reasonable amount of it. And everyone should save time and energy enough for the things that his job requires of him.

Some people find that a change of work rests them quite as much as does play; others require the complete change which comes only with the elimination of responsibility. Those who divide their time among several jobs may require less recreational activity. But few there are who do not benefit most from putting work aside regularly for play.

Some forms of recreation can be enjoyed by oneself; others must be enjoyed in association with other people. Some people like quiet, restful games like solitaire; others like competitive games. Merely being with people may rest you, but tire me. So each must evaluate his individual needs and select what does him the most good.

Recognition of the need for recreation has led to emphasis on *hobbies* for everyone. A hobby is something outside one's regular employment which one likes to do just for the fun of doing it. Everyone should have a hobby. Many people do but don't know it. The greatest benefit is obtained from a hobby which has been selected because of a deep interest in it and the joy which is derived from it. So, every young person should try to develop an interest in some activity to which he can turn in the moments when he is not employed or otherwise engaged in some work or service for himself or others.

When you work, work hard; but not too hard. When you play, play hard; but not too hard. Be moderate in all you do. Don't overdo anything. Know the limit of your powers and keep within it. Work, not because you must, but because you like to work. Play for the same reason. Divide a goodly amount of your time between these two things and you may hope for a long and useful life.

Right now as you approach school-leaving time and a job, check up on the things you like to do and see if one of them can become a hobby that will serve your recreational needs in the years ahead. If you find something that might serve in this capacity, polish it and develop an even greater interest in it, so that you may receive the greatest benefits from it. Label it "My Hobby," and stick to it until you find something better, as you may, with more experience in life and with your vocation permanently chosen.

But be sure that there is no conflict between your job and your hobby; that your hobby doesn't ride you instead of your riding it. This happens when one devotes too much time to a hobby. Quite as much harm can result from overdoing this hobby business as can come from the "all work and no play" habit. Be the master of your own life and let no influence, not even a hobby, keep you from doing what your own best judgment tells you is good for you.

The mechanization of industry, commerce, homemaking, and agriculture have freed much time for activities outside one's regular employment. Consequently, with so much leisure time on hand one needs to consider how it may be used to the best advantage. In many schools students are being prepared for the wise use of leisure time. Few schools consider leisure-time activities as having anything to do with vocational training. It must be remembered, however, that how a person spends his leisure time will have an important bearing on how well he does his daily work. Hence these two types of training cannot be wholly divorced without lessening the effectiveness of each. As a part of any program which seeks to train for vocational efficiency, there should be included courses or activities which focus attention on a well-planned recreational program to accompany plans for a successful occupational career.

The Newton Activity Survey

As a point of departure in your further development of recreational interests, it should be helpful to survey your present accomplishments. For this purpose prepare a form like the one on page 122. Check each activity that you can do fairly well—well enough to get by in the average group as has been clearly demonstrated by participation in it. Space for these checkings at intervals are provided. You should add new ones from time to time.

1. Dance
2. Play bridge
3. Play at least one other card game
4. Play the piano
5. Play one other musical instrument
6. Swim
7. Row a boat
8. Play tennis
9. Play golf
10. Use at least one kind of firearm
11. Drive a car

Item Number	Date	Skilled In	Could Learn	Date	Skilled In	Could Learn	Date	Skilled In	Could Learn
1									
2									
3									
4									
5									
6									
7									
8									
9									
10									
11									
12									
13									
14									
15									
16									
17									
18									
19									
20									
21									
22									
23									
24									
25									
26									
27									
28									
29									
30									
31									
32									
33									

ACTIVITY SURVEY

Score ....
(Number of checks times 3)

12. Build a campfire
13. Raise a garden
14. Cook a meal
15. Make a speech in public
16. Act as toastmaster at a banquet
17. Engage in archery
18. Ice or roller skate
19. Operate a typewriter
20. Ride a bicycle
21. Fish with rod and reel (fly or bait casting)
22. Act in a play
23. Sing, solo or in chorus or glee club
24. Do rough carpentry and household repairs
25. Knit, crochet, or do fancy needlework
26. Ski
27. Play football
28. Play basketball
29. Play baseball (hard or softball)
30. Ride horseback
31. Bowl
32. Play ping-pong, or table tennis
33. Play badminton

Your score is the number of checks multiplied by three. The average score of a group of 130 men and women students in a Michigan college was 69.

At another time in the same college, 97 men students made an average score of 63.21; and 85 women students an average of 51.15. The average for the 182 men and women together was 57.58.

In a college for women in North Carolina, 115 students averaged 60.1, with the juniors and seniors making slightly higher scores than the sophomores.

Compare your score with these averages. If you made a score of less than 57, you are less versatile than the typical college student.

Have you ever known a young man who seemed to consider his good looks sufficient reason for expecting everyone to like him? Or a girl who tried to get by on beauty alone—or clothes—or family reputation? You probably have, and you have found that such a personality is far from attractive. Except for some serious physical disability, is there any good reason why you should not learn to do most of the things on the list?

Some of these activities have more personality-developing value than others. For instance, swimming is a better personality builder than operating a typewriter. Competitive athletics and physical-activity games participated in with other people are more valuable than things that you usually do alone. Bridge will develop your personality more than fishing, especially if you go fishing alone; ping-pong is better for you than carpentry. Probably the best personality developer in the list is social dancing.

One way to make yourself more attractive and more acceptable in the social and business world is to learn to do things. You can if you want to. It may be hard at first. If you shrink from physical activity, you may shy at outdoor games. If you like physical activity, you may reject card games. But you can, if you will, *develop* an interest in activities far beyond that which comes to you quite *naturally*. You will be surprised and pleased at the number of new things you can learn to do well. And you most likely will enjoy them, too, since we usually like what we do well quite as often as we do well what we like.

Look over again the items you did *not* check. Are there some skills in the list that *you could have acquired* if you had been interested? Are there some that you could learn *now?* Remember that every activity listed has some development value. Go back through the list and write YES after each activity you think you can learn within the next year.

Reading Ability and Habits

How you read and what you read will have a most important bearing on your personality and general attractiveness in the eyes of most people. It has been said that "reading makes the full man" while "writing makes the exact man" and "conversation makes the ready man." One who has good reading habits has much to think and talk about. He can hold his own in almost any conversation so far as the range of his knowledge goes. The habit of writing things to fix them in your memory is equally important. Practice in conversing with people is necessary to develop the readiness that will get the conversational ball started and keep it rolling. Having a fund of knowledge, being able to call it up at will, and being at home in conversation with your associates are quite essential elements of an attractive personality.

We have a Survey of Reading Habits for you (page 127). It

deals with *what* you read. But before going on to that, we wish to raise this question. Can you read? Sounds silly, doesn't it? It isn't, though. Suppose we consider this matter further before brushing it off.

Ability to read is a great asset to young people just starting out in life. With books, newspapers, and magazines by the score in almost every home, those who cannot read lose much enjoyment in life; and yet there are many people in this great country who have never learned to read. A country of universal education and yet citizens who cannot read. What an astounding fact!

But it was not of these unfortunate people that we were thinking when we started to write this message. It was of the thousands of boys and girls now in school, and other thousands of adults, who are known as "nonreaders"—people who have had more or less educational opportunity, but who for one reason or another have never really learned to read. Many scientists are striving to find out just why it is that some people never seem to master the relatively simple art of reading, and thus fail miserably in their school work; how young people can drop out of school without their teachers suspecting that they were failing because they were nonreaders; and what teachers can do to remedy this situation.

The "nonreader," of course, may be able to puzzle out ordinary words, or stumble through a printed page. But he takes no end of time to do it and rarely makes much sense out of the words he laboriously repeats to himself. Thus the primary aims of reading are not achieved—knowledge and pleasure.

Now, of course, you are not a "nonreader"; but can you really read? Have you mastered the art to the point where you can quickly and accurately extract from a printed paragraph exactly what the author wished to convey to you? Or do you hesitate as you read? Fail to grasp the meaning of any but the simpler sentences? Glide over hard words or unusual construction? Find that while you have recognized the words one by one you are not quite sure of the writer's message? Finally, do you have to read the words several times before you have captured the complete thought?

Are you one of the fortunate ones who "see at a glance" just what a paragraph contains? Who have what is called a "photographic mind" which instantly registers the meaning of an ordinary paragraph without carefully noting each word it contains? Good eyes, an alert mind, plenty of practice, and a good vocabulary are essential to the achievement of this much-prized ability.

This high degree of reading skill is not indispensable to success in business. But few, if any, nonreaders ascend very far up the ladder of success in the business world. Even to win and hold an office position of moderate importance one must be able to read well. Hence the very great value of this art.

Just where do you stand as a reader? You should find out. If you rate high, you are to be congratulated. If you rate low, you need not be discouraged; that is, if you have the determination to remedy this defect. For each reading defect, there is a reason. For most of these defects, remedies are available. Teachers of English know about them and should be able to help you.

But learning to read well is not the end of your reading problem. Choosing the right matter to read is quite as important. What we really are is in some measure dependent on what we read. If we read only jokes and humorous stories, we are likely to become jokesters; and habitual jokesters rarely achieve any appreciable degree of greatness. If we read only tragedy, we are prone to become morose; and nobody wants a gloomy person around. If we read only emotional stories, we may become emotionally unbalanced; and unstable people are shunned by all. If we read only serious, educational matter, we are likely to become preoccupied and untrustworthy workers. So we must avoid too great concentration in the subject matter of our reading if we would develop the attributes required by workers of the world.

There is another thing about reading in its relation to success in business. Every young worker who hopes to advance to a position of importance in business must read, read, read. If you would know the past of the business concern with which you are connected, you must read about it. If you wish to learn about the history of the kind of business in which you are engaged, you must read. If you would be informed as to the factors which will affect your business in the future, you must read. If you aim to keep posted on occupational trends in your field, you must read. If you want to earn a reputation for alertness and occupational intelligence, you must be able to read and carry out instructions. In short, if you really want to achieve success in whatever field you are engaged, you must know all about that field, and all the worth-while knowledge about it is stored in printed pages which you must read and understand.

So we ask, "Can you read?" On your answer, and what you do about the matter if your answer is, "Not very well," may depend your future as a business man or woman.

A Survey of Reading Habits

DIRECTIONS: Rule a form like the one on page 128. Place a 2 in the first column in Part I, headed *Regularly* for each magazine you read regularly, and a *1* in the first one headed *Occasionally* for each magazine you read only occasionally. Answer the two questions in Part II in the two last columns.

Part I

1. The American Home
2. The American Magazine
3. The American Mercury
4. The Atlantic Monthly
5. Better Homes and Gardens
6. Christian Century
7. Collier's
8. Coronet
9. Cosmopolitan
10. Country Gentleman
11. Esquire
12. Fortune Magazine
13. Good Housekeeping
14. Harper's Magazine
15. Hunting and Fishing
16. Ladies' Home Journal
17. Life
18. Look
19. Mademoiselle
20. McCall's
21. The New Yorker
22. Newsweek
23. Parents' Magazine
24. Photoplay
25. Popular Mechanics
26. Redbook
27. Science Illustrated

28. Reader's Digest
29. The Saturday Evening Post
30. The Scientific American
31. Time
32. Today's Health
33. Vogue
34. Woman's Home Companion

(Add any others that you read)

35. ——————————
36. ——————————
37. ——————————
38. ——————————
39. ——————————
40. ——————————

Part II

How many daily newspapers do you read *regularly?*

About how many books have you read in the last year? (Do not count school textbooks and required school reading.)

You should read *at least* three magazines and one daily newspaper regularly. It is quite common today to find business and pro-

	Part I				Part II	
			Check later for growth		No. daily news-papers read regularly	No. books read last year
Item Number	Regularly	Occasion-ally	Regularly	Occasion-ally		
1						
2						
3						
4						
5						
6						
7						
8						
9						
10						
11						
12						
13						
14						
15						
16						
17						
18						
19						
20 to 40						

A SURVEY OF READING HABITS

Magazine Reading Score ....
(Sum of all 2's and 1's)

fessional men and women who read regularly fifteen to twenty-five magazines.

Book-reading scores vary greatly. Some students read 250 books a year; others read none. The average for a group of 300 college students was twelve books, exclusive of textbooks and required reading assignments. Some teachers read two books *every day*.

You cannot develop a charming personality through the mere reading of magazines and books. On the contrary, if you spend too much time reading, you may miss many opportunities for improvement through social contacts. Nevertheless, a certain amount of reading is essential to the well-balanced personality in modern society. Reading expands your mental horizon, keeps you posted on world events, and steps up your ability as a conversationalist. There is certainly no *disadvantage* in being well informed.

Do not use as an excuse the old chestnut, "I just don't have time to read." We knew a man once who was a United States senator and a college president at the same time and yet read at least one good book a week. No matter how busy you may think you are, you can find some time for reading.

A final word should be that you should not only learn how and what to read, but you also should use different methods and rates for different kinds of reading. Read retentively what is likely to be useful to you in your job or profession. Read less so for pleasure and relaxation. Somewhere between the two intensities read for general information as to what is going on in the world. The whole point is develop several reading habits, not just one. Don't read for retention what you are willing to forget. Don't skim through what you want to remember. Don't treat difficult and easy reading matter just alike. Know what you are reading for and read accordingly, but *read!*

Famous Persons Test

Your adjustment to literate society depends to a great extent on your knowledge about people who are famous. This is a matching test to see how many well-known persons[1] you can identify.

DIRECTIONS: Prepare a form like the one on page 130, and place the numbers in Column 2 in the appropriate parentheses in Column 1.

[1] With the rapid change of world affairs, some of these persons may have abdicated, been assassinated, or changed their jobs before this book gets into print. Such changes, however, need not affect the worth-whileness of the test, inasmuch as all the persons listed have been famous for several years.

FAMOUS PERSONS TEST

COLUMN 1	COLUMN 2
( ) Joe Louis	1. News commentator, radio and screen
( ) Grantland Rice	2. Wrote *Grapes of Wrath*
( ) Walter P. Chrysler	3. Pugilist
( ) Lawrence Tibbett	4. Radio comedian
( ) Lowell Thomas	5. Eminent violinist
( ) Fred Astaire	6. Mexican muralist, artist
( ) John Steinbeck	7. Psychologist
( ) Margaret Mitchell	8. Expert on cancer
( ) Edward Steichen	9. Former Dictator of U.S.S.R. (Russia)
( ) Diego Rivera	10. Physicist
( ) Lily Pons	11. American photographer
( ) Edward L. Thorndike	12. Soprano on screen, stage, radio
( ) Alexis Carrel	13. Prominent Negro leader
( ) William Mauldin	14. Dean of American sports writers
( ) Arthur H. Compton	15. Wrote *Gone with the Wind*
( ) Maude Slye	16. Baritone, radio, stage, screen
( ) Walter White	17. Dancer; stage and screen actor
( ) Joseph Stalin	18. Physician; wrote *Man the Unknown*
( ) Fritz Kreisler	19. World War II cartoonist
( ) Jack Benny	20. Automobile manufacturer

For key to correct answers, see page 214
My score ——
(*Score* is the number correct)

If you get fewer than ten right, you will find yourself at a considerable disadvantage in conversation with informed people when the subject of persons in the news comes up.

If you got fewer than five right, just try to be a good listener until you catch up on your reading.

If you got all twenty right, don't get swelled up—it is an easy test. If you have a high magazine-reading score, you will do well on this test.

Of course these twenty persons are not necessarily the most important or most noteworthy in the world. This test could be extended to include 250 names if space limitations did not prevent. Why not look up accounts of those that you didn't know? That will be as good a start as any in your program of becoming better informed.

A Test of English Usage

A serious deficiency in the field of grammar and word usage may handicap you in your professional advancement. This doesn't mean that you must be letter-perfect in your speech habits. But it does mean that you should not make those common mistakes that distract attention from the topic under consideration, and in many cases irritate people who use good English. The doctor who said, "You aren't photostatic," dropped a peg or two, even professionally, in the eyes of some of his hearers. The saleswoman who said, "Them Dorothy Dodd shoes haven't come yet," had to know more than the other saleswomen about leather, shoes, people, and feet to hold her job.

The businessman who closed nearly every letter with "Anticipating an early reply" got by despite the wrong use of that big word because most people also misuse it. But don't count too much on that fact to get you by where wrong words are used.

The tricky sentences that follow are but a sampling of those you are bound to use and hear. They are given here to emphasize the need for attention to this matter and to help you to appraise your own possible need for improvement in grammar and word usage.

DIRECTIONS: Rule a simple form like the following one. In the parentheses after each number, write the letter representing your choice of the word that correctly completes each sentence.

TEST OF ENGLISH USAGE

1. ( )	10. ( )	19. ( )	28. ( )
2. ( )	11. ( )	20. ( )	29. ( )
3. ( )	12. ( )	21. ( )	30. ( )
4. ( )	13. ( )	22. ( )	31. ( )
5. ( )	14. ( )	23. ( )	32. ( )
6. ( )	15. ( )	24. ( )	33. ( )
7. ( )	16. ( )	25. ( )	34. ( )
8. ( )	17. ( )	26. ( )	35. ( )
9. ( )	18. ( )	27. ( )	36. ( )

1. He went with Tom and (a) *me* (b) *I.*
2. Was it (a) *them* (b) *they?*
3. Between you and (a) *I* (b) *me,* these are the facts.
4. I saw Anson and (a) *him* (b) *he* yesterday.
5. May Tom and (a) *I* (b) *me* go?

6. I don't know (a) *who* (b) *whom* to ask.
7. From (a) *who* (b) *whom* do you come?
8. The rose smells (a) *sweet* (b) *sweetly*.
9. Our team won the game (a) *easy* (b) *easily*.
10. She looks (a) *beautiful* (b) *beautifully* in that dress.
11. Of the two men, I like Jones (a) *better* (b) *best*.
12. We (a) *sure* (b) *surely* enjoyed the party.
13. He is taller than (a) *any* (b) *any other* man in the room.
14. It (a) *was* (b) *were* your letters that were lost.
15. Fido, (a) *lay* (b) *lie* down!
16. He has (a) *laid* (b) *lain* in bed two weeks.
17. His duties (a) *sit* (b) *set* heavily upon him.
18. Our profits have (a) *shrunk* (b) *shrank* lately.
19. The set of books (a) *was* (b) *were* bound in leather.
20. Each of us (a) *were* (b) *was* ready for duty.
21. Neither Jack nor Fred (a) *was* (b) *were* to be found.
22. No one of us (a) *know* (b) *knows* the future.
23. Several of the pipes have (a) *froze* (b) *frozen*.
24. I have (a) *drove* (b) *driven* many kinds of cars.
25. Has the bell (a) *rang* (b) *rung*?
26. Which one of you boys (a) *was* (b) *were* to blame?
27. Every student must bring (a) *his* (b) *their* own book.
28. (a) *Who* (b) *Whom* do you wish to see?
29. Will prices (a) *raise* (b) *rise*?
30. I think it (a) *will* (b) *shall* snow today.
31. (a) *Shall* (b) *Will* we play another game?
32. Neither John nor Bill remembered (a) *their* (b) *his* speech.
33. All of us (a) *could of* (b) *could have* done better.
34. He fell (a) *off of* (b) *off* the horse.
35. Can you see (a) *that* (b) *that there* mountain?
36. She's (a) *to* (b) *too* fat for me.

For key to correct answers, see page 214.

If you missed only four, you did better than the typical college student. If you missed as many as twelve, you need a review of grammar. If you missed as many as eighteen or more, your poor English may handicap you in certain occupations.

The fundamentals of grammar and word usage are not difficult to master. You can do it in a few months by studying in your spare time. Are you willing to try?

Borderline Traits

There are personality traits that are not easily labeled correctly as *good* or *bad*. They seem to be borderline characteristics which, if used properly, enhance one's personality. They are hard to manage and often tell against us if not carefully watched. It should be profitable, here, to deal briefly with a few of these traits as a warning to be on the alert to detect and control them.

EGOTISM

As you all know, this term has something to do with self-esteem. It refers to overindulgence in self-esteem, not to self-esteem that is entirely justifiable. There is another word that signifies the same thing, but a little less emphatically. It is *egoism*. While egotism is used to suggest "offensive self-conceit," egoism is used to suggest a milder form of concentration on oneself.

If you are to become a well-integrated personality, you will have a certain amount of self-esteem. You surely will not be guilty of too much, if any, *self-abnegation;* that is, belittling of oneself in the eyes of others. You will not be forever denying your abilities or good traits. You will admit them, but you will not exaggerate or brag about them. You will not parade them offensively before your friends and other associates.

The long and short of it is that you will possess a high degree of self-respect and show it as occasion may require. You will feel and display a degree of self-confidence that is in accord with the facts as to your actual belief in yourself. If you do not respect yourself and have confidence in your ability to do things, you cannot expect other people to respect and have confidence in you.

Be sure of what you really are and then think and act accordingly. You never should adopt the attitude that you are better than others. It is quite all right to say, "I can do that job to your entire satisfaction"; but it is not quite so good to say, "I can do that job better than anyone else can."

There was a time when *pride of workmanship* was evident in most workshops and elsewhere. People took pride in their jobs and did them as well as they could. Really valuable antique furniture is one result of that quality. Workmen everywhere tried to excel at their trades. Farmers gloried in their fine, big crops. Carpenters built buildings to last for generations. Old colonial mansions so highly valued today are the result of their pride of workmanship.

Pride is a good thing. Self-respect cannot be rated too highly. You should take pride in what you are and in what you can do, but only if you really are and can do what one should be proud of.

Stand on your own feet. Develop good personality traits. Acquire the knowledge, know-how, and skills necessary for good workmanship on any job you undertake to do, and then be unobtrusively proud of yourself. Thus beget the respect and confidence of others.

THRIFTINESS

This is a quality that too often is associated solely with money and other property. It really stands for a trait that can have much to do with one's character development. Thriftiness in the use of time is important as it may play a large part in overcoming such bad traits as laziness, dawdling, and lack of trustworthiness where important tasks are involved. But this quality, even when limited to money matters, may have a lot to do with the *good trait development* with which we are concerned.

It is doubtful if there is any one cause of the breakdown of good personality traits that is more potent than bad management of one's income. Over and over again being badly in debt has led to deceit, lying, theft, and other equally bad things in an attempt to get out of, or to cover up, a bad financial situation.

Too many installment contracts can wreck almost any career. Worry over money matters is admittedly at the bottom of many separations from jobs because of faulty workmanship. No man harassed by debts can be, or even act like, a person at peace with himself and the world. He is bound to violate most of the sound principles of good social conduct.

It has been truly said that living within one's income is essential to that peace of mind which makes it possible to give adequate attention to the thoughts, attitudes, words, and deeds which are the outward expressions of one's real personality. .

A few illustrations of how failure to live within your income may greatly modify your character and lead to wrecking your career may be suggestive of what thriftlessness can do to you in other life situations. What affects you for good or ill in your occupational life is likely to affect you in much the same way in other life relationships.

A young man in one of our big cities received his pay once a week—every Monday. Being a spendthrift, by Friday he faced the week end without funds. This happened every week and soon became embarrassing. What do you suppose he did? He advertised in a daily paper for someone who, being paid on Friday and broke on Monday, would like to lend a little money on Friday in exchange for a loan on Monday. Of course, such a plan was no solution.

And what effect would such money problems have on the work of these young men? Is work likely to be done well by people whose money problems keep them worried at least half of every week? Will they win advancement? Of course not; they will be lucky if they keep their jobs at all. Others will be promoted to jobs which should be open to them, but which are withheld because they give their money troubles more thought than they do their careers.

A young lady wanted a watch. She wanted an expensive one, but her income was small. She could not afford the watch on which she had set her heart, but she would accept no other. So for $60 she bought the one she wanted. Two dollars down and a dollar a week were the terms. She would have little trouble meeting her payments. And what a lot of pleasure she would get out of her watch as she worked from day to day—and paid from week to week.

But let us see just how this affected her work. For a few weeks she was quite thrilled with her new possession. Then new wants appeared. But her small salary would not stand the strain of another purchase, not even on the budget plan. So she became restless and dissatisfied; she wondered why she could not have the things others girls had. She became envious. An envious person is not a happy person. An unhappy person is a poor worker. A poor worker just does not win promotions. She may hold her job, but she is not likely to have much of a career.

Then there was Mary. Her family was well known in the town. She had just begun to work and support herself. She had extravagant tastes and soon let her purchases of clothing empty her purse. When her cash gave out, she followed the example of her more opulent parents and opened a charge account. But the store didn't always have what she wanted; so accounts in others were opened. How easy to get what she wanted! Just charge it! But the day of reckoning came. Many bills were waiting for the contents of her pay envelope—big ones, too. The total amount was far more than she could pay.

Now Mary begins to worry about her debts. What will her parents say? Will her employer learn of her extravagances and disapprove? This worry slows down her work. She makes mistakes. She may learn her lesson, get her affairs straightened out, and turn over a new leaf. If she does not, her career is ruined.

John was a good student in school. On graduation he got a good position, for a beginner. His first week's salary looked big to him. Now he could buy the clothes he always had wanted. So he built up quite a wardrobe of garments that appealed to him, but many of which were not well suited to his needs. However, unlike Mary, he did not run into debt. Neither did he save anything. That was bad, but not what kept him from making good on his job.

John thought too much about his clothes. He talked too much about them. His mind drifted away from his work too often. He lost the confidence of his employer and the good will of his co-workers. One day he found himself without a job.

Martha could not resist candy, sodas, and other sweets. It was her money. Why shouldn't she spend it as she pleased? But her employer noticed her eating habits and expected that her health would be impaired. He was not disappointed. Poor health and good work do not go together. Her daily output of work lessened. She became irritable. She soon lost her position.

What you do with your money will have a lot to do with your success in business. Learn to spend it in ways which will increase rather than decrease your efficiency. How you live will in part determine what you are. What you are will be the measure of your success. Resolve not to let your spending habits ruin your career.

TOLERANCE

This is an essential of good personality. It simply means that you should not impose your views on others. This doesn't mean that you should not defend your views, but simply that you must recognize the fact that others may hold quite different, but equally tenable, ones on the same subjects. This is quite different from yielding to the other person or adopting his views without conviction.

We have urged you not to argue with people. But we didn't mean that you should give in where important issues are raised. Discuss them if necessary, but not with the idea that you are going to win an argument. Rather should it be your objective to make your position clear and to get more facts and other points of view which may alter or confirm it. At the outset make it clear that you are not contending that your position is the only correct one, but merely that on the basis of the information you have it *seems to be the correct one*. At the end of the discussion make it plain that you respect the other person's point of view and can see merit in it—if this is true, of course; and it should be, because you never should get drawn into a discussion of an issue on which you can admit no room for that concession.

The point is that to be a person of good personality you must be a *tolerant* one who can see the merit in the views of others and concede their right to hold them.

Other Personality Tests

In a filing case in one college there are copies of more than fifty different standardized personality tests sold by leading publishing houses. This by no means includes all the tests already in print, and more are appearing each year. In addition to the printed tests there are scores of others made up for specific schools and colleges, and for training courses in business and industry, which are not available to the public. We do not know how many different tests, scales, and surveys there are in the general field of personality and measurement, but suspect there must be several hundreds.

Most of the publishers will sell tests only to colleges and schools, not to individuals. Most of the tests would be of little value to you unless administered and interpreted by a qualified instructor who has had training in this field. In several instances the test alone would be meaningless; it is necessary to buy a manual or a complete book in order to understand it thoroughly.

Perhaps you will want to take more personality tests. There is a solution for your problem if you live in a city where a college or a university or some other organization offers extension classes or night-school work. The classes offered by such institutions depend on the demand. If you can get a number of other persons interested, you can make a request to the proper authority that a course in personality improvement be offered.

It should be pointed out that courses in personality have a variety of names. Some colleges object to the term "Personality Improvement Class" and designate the course as "Practical Psychology," "Psychology of Personality," "Business Psychology," or "Personal Efficiency." But "a rose by any other name would smell as sweet," and your concern would be with the content of the course, not the technical title.

If you live in a large city, there is probably a professional testing service available locally. A number of psychologists have withdrawn from their former occupations as college professors and have set up counseling and guidance offices. At the same time, other persons, not so well qualified, have set themselves up as vocational counselors. A substantial fee is usually charged for their services; so you will want to assure yourself that the man you go to is actually qualified to do what he is doing.

Veterans of World War II have access, at no cost, to the counseling and guidance services offered by the Veterans' Administration in different parts of the United States. Your local veterans' center can give you the address of the counseling guidance center nearest you.

Profile of Your Personality on a Graphic Rating Scale

One approach to personality measurement is through the graphic rating scale. What you think of yourself may not be exactly what somebody else thinks of you; nevertheless, rating yourself is usually interesting and helpful.

DIRECTIONS: Prepare a form like the one on page 139. Place a check mark on the spot on each line that you think best describes you. To the left is low, to the right, high; the middle point in the line is average. Be honest with yourself. Don't be too modest, on the one hand, or too conceited, on the other.

Before you check an item think it over carefully. Don't just place check marks in a more or less casual way on the basis of snap judgment or mere guess.

Items 1, 4, and 5 should give little trouble.

Item 2 is not so easy. Are you really well poised? Do you "fly off the handle" easily? Do you stand erect and squarely on your feet? Do you rely on yourself or run to someone for help whenever decisions have to be made or things have to be done? Do you "fret and fume" at delays of any kind? Are you the touchy, grouchy kind or do you smile easily and act pleasantly toward others?

Item 3 is more difficult. If you know your I.Q., that should help. Are your decisions usually right? Or do you often have to get new facts and weigh them more accurately? Do you have what people call "common sense"? Are you one who reasons things out? Or do you "jump to conclusions"?

Item 6 can be answered on the basis of your teamwork experiences—athletics, clubs, orchestra, family, camp, and others.

Item 7. Are you tactful in dealing with others—not just a few people, but nearly all with whom you deal? Or do you tend to upset, or offend, or annoy people? Is it your habit to be courteous at all times?

Item 8 isn't so easy as some, but you should know whether you do things on your own or often depend on others to tell you what to do when confronted with a new problem or task however simple. Do you tend to copy what others do or say? Or do you do and say things in your own way?

Item 9 will require study. Are you aiming high in your career planning or just drifting along without a clear look ahead?

Item 10 may require some study and even consultation with others who often hear you talk. Don't depend on your marks in English. It is

COMPOSITE SUCCESS TRAITS
GRAPHIC RATING SCALE

		1 Very Low	2 Low	3 Average	4 High	5 Very High
1.	Dress—Neatness, Appropriateness, Attraction					
2.	Poise—Physical, Mental, Self-confidence, Pride, Patience, Good Humor					
3.	Intelligence—Common Sense, Rightness of Decisions					
4.	Honesty—Intellectual, and in Dealing with Others					
5.	Dependability—Promptness, Carrying Through					
6.	Co-operativeness—Doing Your Part, Helping Others					
7.	Courteousness—Tact					
8.	Resourcefulness—Originality					
9.	Ambition					
10.	Speech—Voice, English					

Score = 2.5 + 3.5 + 3.25 + 4.5 + 4 + 3 + 4 + 3 + 4 + 2.75 = 34.5
Top score possible — A paragon of virtue = 50

It should be noted that in this calculation only one checking for each trait is involved. In regular use there will be several on each trait which should be averaged for the final mark for any period of time. How this chart can be used effectively will be explained later.

the English you *use* that is important here—not what you *know about English grammar*. Your voice and speech habits also should be taken into account. Is your voice high-pitched and unpleasant or pleasing to the ear of a listener?

The foregoing comments are not in any sense a complete line of thought in connection with any item. They are intended merely as leads to give you a start in your thinking and as evidence that, to avoid more or less useless guesses in most cases, you will need to do some thinking before checking any item. Some of your check marks may fall in between the degrees of *Very Low, Low, Average, High, Very High.*

Suggestions for Study and Discussion

1. In the tests in this chapter did you in general rate lower than you thought you would? Higher? About as you expected?

2. As a part of your course work to date you have been dealing with your personality assets and liabilities. You have listed both. You have selected noteworthy good traits and equally noteworthy bad ones. Doubtless you have made progress toward the reduction of the bad-trait list. What do you consider your greatest single personality weakness? Ask your instructor if he agrees with you. Ask others if you wish. Be ready to tell why your choice is what it is.

3. Have you been corrected or reprimanded by anyone (especially by a teacher, parent, or employer) within the last month or two about a lack of good manners? In the light of your score on the test on page 116, do you think the criticism was justified?

4. In your notebook jot down briefly any exhibition on the part of your classmates of (1) discourtesy; (2) thoughtlessness of others; (3) vulgar or profane speech; (4) disgusting habits. Don't note the names of classmates observed. Don't discuss with anyone the defects noted unless it can be done impersonally so as not to reach the people involved. All you need to do is to answer honestly this question: Am I free from such exhibitions of bad manners? And then to do something about the matter if in any case the answer is "No."

5. Compare notes with your classmates on reading done. How do your reading habits compare with those of others? Keep in mind the fact that *good taste* in reading does not require that all shall read the same things. There is a wide range of good reading.

6. Do you readily recognize "trashy" magazines and books? Discuss this matter with your classmates and others before deciding what is "trashy" and what is not.

7. Much is said these days about the so-called "funnies" and other cheap reading and picture matter in color which are so dear to younger boys and girls. Also about the "comics" in our daily papers. What do

you think of this kind of reading matter? Did you read it when younger? Do you read it now? Has your taste changed? If you once read it, or still do, do you think it has ever been harmful to you? Justify your answer to this question. Check it against the experience of others. What are your conclusions as to your future reading habits?

8. If you have thought much about your lifework, or perhaps have tentatively chosen it, have you taken into account your temperament and personality type?

9. In your Personality Notebook list the activities and organizations in your community through which you can increase your versatility—church, athletic teams, social, clubs, etc. Make a careful survey before listing these.

10. Select the ones in which you are most interested and those most likely to furnish you the opportunity you need for practice in what will help you to overcome your major personality defects.

11. Investigate the possibilities of joining the associations or clubs or activities of your choice and record your success in each case in your Personality Notebook.

12. Keep a record of your progress in connection with each one actually joined.

13. To stimulate interest in and assure adequate attention to good trait improvement, prepare in your notebook a form exactly like the Graphic Rating Scale on page 139. Think back over each day from here on to discover whether or not you did or said something that was noteworthy either way, good or bad, under any one of the *Composite Success Traits* in the record. If you were grossly discourteous, for example, place a check mark on that scale line near the low end. If you were especially courteous in some situation, place the check mark near the high end. In-between acts of courtesy and discourtesy may be checked at the proper point on the scale.

If you failed to do something rightly expected of you, place the check mark at the low end of *Dependability*. For doing something that was difficult to do, but was done so as not to fail someone, check the line at the right. In-between acts showing dependability of some degree may be checked at appropriate points on the line.

If nothing distinctive happened either way in connection with these two traits for several days, a check mark should be placed near Average to cover your normal acts under these headings.

Proceed in the same way for each of the other traits. There should be something to record for each one, as there should be at least one situation in a period of a week or two to call for the exercise of each trait. This spot-judgment checking is more accurate than checking from memory.

When checkings are done for the selected period (two or three weeks), average them for the final mark on the scale as illustrated on page 139. Place a heavy dot for the average at the proper point on the scale for each trait.

Now take a blue or red pencil and draw a line through the average marks as has been done in the illustration referred to. This gives you a "personality profile" to compare with the one made at the outset in the period covered.

Perhaps you will like to ask someone else to rate you on the same scale. The other person's profile of you can then be drawn in with a different-colored pencil.

A prospective employer could decide what characteristics are most important for his job and then turn to your profile to see where you stand as to these characteristics. He couldn't depend wholly on this evidence, but it surely should be helpful.

We repeat, how you are able to check this list of traits again at the end of a few weeks of sincere effort to improve your personality may count for much more than how you have checked it today.

The period need not always be for a week or two. A monthly one may do as well.

It is not intended that every act of courtesy, dependability, and the others shall be checked; merely those outstanding acts that indicate the need for giving more attention to a certain trait, or that give you special satisfaction because you did the right things in difficult situations.

At the end of several months the numerical values of the check marks used for the construction of the several monthly personality profiles should be averaged to get the final score for the period. Placed on a similar chart and connected by lines, as is shown in the illustration on page 139, this final chart will give you a profile of yourself in terms of these *Composite Success Traits* to compare with the one you made at the beginning of the period covered.

It will be noted that for any period—a week, a month, or a year—a final numerical score can be obtained for each trait, as was done in the illustration on page 139 for a week. Let us suppose that the final average scores for the ten traits listed were in the order named as follows: 3.5, 4, 2.25, 4.25, 5, 3, 1.5, 4.5, 3, 2. The average would be $33 \div 10 = 3.3$.

The mid-point of the scale is at 2.5. Hence a final score of 3.3 shows a personality a little above average. But this *average* is not what is important. It is the separate traits that are of most importance to the employer. A person might attain a *high average* by reason of high scores on the traits that for a given job matter least. What the prospective employer wants to know is where the applicant rates on those traits that he regards as essential to success in the job to be filled. So do not be too much concerned with *average* scores. Try to raise the score on each trait.

There is not nearly so much work involved in keeping such a record as at first may be thought. Even if there were, it would be well worth while. Before giving up on it, try it for a time. You may be surprised to find how interesting and helpful it can become.

Personality Reminders

1. Did you let the other fellow do his share of the talking today?
2. Have you refrained from faultfinding today?
3. Have you taken the initiative lately in organizing any kind of group activity?
4. Have you taken a bath in the last twenty-four hours?
5. Did you take any vigorous exercise today?
6. How are your manners in general today?

Special References

Slavson, Samuel Richard. *Recreation and the Total Personality*

Thornton, Francis Beauchesne. *How to Improve Your Personality by Reading*

Laird, Donald Anderson. *Technique of Personal Analysis*

Broadley, Charles V., and M. E. Broadley. *Know Your Real Abilities*

Kuder, George Frederic, and Blanche B. Paulson. *Discovering Your Real Interests*

CHAPTER SEVEN

Systematic Plan for Improvement

YOU MAY HAVE OBSERVED personality changes in people who apparently were making no attempt to bring about such changes. Sometimes these unintentional changes are in the direction of improvement; sometimes, the opposite.

How Changes in Personality Come About

Personality changes may come about through a variety of causes. Here are some of the commonest.

ACCIDENTS

Accidents may upset the individual's glandular balance and effect changes in his size, voice, growth of hair, mental alertness, etc. Such physiological upsets radically modify personality and temperament. One woman who was thus affected began developing such masculine characteristics as a deep voice and a heavy growth of hair on her face. Another began to gain greatly in weight, in spite of her frantic efforts to reduce. These sudden, and in many cases unexplainable, changes in a person's body build and physical traits are enough to disorganize the entire personality. The individual tends to become sensitive about his appearance, to retreat from his normal associations with people, and, in general, to develop a withdrawn personality.

Accidents may also mutilate a person's face, or cripple him, thus changing his pattern of living and his whole perspective on life.

A pretty and popular college girl was involved in an automobile accident that badly disfigured her face. Whereas she had, both in high school and college, been active in numerous social and athletic enterprises, she now became so sensitive about her face that she left college and remained in her home most of the time. Her whole life pattern was thus radically modified.

A man who was once an aggressive, athletic, energetic extrovert, engaged in all manner of sports and physical exercise, always on the move—a typical "go-getter" type—suffered a serious accident, which permanently crippled him. After several months in the hospital it became necessary for him to reorganize his entire life. The first year in the unaccustomed and dreary routine of his new office job was an intensely unhappy one. Gradually, however, he became interested in the movies, in playing bridge, in reading books and magazines, and in other pastimes that involve little physical exertion. Now he is well adjusted and has successfully transformed his personality from extroversion to introversion.

ENVIRONMENT

Personality change may result from radically changed environment. A person may move or be moved into a different environment, or his old environment may undergo striking changes. Children taken from below-average orphans' homes and adopted into upper-class private homes, for example, will undergo remarkable personality modifications. These children do not voluntarily change; the change is gradually brought about through a better type of surroundings. To a lesser degree, adults will be unconsciously modified in personality when they move to a new and different place.

Personality changes, usually in the direction of disorganization, have been observed where an isolated village has suddenly become a boom town through the discovery of oil or gold. Boom towns are, generally, poor places in which to raise children. There are too many disorganizing influences, too many drifters and itinerant workers, too many sociological "growing pains."

If we know in advance that our environment influences to a marked degree our personalities, then it is only common sense, when possible, to choose an environment that will develop desirable traits.

EMOTIONAL CRISES

Emotional crises account for some cases of changed personality. An unhappy love affair may sour a person on the human race. A happy one may tame down and reform an unruly and unconventional individual.

Psychic shocks, especially terrifying experiences, may make a formerly bold child timid and fearful. A narrow escape from death makes a lasting impression on any individual. A child badly frightened by a dog may retain part of the fear all his life. Any sort of fearful or awe-inspiring experience leaves its imprint on the personality, whether one wills it or not. In Chapter Nine we shall learn more about how fear affects men and women and children.

Religious conversion, in thousands of instances, has changed individuals so radically that they were hardly recognizable by their former associates. Individuals whose personality pattern was one of drunkenness, theft, and vice have, through the impact of a deep religious experience, been literally transformed to personality patterns of sobriety, honesty, and virtue.

NORMAL MATURATION

Normal maturation explains still other instances of personality changes. Most boys experience noticeable, and sometimes alarming, personality changes when they begin to mature physiologically. Girls undergo comparable changes as they mature. Little boys and girls go through a stage in which they appear to dislike the opposite sex. This stage is followed, however, by a stage in which they are attracted to each other. These stages are characterized by certain rather definite personality traits.

As people grow older, they characteristically grow more conservative; part of this personality modification is due to bodily changes.

VOLUNTARY EFFORT

Personality changes are sometimes voluntary changes, largely under control of the individual himself. With that kind of personality modification this book concerns itself almost entirely.

The individual senses a need for improvement, experiences a strong desire for improvement, takes inventory of his strong and weak points, and finally undertakes a systematic plan for self-improvement. This systematic program, if assiduously carried out long enough, inevitably leads to personality improvement.

The remainder of this chapter deals with some additional character traits that have much to do with life adjustments. There will be brief discussions of these traits, followed by specific suggestions for doing something about them if you possess them in any degree. After what has been said in the preceding chapters, and you have considered the results of the tests you have taken, you should have a pretty good idea of the personality areas in which you need improvement.

In the next chapter *grooming* and *general appearance* will be dealt with. In Chapter Nine the following detrimental, but easily overcome, traits will receive attention: fear, stage fright, excessive shyness, timidity, egotism, and self-abnegation.

Throughout these chapters we have tried to be as practical as possible. We have tried to make suggestions that will work for you, that have already been helpful to others, that are based on experience rather than theory. If a few of the suggestions seem bizarre and unreasonable, remember that, as Shakespeare said,

> . . . . diseases desperate grown
> By desperate appliance are relieved,
> Or not at all.

In other words, if your personality is very poorly developed and full of serious defects, you will have to take drastic steps to improve yourself.

Inferiority Complex

Probably the most overworked, misused, and abused term in psychology is "inferiority complex." Most of those who use it don't really know what it means. Too frequently it is made to serve as a rationalization for getting out of unpleasant duties or as an excuse for sheer laziness.

Recently a young woman was asked to assume the responsibility for selling tickets to a hospital benefit party. She said, "Oh, I really couldn't do that. I have the most terrible inferiority complex." What she should have said is, "I am too lazy to do that, but it is such a worthy cause I can't afford to refuse, so I'll have to find some excuse. Now, let me see, what excuses can I cook up? A broken leg? Sick with the measles? A touch of angina? No, they're all too messy. Oh yes, of course, my inferiority complex! Why didn't I think of that before?"

The poor old inferiority complex has had to cover a multitude of sins—much more than its share.

Students have spoken almost reverentially of their "inferiority complex," as though it were something of which one should be proud, as though it set its possessor apart from the common herd and marked him as an outstanding person.

The world would be better off if everybody would agree never to use the term again.

Our first advice, therefore, to those who think they have an "inferiority complex" is: *Don't tell anybody*. Keep it a dark secret; maybe nobody will notice it.

However, if you really are lacking in self-confidence because you honestly believe you are inferior to other people, here are some worth-while suggestions.

1. If you think yourself inferior to others in intelligence, get your principal, vocational adviser, or a psychologist to give you an intelligence test. This test will yield an intelligence quotient (I.Q.) or a percentile rank that will reveal whether you are average, below average, or above average in mentality. Then you will at least know the facts.

2. If you feel inferior because your associates play a better game of bridge, golf, tennis, etc., than you do, bear in mind that your game can be improved immensely by practice.

3. If you feel inferior because others are better looking or prettier than you, first see how much you can improve your appearance. If you are still doomed to be the ugly duckling, try to develop in other fields as a compensation. Improve your conversation, your skills in games, your tact, your pleasantness. You may be farther ahead in the long run than the naturally handsome or pretty person who tries to get by on beauty alone.

Educational Inferiority

If your feeling of inferiority comes from the fact that you dropped out of school in the eighth grade whereas your associates are college graduates, don't let *that* worry you. If you only knew what we know about college graduates! A college degree is no guarantee of an education. Some of the most ignorant people have college diplomas framed and proudly on display in their homes. Many of the best educated men of our times never finished high school.

If you feel inferior because your family is obscure and none of them ever amounted to much in the world, remember that now, as never before, the world judges a person by *his own standards, his own ambitions,* and *his own achievements.*

We sometimes think that feelings of inferiority, if they do not become permanently fixed, are good for us. They act as stimuli prodding us on to learn more, to achieve more. A very versatile student once said that he acquired most of his versatility simply because it irked him to see anyone doing anything that he couldn't do.

Don't let your feelings of inferiority become ends in themselves. They will only make you unhappy. Use them as motives—as starting points for self-improvement. Why not take the point on which you have your greatest feeling of inferiority and make that your strongest point in personality?

The suggestions in the following section are for persons who were unable to complete their formal education and have begun to feel a need for a more adequate general education. It also is for those who know that however complete their schooling, there is much left to be learned.

1. Read a good news magazine like *Time* or *Newsweek.*

2. Read The *Reader's Digest* from cover to cover every month. Familiarize yourself with the other magazines listed on page 127. Don't be satisfied to nibble at the picture magazines—bite into the *Atlantic* and *Harper's* occasionally.

3. Visit an art museum occasionally. Secure the catalogues or guidebooks explaining the displays, and make a sincere effort to find out what it's all about.

4. Get a record player and start building a collection of classical

Be zealous in your efforts at self-improvement. Find new ways to broaden your interests.

records. Try to figure out for yourself what the music means. Refer to the manuals which frequently accompany albums of such records. Supplement this activity by choosing one or two radio programs each week that feature classical music. Musical knowledge and appreciation are acquired more easily and at less cost now than ever before.

5. Get yourself a good dictionary and use it every day. If you can afford it, buy a set of the *Encyclopaedia Britannica* and read from it regularly.

6. Buy a practical book on grammar and improve your English.

7. Select two or three radio programs a week that have to do with cultural development and general education. Listen to news broadcasts.

8. One of the best sources of a liberal education is a set of books known as the Harvard Classics. Your librarian will show them to you and explain how they should be used. You may want to add a set to your personal library.

9. Build a personal library. We have already recommended a dictionary, a set of encyclopedias, a grammar book, and the Harvard Classics. Add a complete one-volume Shakespeare, a Bible, Roget's *Thesaurus,* Van Loon's *Story of the Bible,* and Van Loon's *Story of Mankind,* and you will have a library that can give you more education than many college graduates ever acquire.

To establish a personal library does not mean a heavy investment. Books are relatively cheap nowadays. The only expensive items we have mentioned are the *Encyclopaedia Britannica* and the Harvard Classics. Most bookstores handle a series of dollar books comprising the world's greatest literature. A series of 25- and 35-cent books has been placed on the market. Many of the best books are printed in these low-priced series.

Don't neglect to add one or two technical or professional books in your particular field. Any librarian will be glad to advise you.

You may want to join one of the book clubs advertised in the magazines. There are many of these clubs, but they are somewhat alike in that you are expected to buy a certain number of books each year; in one instance, one each month. They are valuable in helping you to keep up with some of the best new books.

If you want to build a larger library, one that will include the great books of all time and all nations, A. D. Dickinson's *One Thousand Best Books*, published in New York by the H. W. Wilson Company, can be recommended as a guide. Dickinson's volume lists the greatest literature from the thirteenth century B.C. up to modern times. His choices are not based on any one man's judgment of what is a great book, but on the composite judgments of a large number of competent individuals and groups. Even if you feel that you cannot afford to invest in many books, Dickinson is a good guide for your selection of books to read.

10. Go to public lectures, panel discussions, and lyceum programs.

11. Most cities and many small towns now have night schools and extension classes, the charges for which are unusually low. Correspondence courses are available on a variety of subjects. These classes are usually advertised in newspapers and by posters in libraries. Nationally known correspondence schools advertise in magazines.

12. As you investigate the matter, you will probably discover in your community other educational opportunities not mentioned here.

A good education is considered the birthright of every American. There is no excuse for any person's living his life through in ignorance if he really wants an education.

How to Make Your Personality Stand Out

You may find that, even though you have improved your personality greatly, some people still will not like you. Some others will not even notice you.

It is impossible to develop a personality that *every* individual you meet will like. To some, your dark hair, for instance, or the shape of your chin, may be a reminder of an unpleasant person they knew years ago. The arch of your eyebrows may remind them of a cranky schoolteacher they once knew.

Your posture or walk, regardless of how free it is from whatever might make posture or walk unattractive, may remind them of an overbearing bully in their grade-school experience. Your name even might be the same as that of a person who defrauded them a long time ago.

There is little that you can do to overcome completely such deep-

The give-and-take of friendly conversation enriches one's education and prevents narrow-mindedness.

rooted prejudices and conditioned emotions in people. You may as well resign yourself to the fact that somewhere, sometime, you will find somebody who will not like your personality.

Your job is to develop and nurture as many as possible of those traits and characteristics that are generally liked by most normal people. Those traits have been pretty well analyzed in Chapter Four.

There is something further, however, that you ought to do. You should engage in what might well be called a program of personal publicity. You must find ways of calling attention to yourself; but it must be done in an indirect, unobtrusive manner—in a manner that will not offend anyone or give the impression that you are too forward or brazen.

The following activities will help you to create a good impression of yourself among people who count. They are particularly helpful to young people who go into a new community to work. If you will do these things, you will gain the respect, good will, and admiration of a constantly increasing circle of acquaintances.

Here are some things that you should do:

1. Start a savings account. If possible, deposit in savings a small part of your *first* pay check and part of every succeeding one. Do not allow an exception to occur. Start your account in a bank frequented by the people you wish to cultivate. Make your deposits at a time when some of these people are in the bank. Don't obtrude yourself on their attention; be quiet and unassuming in your manner. But manage to be seen making deposits. Successful businessmen admire young people who are thrifty.

2. Start a charge account in one or two local stores if you have a regular income or allowance. Do this even if you have the money to pay cash for all your purchases. Pay your bills in full on the exact day they are due. The way to build up your credit is to become known as a good credit risk. Use judgment in your choice of a store or stores in which to start charge accounts. One good place is in a high-quality clothing store.

3. Room at a "good address." Before you settle permanently in your new work environment, get the lay of the land. Select a desirable section of town; rent a room or an apartment in the home of a well-thought-of family. Avoid sections of town, streets, or apartment houses frequented by persons of doubtful moral reputation. Get a room or an apartment where you will be thrown with people of culture and good reputation. In almost every town or city, rooms are available in the homes of people whose friendship can be helpful to you.

4. Join at least one business or professional association or service club as soon as you can; for example, Rotary, Kiwanis, Business and Professional Women's Club, Junior Chamber of Commerce, Lions Club. Rotary is harder to get into than Lions. Lions will bring you into contact with the younger men of the community; Rotary with many of the older, better established men. Whatever you join, pay your dues promptly, attend all the meetings, and accept willingly the duties and responsibilities that may be placed upon you. For instance, as chairman of the committee on the Christmas party for poor children, you will have entree to the offices of business executives. You will also get invaluable experience in managing programs

and, incidentally, some worth-while personal publicity in the local newspapers.

5. Go to church regularly, and support your church with donations of both money and time. The chief value here is your own spiritual and character development, but everyone is aware of other values. Many of the leading people of your community will be found in church every Sunday. They will see you there. They will consider you one of them. There is every reason for you to tie up with a church.

At this point we want to make it clear that we do not advocate church membership and attendance for the purpose of pushing yourself forward socially or professionally. Anyone who goes to church just for this purpose is unworthy of any real benefits that might accrue to him from such attendance. As a matter of fact, anyone who goes to church exclusively for such selfish reasons is beneath contempt.

Nevertheless, if we face facts realistically, we know that church affiliation and participation *will* gain for you the attention and respect of many people who are worth knowing and whose good will we should all covet.

6. Dress as well as you can afford. If necessary spend a considerable portion of your income on your clothing and appearance. No better advice on this subject can be found than that given in Shakespeare's *Hamlet* by Polonius to his son, Laertes:

> Costly thy habit as thy purse can buy,
> But not express'd in fancy; rich, not gaudy;
> For the apparel oft proclaims the man . . .

Always keep your clothing freshly cleaned and pressed, or laundered. When in doubt, dress conservatively. You will never be criticized for that; you may be criticized for sponsoring every new fad or gaudy accessory in clothing.

7. Be seen in the "right places"; do not be seen in the "wrong places." You can soon learn the difference in your new environment. Among typical "wrong places" are certain types of rowdy dance halls, poolrooms (generally), most beer parlors, burlesque shows, meetings of radical or suspect political groups. Typical "right places" include church, Sunday school, high-grade theaters, bowling alleys (in some communities), church suppers, respectable and respected

political and social group meetings, country clubs, municipal and private golf courses.

8. Go to the library at least once every two weeks. Here you will see and be seen by a different group of worth-while people from those that you will meet in most other places. Get acquainted with the librarian. Get a library card and draw out at least two books a month. Keep tab on the best cultural magazines on the racks.

9. Attend amateur theatricals (no matter how hammy they are), benefit performances, concert series, lectures, etc. Some of this may be slightly out of your field, but notice the class of people who attend such events! They are the people you want to know. If you have any interest in it, you will profit by participating in home-talent performances.

10. Act on committees whenever you can, for example, those of the Red Cross, Community Chest, hospital benefits, Old Newsboys, March of Dimes, etc. Through such activity you will be rendering a worth-while public service, developing your own self-confidence, and getting better acquainted with leaders in your community.

11. Buy some life insurance, even if it is only a minimum-sized policy. Buy it from an agency that is outstanding in the community. Buy it from an executive of the agency or the most prominent salesman in the agency. Ask his advice about the different types of insurance. He will be a walking advertisement of your business judgment, progressiveness, and general common sense. The smaller the town, the more personal publicity you will get.

12. Buy some real estate as soon as you can; it doesn't matter much how small the parcel of land or how little you really need a parcel of land. Owning real estate makes you an honest-to-goodness taxpayer. Of course, you've always paid taxes of one sort or another, but now you become a special kind of taxpayer. You now belong to the elite of the taxpayers. You own part of the good earth. This establishes you as a very solid citizen indeed. In many communities you can't borrow books at the public library without a card signed by a "dirt taxpayer"; you can't vote in certain kinds of elections. But as soon as you get your first real-estate tax receipt, you automatically are classified as a person who counts in the community.

13. Be seen with community leaders (but don't be servile and sycophantic about it), and don't habitually be seen with the wrong crowd. In towns and small cities it is as easy and natural to talk

with a bank president as with the village loafer. Important persons are really quite friendly and helpful if you approach them in the right way. Mingle socially with people who are cultured, decent, and respectable, but not necessarily rich or members of the "best families."

In your new environment you will find that people pretty generally accept you at your own evaluation of yourself. If your dates are with casual street-corner and beer-hall pickups, you will be classified as such a person. It's just as easy to have dates with sons or daughters from the homes of leading citizens.

14. When the proper time comes, join some fraternal order if it seems to be the thing to do in your particular community. Some communities almost ignore fraternal organizations; in others, if you aren't an Elk, you are nothing but a nothing. Be guided in this matter by the sentiments and practices of the better element in the community.

Do not do any of these things merely to "make your personality stand out." Each is good in itself. It might be better to say that one who has a fine personality (not in outward appearance alone) will do most of the things suggested. He will be thrifty, and save. He probably will buy enough to justify a charge account. He will want to, and be able to, live in a good residential district. He will have a variety of interests and probably belong to local groups. He no doubt will want a church affiliation. He will dress well because he cares about his personal appearance. Naturally, being a good sort of person, he will want to be in good places and of course will shun bad ones. He will seek more education and thus require books. Lectures and other good entertainment will interest him. Being the right sort, he will be interested in social-betterment activities. He will understand the value of life insurance. He will want to own his own home.

Being a man of some civic and economic standing, he will meet community leaders. He may not be what is called a "joiner," but some fraternal organization may appeal to him. In short, you see, people of strong personality just naturally do the things you are advised to do. Yet, on the other hand, doing these things may be counted on to help you to develop into the kind of person who just naturally does them. They are both the outward evidences of your goal (a fine personality) and aids in achieving it.

Suggestions for Study and Discussion

1. You are relatively young, and as yet your personality may have undergone no great change due to any of the causes listed in this chapter. It is assumed that there have been changes, but only those representing usual growth changes for better or for worse. It may be helpful, however, to think back two or three years to see if you can detect and account for any unusual change that may have taken place. Your check lists should help you do this. Ask yourself this question: Am I greatly different in any of the attitudes and traits already entered in my notebook from what I was, say, two or three years ago? Discuss this matter with members of your family and your intimate friends. They may have noticed things that escaped you.

2. You have listed the community activities in which you have or might have participated for the purpose of improving your personality. Now list every activity in your school or college that is open to you. A form in your notebook like the following should be ruled for this list:

STUDENT ACTIVITIES				
Date				
Activities	Have actively participated in	Have joined but not active	Will join	Date new ones joined

There probably are more than you think. Don't overlook any—camera club, chorus, football team, secretarial club, rifle club, dramatics club, fraternities, sororities, foreign-language club, band, etc.

Compare your score with others in your class.

3. Have you any strong personal interest, or interesting hobby, not represented in the list of activities you have compiled? If so, see if there are others in your class who may be interested in starting a club for mutual helpfulness in connection with this interest or hobby. Such a club does not have to be large. A very small group often will serve as well or better. Keep in mind the fact that personality development is, or may be, furthered by this activity.

4. The groundwork for personality development may be laid in activities which one does alone—reading, thinking, self-criticism, observa-

tion, attending movies, etc. But personal-trait development is best accomplished in association with others. The personal traits of hermits are far less important than are those of people who are living in close association with other people as most of us do.

For a period of two weeks record in your notebook under an appropriate heading the things you do alone—hiking, skating, attending movie, reading, etc.

Then list the things you do with others—playing cards, singing, tennis, etc.

In each case list only the things you do of your own volition, not such things as attending class, or reading an assigned book, or studying a lesson, etc.

5. In the next week add some things to the list of things voluntarily done with others.

6. You have been asked to consider whether or not your personality has undergone more than usual change recently. Can you detect any sudden and somewhat unusual change in anyone whom you know intimately? If so, can you suggest a possible reason for it? We frequently say, "He didn't seem to be so quick-tempered last school year." Or, "She seems to be a lot more shy than she used to be." Do you know anyone about whom you might make some such comment? Trying to find one about whom such a comment can be made is a personality-development exercise. It requires *observing* and *thinking*, two essentials of personality development.

7. Often people say of someone recently met, "He is hard to get acquainted with, but the longer you know him the better you like him." Or, "He seems like a mighty nice chap at first, but the longer you know him the less you like him." Or, "She is a fine person, who wears well."

What do these sayings represent as to the personality of people thus described? They mean something. Could any of them be said of you? Which would you prefer to be said of you? Is there something you would prefer to have said about you by people whom you meet for the first time? If so, tell what it is, why you prefer it, and how you may best merit it.

8. Think about yourself carefully. Have you at least a tiny bit of *inferiority complex?* Do you ever, without much thought, say promptly, "I can't do *that*"? Or, "He can, but I can't"? Be honest. If you even occasionally get out of doing something without trying to do it, put yourself down as a little dishonest or a victim of inferiority complex.

9. Have you ever taken an *intelligence test?* If so, do you know the I.Q. it revealed? If you haven't taken one, should you do so? We don't know. You alone should know whether you have any doubt as to your mental equipment. Perhaps your school or college grades are enough to tell you what you want to know. At any rate, you should do something about the matter if you aren't doing good work and think you can't do any better.

10. Do you feel inferior to others in any outstanding respect? Should you really feel that way? How do you know? What have you done to overcome your inferiority? Of course, you are inferior to certain other people in some things. We are not all equal in all respects. Our whole educational system is based on the theory of *individual differences*—that our *aptitudes, interests,* and *over-all abilities* differ greatly. You must not jump to the conclusion that differences may not be wholly or partially overcome. So check carefully any feeling of inferiority in order to find out whether it is well founded or not. This takes in quite a bit of territory—scholastic standings, or skill in games, or physical appearance, or lack of family traditions, or extent of education.

11. In your notebook list two or three specific things in addition to those listed here which one may do to overcome a feeling of inferiority as to educational status.

12. In your notebook make a list of things you can do *now* to "make your personality stand out." Some of those mentioned in this chapter, of course. But others, like them, that are within your reach. It is from your quest for helpful things of this kind that you may get real help in developing your personality. Such study of the problem keeps one *personality-conscious,* an essential of the personality-development period. Later you should have so habituated good traits as to think very little about your own personality.

Personality Reminders

1. Are you a good listener? Or do you interrupt people?
2. Have you learned a new game or skill in the last six months?
3. Have you done anything in the last week to make anyone happy?
4. Did you refrain from getting into pointless arguments last week?
5. Have you done anything recently to bring yourself favorably to the attention of your superiors?

Special References

Hunter, Estelle Belle. *Personality Development*
King, Eleanor Helen. *Glorify Yourself,* Revised Edition
Ryan, Mildred Graves. *Cues for You; Guidance on Manners, Appearance, and Personality Growth*
Smith, Edna Barbara. *Personality Improvement for All*
Diehl, Harold S. *Textbook of Healthful Living,* Fourth Edition
Liebman, Joshua Loth. *Peace of Mind*

CHAPTER EIGHT

Good Appearance—Grooming

GROOMING IS A RATHER difficult subject to cover adequately in limited space; especially that part of it which has to do with clothes. There are so many views on this subject; so many different tastes to cater to; so many greatly different situations of time, place, and activity to be considered. Then, too, some allowance should be made for different ages and the prevailing styles or habits that are dominant in different age groups.

We could brush this most important subject off by urging you to dress appropriately for every time, place, and occasion, taking into account your age and station in life. That would be easy but not very helpful.

It has been pointed out in more than one place already that grooming, clothing, and general appearance are among the most important factors in the impression we make on other people. The world judges us more and more on external appearances. At any rate, the first impressions, and frequently the most lasting ones, are made by our appearance. Whether or not this is fair is of no importance here.

We must face the fact that the well-dressed person makes a better first impression than the poorly dressed one. The neat, trim-looking person creates a better impression than the dowdy one.

School boys and girls, like most adults, don't want to be far out of line with the prevailing dress habits of their associates. Thus it comes about that some one of the leadership type of girl comes out with saddle-back shoes, dungarees, and other items of wearing apparel that may be far out of line with good taste, or comfort, or appearance. A few girls immediately follow this leadership, and soon the whole female student body comes out dressed exactly alike.

At the college level it is much the same, but not quite so extreme as at the lower level.

We are not concerned here with either school or college dress habits. We don't know how prevailing styles got started. We don't condemn them. We don't even understand them. What we do know is that the average person, be he a school boy or girl, a college student, or an adult fully settled in his or her niche in life, just naturally falls in with the prevailing mode of dress in his set and fears nothing more than he does the eyebrows likely to be lifted at him if he were to show a conspicuous degree of individuality. This is a fact; so we may as well accept it and deal with our subject accordingly.

What we have to say about dress as an important phase of grooming is addressed to you who are not so firmly rooted in the habits of your present associates that you cannot look forward to breaking with dress habits of the present when you begin your lifework as an adult who must make his way among other people of quite different dress habits. In short, we are dealing with clothes on the adult level. But don't interpret this as being a criticism of the dress habits of young people, and above all don't assume that how adults dress is of no concern to you.

Your good appearance is not wholly dependent on the clothes you wear. There are other important factors, and these will be discussed. They apply to all alike—school boys and girls, college students, and adults in all walks of life. Mark them well! They surely apply to you right now whatever your present status in life may be.

Suggestions for Men

1. Take a bath every day. This means an allover bath, tub or shower, *every* day, with plenty of lather. Most men don't bathe often enough.

2. Shave every morning. If you have a heavy beard, you may need to shave again for an evening engagement.

3. Use a deodorant after bathing. Get over the notion that deodorants are for women only. B.O. is just as bad in a man as in a woman!

4. Every morning put on a fresh pair of shorts and a fresh pair

*"Do I look my best?"
is the question she asks
herself before starting
out.*

of socks. If you haven't enough pairs, either buy some more or have
your laundry done more often. And don't let your socks sag. Either
wear garters or buy the elastic-top socks.

5. Be sure that the shirt you are putting on in the morning has
clean collar and cuffs and is free from perspiration odor. Have your
"dress-up" shirts done at a professional laundry, to avoid that wilted-
collar look.

6. Keep your necktie clean, free from wrinkles, neatly tied,
straight in your collar, and appropriate to the suit you are wearing.

7. Keep your suit and coat cleaned and pressed and your hat
brushed and blocked. Occasionally, air your suits before putting

them away. If you can do so, avoid wearing the same suit on successive days.

8. Polish your shoes regularly. Keep them in shape by using shoe trees. Have new lifts put on as soon as the heels begin to wear over. People judge you more than you supect by the shapeliness, cleanliness, and general appearance of your shoes.

9. Have a special place to keep your clothesbrush and shoe-polishing things, and always put them back after using them. Be sure that they are in a handy place where a minimum of effort is required to reach them. Get into the habit of using these utensils *every day.*

10. Brush your teeth thoroughly three times a day (with gum

"Is my tie straight and correctly adjusted?" asks the young man who is careful about the details of grooming.

massage) and use a mouthwash regularly. Clean between your teeth at least once a day with dental floss. If halitosis persists, have your teeth and tonsils checked as possible sources of odor. Excessive use of tobacco also causes bad breath.

11. Have your hair cut and shampooed about every ten days. Keep a *clean* comb and brush in a convenient place, and use them frequently. The appearance of your hair will be greatly improved by vigorous daily brushing. Don't slick your hair down, but use a good hair dressing to keep it in place.

12. Keep your fingernails clean and clipped or filed down to a

CORRECT DRESS

	Jacket	Waistcoat	Trousers	Shirt	Necktie	Hose
Formal Day Wear	Cutaway in black or oxford grey; worsteds, cashmeres or cheviots.	To match coat, or washable or finished material; white, grey or buff.	Black and grey striped worsted or cheviot; checks. Cuffless.	Stiff or pleated bosom, white; bold wing or fold collar.	Ascot, four-in-hand or bow tie; grey figures, stripes or checks.	Black, lisle or wool; ribbed, plain or clocked.
Formal Wear after 6 p.m.	Tailcoat in black or midnight blue worsted.	Single or double-breasted white pique, V-front.	Same fabric as coat—two braids at sides.	Starched bosom white piqué, single cuffs; bold wing collar.	White pique—may match bosom and waistcoat; bow tie.	Black or midnight blue nylon, wool or lisle.
Semi-formal Wear after 6 p.m.	Dinner jacket, single or double-breasted, black or midnight blue. Summer, white lightweight.	Single or double-breasted midnight blue or black; Cummerbund with Summer jacket.	Same as jacket—one braid at sides. With light jacket, midnight blue trousers.	White piqué with single cuffs, pleated bosom with double cuffs, wing or fold collar.	Plain black or midnight blue bow tie. Maroon with Summer jacket.	Plain black or dark blue nylon, wool or lisle.
Business Wear	Single or double-breasted jacket of plain or fancy worsteds, Saxonies, cheviots, etc.	Single or double-breasted to match or contrast with jacket, or no waistcoat.	To match jacket, with or without cuffs.	Broadcloth, madras or oxford. White or colored starched collar or attached collar.	Four-in-hand or bow tie. Stripes, figures or plaids. Solid colors.	Wool, rayon or lisle to harmonize with ensemble.
Campus, Country and Resort Wear	Single or double-breasted jacket; Homespuns, tweeds, Shetland, gabardine, cashmeres.	Like jacket, solid color or Tattersall checked flannel, soft leather; pullover.	To match or odd slacks of flannel, gabardine, covert, checked tweeds.	Soft white or colored flannel, oxford or gabardine.	Four-in-hand or bow tie. Woven or crochet, printed wool, stripes, rep.	Small pattern Argyle plaid or solid color wool.

reasonable length. Keep clippers, nail file, and a small hand brush in a convenient place.

13. Wear clothes that are appropriate to the place and time. Keep tab on *Esquire* magazine. The chart shown on pages 164 and 165, reproduced through the courtesy of *Esquire,* is a reliable guide for men as to what to wear and when to wear it.

OTHER APPEARANCE FACTORS IN MEN

If your physique, complexion, voice, speech, habits, carriage, or general behavior in the slightest degree suggests effeminacy, do

FOR MEN[1]

	Footwear	Hat	Gloves	Outercoats	Accessories	Jewelry
Formal Day Wear	Black calf low shoes. White or grey linen spats may be worn.	High silk hat, wide felt band.	White, grey or buff lightweight mocha to harmonize with waistcoat.	Single or double-breasted black, navy blue or Oxford grey.	White or grey muffler, white linen handkerchief, white carnation, grey braces.	Pearl stickpin, gold, pearl or stone cuff links and studs, pocket watch, key chain.
Formal Wear after 6 p.m.	Patent leather low shoes; long vamp patent leather pumps.	High silk, high collapsible opera.	White kid, mocha or chamois.	Black, oxford grey or dark blue single breasted fly front; double-breasted.	White scarf, handkerchief, white or red carnation, white braces.	Studs of pearl or precious stones, cuff links to match, pocket watch, key chain.
Semi-formal Wear after 6 p.m.	Patent leather low evening shoes; patent leather pumps.	Black homburg. Straws in season.	Grey mocha, chamois or buck.	Black oxford grey or dark blue single or double-breasted.	White scarf, handkerchief, red or white carnation. Black and white braces.	Studs and cuff links of mother-of-pearl, enamel, plain gold or colored stone; watch; key chain.
Business Wear	Black or brown calf low shoes, plain or perforated toe caps.	Homburg, derby, semi-Homburg, snap brim. Straws in season.	Natural chamois, tan capeskin, grey mocha, pigskin. Buttoned, snap or slip-on.	Single or double-breasted woolens or worsteds. Processed fabric raincoat.	Scarf to harmonize or contrast. White or colored linen handkerchief. Belt or braces.	Collar pin, cuff links of modest character, tie holder, wrist or pocket watch, key chain.
Campus, Country and Resort Wear	Brown or black brogues, reverse calf, moccasins, white with or without trimming.	Soft felt pork pie, tan cotton. Native straws for summer. Tweed cap.	Pigskin or buck, soft wool or string.	Raglan or set-in sleeve single breasted, tweeds and coverts; double-breasted polo coat; raincoat.	Cotton or printed foulard handkerchiefs; and neckerchiefs; sports leather or ribbon belt.	Collar pin, tie holder, wrist watch.

[1] Copyright, by Esquire, Inc., Esquire Building, Chicago 1, Ill. Used by permission.

everything in your power to create an impression of masculinity. Pitch your voice lower. Develop your arm muscles and your chest expansion. Avoid pet expressions and exclamations commonly used by women. See that your posture and walk are masculine: hold up your shoulders, throw out your chest, take longer steps. Think masculine, and act masculine.

Here is a list of gestures commonly associated with women and another list commonly associated with men. If you use any of the feminine gestures, stop at once and substitute the corresponding masculine gestures. You'll have to watch yourself pretty closely on this.

FEMININE GESTURES	MASCULINE GESTURES
1. Hand on hip	1. Hands folded over chest or clasped in back
2. Head tilted to one side	2. Head straight and held high
3. Feet close together, one slightly ahead of the other	3. Feet spread apart about twelve to fifteen inches
4. Edge of hand held against face, with finger bent slightly	4. Fist clenched
5. Tapping front teeth with fingernail	5. Clenched fist under chin or jaw
6. Short, mincing steps	6. Long steps
7. Looking at people from corner of eyes	7. Direct look; entire head turned toward person
8. Waving to friends; wrist and fingers flexible	8. Any form of salute; wrist and fingers stiff
9. Standing with one knee bent and slightly in front of the other	9. Standing with both knees rigid
10. Putting one hand up to back of head to touch hair	10. Clenching fingers of both hands together firmly at back of head

How do you laugh? Are your laughs pitched high, like a woman's? Lower the pitch—develop a masculine laugh. Chuckle. Laugh from the depths of your chest and stomach. Roar. Bellow. Do anything but giggle! Don't be guilty of a high, hysterical laugh. Listen to Edward Arnold and Clark Gable in the movies. Imitate their laughter. You can't do it, but you can at least try.

Suggestions for Women

1. Take a bath every day. Never miss a day except for reasons of health. In summer bathe twice a day.

2. Use a deodorant after your bath. There are two schools of thought about deodorants. One says that a deodorant should stop perspiration in the areas where the deodorant is applied and thus prevent perspiration odor. The other says that it is healthier to perspire and that the function of a deodorant is to prevent perspiration odor without interfering with the normal functioning of the sweat glands. Deodorants of both types are widely sold.

3. Brush your teeth at least twice a day, and use a mouthwash freely. Use dental floss to clean between your teeth.

4. Protect yourself from halitosis as you would from the plague. Check all possible sources of bad breath: tonsils, decayed teeth, stomach disorders, catarrh, overindulgence in tobacco, etc. The advertisements about the disadvantages of bad breath are certainly not exaggerated.

5. Keep your neck, hands, ears, and face clean. This should be an unnecessary warning in an age of plentiful soap, cleansing cream, and water; but we know from observation that many an otherwise fastidious girl offends in these particulars.

6. Shampoo your hair as often as it needs to be shampooed. No one rule will be right for all types of hair and scalp. When in doubt, consult your physician or a properly qualified beautician. Brush your hair every day.

7. Take whatever steps are necessary, regardless of the trouble and expense, to clear your complexion of unsightly blemishes of whatever nature. There is hardly a facial blemish that will not yield to the proper treatment. Even large birthmarks can be scientifically covered so that they are not noticeable.

8. Keep your hands smooth and your nails well manicured. Remember that men still dislike a too-vivid nail polish and long claw-like nails.

9. Use discretion, restraint, and common sense in applying rouge, lipstick, and face powder, and in plucking your eyebrows. Don't be a freak. When in doubt, be fairly conservative.

The real purpose in using cosmetics is to add to your attractiveness, a fact which many young women blandly ignore. By far the most serious mistake that women make in this field is in using too much make-up. The ideal make-up is one of which the observer is not aware. The rouge should be skillfully blended into the skin, not daubed on in spots. The powder shouldn't show at all. Lipstick shouldn't remind one of a surgical incision or look like a gooey smear. Rouge may be used for two purposes: to give you a healthy, vital appearance and to change the apparent shape of your face.

Rouge properly applied can make a round face appear longer, or a too-long face appear more plump. Keep in mind the old rule about lines in clothing. Up and down lines make a figure or a face appear longer. Horizontal lines create an illusion of width.

If your teeth are too prominent or are unattractive, use lipstick very sparingly, for the bright red attracts attention to your mouth.

Lipstick properly applied can make a wide mouth appear smaller, a small mouth appear wider, a thin lip appear fuller, or a too-thick lip appear relatively thin.

Use lipstick that harmonizes with the color of your rouge and with the color of your skin. For example, if you have a "rosy" complexion, do not use a vivid red lipstick.

In arching your eyebrows, do not pluck them in a too-high arch and do not reduce them to a thin line. It is best to arch them along the line of natural growth.

Never pluck out or shave off all the eyebrow and then pencil one on. This not only looks artificial but also detracts from the attractiveness of your eyes. Your eyebrows are meant to make an attractive frame for your eyes and emphasize their beauty. Unless you know how to apply mascara and eye shadow properly, don't use them at all.

10. Study your face shape and features and choose your hair-do accordingly. Beauty experts tell us that the ideal face is oval in shape. In choosing your hair-do, choose one that will make your face look oval. Particular care is necessary in the case of women with large jaws, oblong faces, round faces, or any shape that deviates noticeably from the oval.

Unless you are a lady of leisure, wear your hair in some simple style, except for formal occasions. A too-elaborate hair-do is hard to keep looking right without spending much time on it. Change your hair-do frequently. Hair styles change almost as rapidly as styles in women's clothing.

Strive for individuality in your hair style. A hair-do that is very becoming on another person may be very unattractive on you. Seek the advice of your hairdresser and experiment by yourself until you find the types that best suit your particular face shape.

11. Don't use heavy perfume at school or in a business office. Colognes and very light perfumes are the only ones acceptable in such places. Never substitute perfume for a good bath.

12. Get a complete kit containing a clothesbrush, a brush for suède shoes, cleaning and polishing liquid or paste for each color of shoes you wear, and an adequate supply of brushes and cloths for shoe cleaning and polishing. Keep these materials in a handy place where you can reach them from any part of your room in two seconds. Make it *easy* to keep your hats, shoes, suits, coats, and accessories clean.

13. Brush your hat, shoes, suit, collar, and coat just before you go out. Watch out for dandruff or fallen hair on your shoulders, powder on collars, neckline, etc.

14. Keep your suits, skirts, coats, and dresses cleaned and pressed. Air your clothes before hanging them in the closet. If you detect the slightest perspiration odor when you open your closet door, take *everything* out and have it cleaned, aired, or laundered.

15. Keep all accessories in good order: collars, gloves, cuffs, purses, galoshes, belts, clothing decorations, etc.

16. Keep your shoes cleaned and brushed or polished. Keep the heels straight.

17. Wear fresh underclothes every day. Wash your girdle often.

18. Wear fresh hose every day. Beware of crooked seams. Men notice them even if you don't. Wash your hose out at night. Keep them free from runs, snags, and holes.

19. Do not attempt to lose weight rapidly by means of a rigid diet. If you are overweight or underweight, consult your physician for information about diets. By means of a scientifically planned diet and systematic exercise, keep your figure trim and pleasing to the eye.

20. Wear good foundation garments to trim your figure. Even if you are slim, they are necessary for your posture and poise. Your clothes will fit better and look neater. Don't think that girdles and uplift bras are meant just for overweight women. They are designed for every type figure.

21. Be sure your clothing is appropriate to the time and place. If possible, have enough variety of clothing so that you will have the proper attire for any occasion. If you are budget-conscious, be

Typed for You: TOO TALL

REPRODUCED BY ARRANGEMENT WITH EDITORS, *Mademoiselle*, 122 E. 42D St., NEW YORK 17

Self-Portrait

Potentialities. You can wear the widest brimmed hats, the bulkiest tweeds, the furriest jackets, the biggest jewels. You can lounge in slacks. You can wear either flat heels or high heels (depending on the occasion, of course) and look wonderful. They'll call you Junoesque, willowy, or streamlined, according to your basic structural plan. And "queenly" is the word for you when you walk down the aisle in your regal white wedding gown.

	SILHOUETTE	FABRICS AND COLORS
IN PRO-PORTION	1. You can wear— a. Slim fitted dresses and suits and coats b. Or, the most dramatically sweeping lines c. Classic, sculptured, or waltz-skirted evening dresses 2. You should cultivate— a. Normal, easy shoulders b. Full bishop sleeves c. The two-piece look: blouses and skirts	1. You can choose— a. Fabrics with body b. Jerseys and woolens and tweeds c. Brocades and satins d. Big prints 2. You should avoid a complete outfit of one shock color (as fuchsia, chartreuse, bright royal)
TOO FAT	1. You should wear— a. Slightly bloused tops b. Straight or flaring skirts—in any case, worn as long as is becoming and always easy through the hips c. Deep V necks (for evening, halter décolletages) d. Moderately padded shoulders e. Long, loose sleeves f. Swagger rather than fitted coats 2. You'd better avoid— a. Short sleeves b. Any plastered-to-the-body effect in fitted clothes	1. Your best bets are— a. Mat-textured dark woolens and tweeds b. Faille, moire taffetas c. Velvet d. Tiny prints, geometrics, on dark ground 2. You'd better skip— a. Shiny fabrics b. Two-color, two-piece outfits
TOO THIN	1. Your forte is— a. Soft, bloused bodices and very full, long cuffed sleeves b. Very full, gathered skirts c. Evening dresses with covered tops, billowy skirts d. Dramatic capes, bulky polo coats 2. You'd be wise to— a. Round out shoulders with slight padding b. Accent the littleness of your waist	1. Yours the right to wear— a. Shiny fabrics b. Hand knits, nubby tweeds c. Stiff fabrics 2. Play around with a. Bold prints and plaids b. Stark-white outfits
TOP HEAVY	1. Your best rules are— a. Gently bloused bodices b. Butcher-boy jackets c. High or narrow V necks d. Dropped waistline, perhaps cuffed around hips, or an unaccented waistline e. Flared or full skirts, with fullness starting at waistline or a little below f. Swagger coats, flaring slightly 2. Beware of— a. Padded shoulders b. High waistlines c. Short sleeves, especially short puffed sleeves	1. You can wear two-piece combinations; for instance— a. Dark top over light skirt b. Plain top over patterned skirt 2. Keep away from— a. Printed blouses b. Thick fabrics, especially above the waist
PEAR-SHAPED	1. You can wear— a. Short fitted jackets b. Flared skirts c. Evening dresses with deep decolletages and billowy skirts d. Flareback swagger coats—full length and sweeping, or very brief, boxy boleros 2. You should wear— a. Big collars, wide necklines, other top interest b. Slightly padded shoulders	1. Your two-piece combinations will be— a. Light top over dark skirt b. Patterned top over plain skirt 2. Better skip— a. Too-bulky skirt fabrics b. Any accents of a different fabric or color on skirt (as ruffles, bands, pockets)

170

Self-Portrait

Pitfalls. When you should stand and sit tall, you slump self-consciously, inevitably calling more attention to your height. You are apt to fall for certain trivia that you should avoid— little bows, tiny blossomy hats, little-girl clothes. And if you aren't wise, you'll be harassed by too-short girdles, slips that ride up, bra straps that cut into your shoulders, and toe-stubbing shoes.

	FOUNDATIONS	SLIPS

IN PRO-PORTION	1. You require a smooth all-in-one for special occasions
	2. And always you want—
	  a. A girdle proportioned to your elongated self
	  b. Carefully fitted bras, perhaps long-line ones
		1. Seek out a slip sized for taller women
		2. Wear petticoats

TOO FAT	1. You'll definitely want an all-in-one, fairly long in thigh 2. Be warned—don't attempt strapless bras	1. Have a slip with a bra-shaped top 2. Always wear easily cut slips that refuse to ride up and bunch
TOO THIN	1. Have lightweight restraint by way of an elastic-woven pantie-girdle 2. A padded bra, if you need it	1. Try petticoats to puff out full skirts 2. Wear lacy, ribbony camisoles for an illusion of more up top
TOP HEAVY	1. Choose an all-in-one with particularly well-built bra 2. Or, pick a firm, longer-line bra and a separate high-waisted girdle that meet each other	1. A must is the slip with well-fitted bra top 2. A petticoat for under your fuller skirts

PEAR-SHAPED	1. Wear a competent girdle with tummy and *derrière* control
	2. Wear a padded bra, if needed, for balanced proportions
		1. You can wear a camisole-top slip, bias cut front and back, straight at the sides, to avoid "sitting it out"
		2. For special occasions, wear—
		  a. Camisoles
		  b. Low-flared petticoats

171

	SHOES	STOCKINGS

IN PRO-PORTION	1. You're the lucky one who can wear—
	  a. Flat heels *or* medium high-heeled pumps
	  b. Wide straps
	  c. Polished Cuban-heeled walking shoes
	2. Goes without saying you don't need—
	  a. Spike heels
	  b. High platform soles
		1. You need—
		  a. Stretchy Lastex-topped stockings
		  b. Stockings made for your lengthy limbs
		2. Your extra dividends for fewer runs—mesh stockings

TOO FAT	1. You should consider—
	  a. Custom-made shoes
	  b. Shoes with unusually efficient arch support
	  c. Moderately low vamps for a slimming effect
	2. But you won't choose—
	  a. Deeply cut (bulge-making) opera pumps
	  b. Very high heels
	  c. Very flat heels
		1. For you—
		  a. Elasticized tops and reinforced heels and toes
		  b. Absolutely straight seams at all times
		2. Have high, slim, darker heels to trim look of ankles

TOO THIN	1. You may have—
	  a. All the straps you want
	  b. Colorful evening opera pumps
	  c. D'Orsay cut street pumps
	2. But beware of—
	  a. Buying shoes carelessly, settling for less-than-perfect fit
	  b. Teetering on spiky heels
		1. Wear high-luster stockings for curvier-looking legs
		2. You can have—
		  a. Seamless stockings
		  b. Lighter shades

TOP HEAVY	1. Your best bets are—
	  a. Medium-high heels
	  b. Wedge-heeled sport shoes
	  c. Low, slimmingly cut vamps
	  d. Shoes that blend with your costume—lengthen waist-to-toe effect
	2. You wish to avoid—
	  a. High-cut shoes
	  b. Flat heels
		1. Wear stockings fitted as to ankle, leg, and welt, as well as to length
		2. Do try seamless stockings, blended with your dress

PEAR-SHAPED	1. Your choices are—
	  a. Opera pumps
	  b. Medium to high heels
		1. Select—
		  a. Dull, darker hosiery
		  b. Inside-out woven stockings
		2. Stress straight seams

172

	ACCESSORIES AND HATS	SPORTSWEAR

IN PRO-PORTION	1. Say a definite "yes" to—
	  a. Big handbags (for casual wear, shoulder bags)
	  b. Wide belts
	  c. Multistrand necklaces, dangling earrings
	  d. Gauntlet gloves
	  e. Dramatic cartwheel hats, big sailors, etc.
	2. A definite "no" to—
	  a. Tiny calots
	  b. Small flower hats
	  c. Winsome bonnets
		1. You'll play around in—
		  a. Slacks
		  b. Contrasting sweaters or shirts
		  c. Two-color dressmaker swim suits
		  d. If perfect figure, a white satin suit
		2. You'll give a wide berth to—
		  a. Kittenish play dresses
		  b. Brief shorts

TOO FAT	1. You should acquire—
	  a. Flat, neat, but fairly large handbags
	  b. Dramatic clips for bottom of plunging V necklines
	  c. Cartwheel hats, outsize berets
	  d. Narrow belts (preferably self-belts)
	  e. Loose gloves
	2. You'd best not play around with—
	  a. Choker necklaces
	  b. Halo hats
		1. You'll go outdoors in—
		  a. Well-cut golf dresses
		  b. A dressmaker swim suit (dark, dull fabric) with important inside slimming apparatus—possibly custom made
		2. You'll rule out—
		  a. Slacks
		  b. Shorts

TOO THIN	1. Yours by all rights—
	  a. Massed jewelry at neck and wrist
	  b. Large gathered bags
	  c. Asymmetrical cartwheels and visor hats
	  d. Wide, fantastic belts and crushed cummerbunds
	  e. Brilliant scarves
	2. Not half so effective—
	  a. Tiny, delicate jewelry
	  b. Envelope bags
		1. You can have—
		  a. Slacks
		  b. Bare midriff outfits
		  c. A dressmaker swim suit—splashy print, bold color, or shiny fabric
		2. You'll snub—
		  a. Shorts
		  b. Strapless sun dresses
		  c. Maillots

TOP HEAVY	1. You might choose—
	  a. Small pins, bracelets, earrings
	  b. Casual shoulder bags
	  c. Small, narrow-brimmed hats—as a cloche, a briefly brimmed sailor, etc.
	  d. A bright scarf to dangle from your handbag
	  e. Smooth, classic gloves
	2. You should ignore—
	  a. Cartwheel hats
	  b. A lot of ornamentation above your waist
		1. You'll play in—
		  a. Slacks
		  b. Longish golf dresses
		  c. A dressmaker swim suit with good midriff control
		2. But you won't play in—
		  a. Bare midriff outfits
		  b. Shorts

PEAR-SHAPED	1. You can go in for—
	  a. Big, beautiful pairs of clips—one for either side of a square or heart-shaped neckline
	  b. Clumpy jewelry
	  c. Large brimmed hats—bretons, garden-party hats, etc.
	  d. Cummerbunds
	2. But don't indulge in—
	  a. Pinhead hats
	  b. Long necklaces dangling down to your waist
		1. For you—
		  a. Flared golf dresses
		  b. Dirndl sun dresses
		  c. Princess swim suit
		2. But not for you—
		  a. Slacks
		  b. Pedal pushers

173

Typed for You: TOO SHORT

REPRODUCED BY SPECIAL ARRANGEMENT WITH THE EDITORS OF *Mademoiselle*, 122 EAST 42ND STREET, NEW YORK 17, N. Y.

Self-Portrait

Potentialities. You can wear flowery little bonnets, fluttery chiffons and tulles, small-girl dresses, and severely tailored suits—the last without looking mannish, somehow. You can scamper around in brief shorts. You can walk on high heels without eclipsing your man. They'll call you petite, ethereal or *gamine* according to your basic structural plan. And "angelic" is the word for you when you walk down the aisle in your misty white wedding gown.

	SILHOUETTE	FABRICS AND COLORS
IN PRO-PORTION	1. You can wear— a. Accordion-pleated skirts b. Fitted, beltless princess lines c. Long, fitted sleeves d. Bellboy jackets and boleros e. Short capes for evening 2. Steer clear of— a. Too-voluminous coats b. Too much shoulder padding	1. Definitely for you— a. Chiffon and tulle b. Crisp faille and taffeta c. Colors, colors, colors 2. Instead of nubby tweeds, pick— a. Flannels and thin woolens b. Mat jerseys
TOO FAT	1. You are at your best in— a. Vertical lines b. Redingotes c. Straight full-length coats d. Straight or slightly flared skirts e. One-piece dresses f. Shoulders with a bit of padding 2. Beware of— a. Flying scarves, contrasting panels that distract from smooth overall effect b. Tight fit through hips	1. You should choose— a. Dark, simple fabrics (always, always your best friend is black) b. Single-color dresses c. Tiny tie prints, if a print you must have 2. Be sure to shun— a. Clinging fabrics b. Harsh loud colors c. White
TOO THIN	1. Yours the privilege of wearing— a. High-waisted ballerina skirts b. Soft, romantic blouses c. Short boleros and brief flaring jackets d. Short or long puffy sleeves e. Evening skirts and blouses 2. But avoid the two extremes of— a. Fussy (instead of soft) clothes b. Severely tailored suits	1. You can wear— a. Soft tweeds and flannels b. Chiffon, silk, bouffant fabrics c. Small checks and prints d. Satin and other lustrous fabrics 2. Avoid— a. Too-bulky fabrics b. Outsize plaids
TOP HEAVY	1. You are prettiest in— a. Unadorned bodices b. High or V necks c. Evening dresses with shoestring straps d. Normal or dropped waistline, then full or flared skirt 2. Remember to have— a. Normal or raglan shoulders—utterly padless, if becoming b. Skirts as long as practicable	1. You should pick— a. Smooth woolens b. Mat rayons 2. Steer clear of— a. Ruffles or other doodads above the waistline b. Two-color combinations, skirts and shirts c. Bold prints
PEAR-SHAPED	1. You should wear— a. All extraneous details at waist or above (vertical tucks or ruffles to plump out bosom, etc.) b. Full or flared skirts to conceal bulges c. Shoulders slightly padded d. For evening, a long, full, dark skirt plus a light bodice 2. Beware of— a. Swags, draperies, floating panels on skirts b. Tight-fitting long jerkins, overblouses, etc.	1. For you— a. Lingerie touches on bodice b. Dark smooth-fabric skirts c. Small flower or geometric prints 2. Not for you— a. Brightly colored skirts b. King-size plaids and prints

174

Self-Portrait

Pitfalls. When you should make it a point to stay small and sweet, you clamber up on too-high heels and platform soles and you build up your forelock into an overwhelming pompadour. You have a yen for things you'd best leave strictly alone—the big cartwheel hat, the huge dashing shoulder bag, the wrapped three-quarter length coat. And if you aren't careful, you'll be tortured by slips that always show, girdles too long for your stockings and stockings too tall for your girdle.

		FOUNDATIONS	SLIPS
	IN PRO-PORTION	1. Wear a brief girdle or pantie-girdle 2. Pick good uplift bras	1. Try the snip-off-at-proper length slip 2. And with princess-line clothes, a princess-line slip
	TOO FAT	1. You'll want an all-in-one, not too long in waist and thigh 2. Remember to look for half-size underthings best for shorties	1. Your choice is a bra-top slip: to be had in shorter than average length 2. And always you'll want half-size slips, to make tucks unnecessary
	TOO THIN	1. Select an all-elasticized knit pantie-girdle 2. And wear a well-fitted light-duty bra, padded if necessary	1. For you—a half-size bias-cut slip 2. Wear camisoles and petticoats under full skirts and blouses
	TOP HEAVY	1. You'll want perhaps a custom-made bra 2. You'll want, too, a high-waisted, boned girdle	1. Pick a bra-top slip 2. Under frilled skirts wear a petticoat and a long-line camisole-strapped bra
	PEAR-SHAPED	1. Wear a girdle with diagonal control for tummy and *derrière*, with a high, lightly boned waist 2. Choose a longer-line bra for a smooth diaphragm	1. Select a camisole slip, easy above the waist, flared from there down

175

	SHOES	STOCKINGS

IN PRO-PORTION	1. You can walk on—
	  a. High, slim heels
	  b. Opera pumps
	  c. Colorful play shoes
	2. You won't want—
	  a. Ballet slippers
	  b. Too many straps
	  c. High platforms
		1. Yours the pleasure of—
		  a. Stockings blended to your ensemble
		  b. Seamless stockings
		  c. Lacy evening stockings
		2. Yours the necessity of searching for shorter stockings for smaller feet

TOO FAT	1. You'll look for—
	  a. Slightly pointed vamps
	  b. Good arch support
	  c. Medium heels (never allowed to get run-over)
	2. You'll refuse—
	  a. Odd colors
	  b. Spiky heels
	  c. Straps
		1. Always choose—
		  a. Length proportioned to foot size
		  b. Stockings with stretchy tops
		2. You might try dark stockings, blended with your dark costume

TOO THIN	1. You can wear—
	  a. The dressier shoes—small bows, gilt touches, etc.
	  b. Moderate platforms
	2. But you won't want—
	  a. Ballerina slippers (you'll never find them narrow enough, anyway)
	  b. Intricately cut-out sandals
		1. You can wear—
		  a. The newest light shades
		  b. Seamless stockings
		  c. For evening—all the frivolities, as lacy stockings, clocks, etc.
		2. Be sure your stockings are the right size—beware of bunching at the ankle

TOP HEAVY	1. You may choose—
	  a. Opera pumps
	  b. Medium-heeled walking shoes
	  c. Wedge play shoes
	2. But shun—
	  a. The spikier heels
	  b. High-strapped shoes
		1. You can have dark, blending stockings

PEAR-SHAPED	1. Your best choices are—
	  a. Opera pumps
	  b. Dark, simple shoes
	2. Don't attempt straps, bows, etc.
		1. Try stockings with darker seams and tall heels to slim ankle and calf
		2. Don't attempt pastel colors or seamless stockings

	ACCESSORIES AND HATS	SPORTSWEAR
IN PRO-PORTION	1. Yours for the having— a. Pearls and pearls and pearls b. Small button or short dangle earrings c. Dull stones in small settings d. Little pouch bags e. Short snug gloves f. Small cloches, flower bonnets 2. Yours just for looking at— a. Big knapsack bags b. Huge glittering masses of costume jewelry	1. You should play in— a. Brief shorts b. Little-girl play dresses c. Maillots or soft dressmaker suits d. Pedal pushers 2. Leave slacks for your leggier sisters
TOO FAT	1. You can wear or carry— a. Narrow flat bags b. Baguette clips at base of plunging V neckline c. Wedding-ring earrings d. High-crown, sharply slanted brims on hats; medium berets 2. You'd better shun— a. Boxy bags b. Hats with bows and veils, especially chin veils c. Necklaces	1. You can wear— a. Golf dresses b. Dark or neutral play suits c. Dressmaker swim suits 2. But avoid— a. Slacks and shorts b. Bright colors
TOO THIN	1. You may have— a. Lots of pearls b. Squashy bags c. Wide belts d. Softly veiled and flowered small hats e. Long white kid evening gloves f. A silk scarf for your neck or waist 2. But not for you are— a. Big costume jewelry pieces b. Cartwheel hats	1. For you— a. The hard-to-wear, straight, long shorts b. Shiny swim suits c. Skinny blue jeans d. White; large prints 2. But don't swim in skin-fitting maillots
TOP HEAVY	1. You can choose— a. 4-button white gloves if your arms are longish b. Small, trim handbags c. Almost brimless sailors, cloches 2. You'd best avoid— a. Wide-brimmed hats b. Too much jewelry	1. Wear— a. Well-cut medium-length shorts b. Dark shirts c. Rather long golf dresses d. Bra-control swim suits 2. Don't wear slacks or short shorts
PEAR-SHAPED	1. You can revel in— a. Lapel doodads b. Chin bows c. Cummerbunds to bind a small waist d. Small, rather flat handbags e. Bretons, veiled sailors or bonnets 2. But skip— a. Shoulder bags b. Too many fussy details, even above waist	1. You're pretty in— a. Flaring play dresses b. Princess swim suits 2. Better shun— a. Slacks b. Jeans

conservative in the styles you buy. Some of the up-to-the-minute fads in clothing soon become outdated, whereas most suits, tailored dresses, and other conservative clothes remain fashionable much longer.

Don't wear slip-over sweaters, low-cut necklines, or fancy oddments in the office. Don't overdress or wear an excessive amount of jewelry. When in doubt, be conservative.

Every woman who takes pride in her appearance should keep tab on such magazines as *Mademoiselle, McCall's, Women's Home Companion,* and *Ladies' Home Journal.*

22. The charts on pages 170 to 177, reproduced through the courtesy of *Mademoiselle,* will be helpful to women who have a figure problem. You will notice that the charts have to do with two major deviations from the "normal" or "average" figure—the girl who is *too tall,* and the girl who is *too short.* These two main categories are broken down into five subcategories each. Thus there is a discussion of the *too-tall* girl who is in proportion, or too fat, or too thin, or top heavy, or pear-shaped. The *too-short* girl is then discussed under the same subcategories: in proportion, too fat, too thin, top heavy, and pear-shaped.

The easiest way to use these charts (if you have a figure problem) is to find the silhouette, under either "Too Tall" or "Too Short," which most nearly resembles your own, and then read across the charts. You will find, in order, suggestions on these topics: silhouette, fabrics and colors, accessories and hats, foundations, slips, shoes, stockings, and sportswear.

One further word on the subject of dress. Repetition for sake of emphasis may be desirable. Do not dress like a fashion plate at all times. Dress suitably for the occasion. We have written mostly about business dress. We may have left the impression that one should be *dressed up* all the time, or that under any and all conditions one should dress so as to make the *best appearance.* Not so; at a party, at the golf club, at the beach, at home, on a motoring trip, on vacation, and at many other places a wide range of choice of clothing is permitted without ignoring the stated controls of appropriate dress— health, comfort, good taste, and attractive appearance. If you take pains with your attire wherever you are, you will not be a slovenly, unattractive person in any company.

Suggestions for Study and Discussion

1. On the assumption that one should dress appropriately for the occasion, list in your notebook the principal activities in which you engage regularly. Include such things as tennis, golf, bridge, evening parties—formal, semiformal, and business-dress—motoring, winter sports, swimming, and others of like nature in addition to your school or college or business or home activities.

2. List for each what you consider the kind of wearing apparel that is comfortable and in reasonably good taste.

3. Check off the items in the list which you have in sufficient supply.

4. Indicate the order in which you should add to your wardrobe items you do not now have by placing a figure 1 after each needed most, and a figure 2 after those to come next. This assumes, of course, that you may not be able to supply all your needs at once.

5. Why are certain items of dress approved for different activities? Do you remember "plus-fours" that golfers once favored? Or the feminine bathing suits once considered the thing? At least you have seen pictures of many outmoded items of dress. Why have so many changes come about? The preference for the *tuxedo* over the "swallow-tail" full-dress suit, for example. The answer is not so simple as it seems. There is a good lesson for you in a complete answer. Trying to think it out should be a rewarding exercise. You will better understand the reasons for current usage in the matter of dress if you can account for changes in customs. When you have thought this matter through, list the reasons for the radical changes in dress that have come about.

6. Clothes alone are no guarantee of good grooming. Many auxiliary tools and materials are necessary. List the tools and materials needed if you are to keep up a good appearance without prohibitive cost.

7. Why use a deodorant after bathing? To kill B.O.? Why use it at any time?

8. Voice plays a large part in the way one impresses others. List the qualities of your voice and manner of speaking and laughing normally. Also, when under pressure, or in a hurry, or on the telephone, or in any unusual situation. Check the things that need special attention. Ask friends and relatives for their opinions of your listing; even for their help in overcoming defects.

9. List your posture defects, your walking habits, your lounging habits. Check those needing special attention. Here again ask others to help keep you up to the mark in your efforts to improve your appearance in these respects.

10. Actors and actresses often are imitated by others in the things they do to enhance their "stage presence." Consider this matter carefully. You may reach conclusions that will modify your own practices, or prevent questionable ones.

Items	First Week								Second Week								Third Week							
	S	M	T	W	Th	F	S		S	M	T	W	Th	F	S		S	M	T	W	Th	F	S	
1. Teeth brushed (3)																								
2. Thorough bath																								
3. Men: Shave Women: Proper make-up																								
4. Hair combed and brushed																								
5. Fresh pair hose																								
6. Nails cleaned and trimmed																								
7. Hands washed																								
8. Clothes pressed and clean																								
9. Clothes free from odor																								
10. Shoes cleaned and shined																								

11. List some fads that are currently observable, and others that have passed. Then state your conclusions as to the wisdom of following faddists in matters of grooming.

12. Assume that you are about to apply for, or enter upon, your first important permanent job. How do you measure up to the requirements in the matter of approved business dress and general grooming? What do you need to add, or do?

13. Check the current issues of such magazines as *Esquire, Mademoiselle, Ladies' Home Journal,* etc., for new suggestions on dress and grooming.

14. Rule in your notebook a record form like the one on page 180, and for a few weeks keep a record of your grooming habits. Under each day of the week put a check against each item on which you were fully up to the mark set by good-grooming standards.

Too much work? Remember that you must *work at* personality development if you would achieve an outstanding personality. Also, that habit-forming is a part of the process. Recording these details for a time will greatly assist you in forming good habits.

15. After the record-keeping period is passed, turn back to your record from time to time and check your standing that day on these items. If you don't rate high, resume the habit-forming practice of recording your daily appearance.

16. Make a shopping tour to determine the cost of good grooming. You needn't buy at the moment unless you wish to. Inquire about styles, fabrics, and prices. You may be surprised to find that it costs no more to be well dressed and generally well groomed than it does to be carelessly attired and unprepossessing in appearance.

Personality Reminders

1. Do you need a haircut *now?*
2. Did you remember to stand up straight yesterday?
3. When was the last time you washed your hair?
4. Do you use a deodorant regularly?
5. Are your neck and ears clean *now?*

Special References

Bennett, Joan. *How to Be Attractive,* Second Revised Edition
Kettunen, Marietta. *Fundamentals of Dress*
Morton, Grace Margaret. *Arts of Costume and Personal Appearance*
Ryan, Mildred Graves. *Your Clothes and Personality,* Third Edition
Stote, Dorothy. *Men Too Wear Clothes,* Revised Edition
Cotten, Emmi. *Clothes Make Magic*
Williams, Beryl. *Fashion Is Our Business*
Fenwick, Millicent: *Vogue Book of Etiquette*

CHAPTER NINE

Overcoming Fear and Stage Fright

SHAKESPEARE, in Act II of *Julius Caesar*, has Caesar say to his wife, Calpurnia, on the day of his assassination,

> Cowards die many times before their death;
> The valiant never taste of death but once.
> Of all the wonders that I yet have heard,
> It seems to me most strange that men should fear;
> Seeing that death, a necessary end,
> Will come when it will come.

Here Caesar was thinking of a particular kind of fear—the fear of death. He had been warned not to leave his house that day because the signs and portents hinted at the imminent death of a great man. But Caesar scoffed at the thought of fear—with a result that everybody knows.

The Universality of Fear

If Caesar actually knew no fear, he was truly a remarkable person. Fear is probably the most universal of all experiences. It has plagued and tortured the human race since the beginning of time.

Our primitive ancestor shivered in his dark cave, terrified by the flashes of lightning and the distant booming of thunder, or gazed with superstitious dread at an eclipse of the sun or a meteor in transit. Contemporary man sits in his well-appointed office and shivers in fear over the horrors of war or looks forward with dread to the speech he must make tonight.

These two men are thousands of years apart in time. A great gulf separates them in their culture levels. One is ignorant; the other is educated. One is unkempt; the other, clean and well dressed. One understands none of the most elementary facts about the world; the other may have a college degree in engineering.

But they are both afraid.

Fear is a great leveler. It puts kings and slaves on the same plane. The peasant and the lord, the worker and his boss, the dictator and his subjects, the conqueror and the conquered, the great and the small, the young and the aged—fear is at some time the master, the universal oppressor of them all.

Fear is the great common denominator of all mankind. We may disagree as to its exact definition, but we all understand how it feels.

Fear hampers personality development. It makes us hesitant, uncertain, shy. It keeps us from striking out boldly to accomplish our destiny. Stage fright is a stumbling block to the career of many a promising young man or woman. If we are to develop our personalities adequately, we must know some way to conquer fears or at least to decrease their number and force.

Look about you at the people you know. Observe how fear, timidity, shyness, and stage fright regulate their lives, beat them down, keep them from doing the things they should do, from accomplishing what they should accomplish.

Here is a brilliant young woman of twenty-two, a college graduate. She has a good job and is apparently well adjusted socially. What is she afraid of? She is so terrified of the darkness that she will not walk from her car at the curb across some twenty feet of lawn and sidewalk to her front door unless someone is with her. She will not enter her own home at night if her parents are away and the lights are off. She will not walk down a well-lighted street at night alone. She cannot remember a time when darkness did not terrify her. Nothing has ever hurt her in the dark. So far as she can remember, no person or animal has ever frightened her in the dark. Nevertheless, she is afraid of the dark. This particular woman will probably never overcome her fear.

Here is a college sophomore who turned down a bid to a fraternity that he had long wanted to join, a fraternity that would have been of great value to him, not only in college but also in his career after graduation. The reason? One of the requirements is that initiates must make a speech before all the members. He couldn't do it. The thought of talking before a group fills him with such dread that his hands sweat, his heart pounds, his mouth gets dry, his knees literally shake. He wouldn't make a speech if he never joined a fraternity. He wouldn't make a speech if his whole future career hinged on it.

This young man is fearless in most circumstances. He dives from the high board, fights anybody who will put on the gloves with him, and plays football. But he is afraid to speak in public.

Here is a little girl in the second grade who developed an unreasonable dislike of school. Her parents and teacher were baffled at this change because the child seemed to get along nicely in her classes. She was well behaved in school and on the playground. She was moderately extroverted and did not seem to fear any of the other children. Her dislike of school was finally traced to a terrifying experience she had had with a large dog when she was in the first grade. She was walking to school alone, some four or five blocks away, when the dog blocked her path and growled at her. She retreated, screaming, to the porch of a near-by house, with the dog in full pursuit. Some college students chanced by, drove off the dog, and walked to school with the child. Later that year she had nightmares about dogs, and in this manner the fear was aggravated. Fear of being teased caused her to suppress any expression of her real fear and to develop an intense dislike of school.

Look around you anywhere and you will see people working and living in fear. The child is afraid of his school examinations. The girl is afraid of losing her popularity. The business head is afraid for his business. The teacher is afraid that she will lose her job. The minister is afraid that he will be moved to a less happy place of work. The farmer is afraid that the price will go down before he can sell his produce.

In every factory, farm, home, business, and school, there are miserable people constantly haunted by fear. We can't seem to rid ourselves of it.

There is hardly a thing in the world that someone is not afraid of. People are afraid of worms, bugs, spider webs, darkness, strangers, rain, lightning, dark clouds, furry animals, dead bodies, bones, fish, doctors, medicine, knives, high places—the list could go on indefinitely. As if this were not enough, man has conjured up in his mind countless creations of the imagination to be afraid of:

witches, goblins, ghosts, demons, spirits, giants, elves, wicked fairies, and a host of other things.

From time to time attempts have been made to give impressive-sounding names to our more serious fears. Here are a few of them.

Zoophobia—fear of animals
Pathophobia—fear of disease
Claustrophobia—fear of closed places
Peccatiphobia—fear of sinning
Monophobia—fear of solitude
Phobophobia—fear of being afraid
Misophobia—fear of contamination
Ereuphobia—fear of blushing
Astraphobia—fear of thunderstorms
Botophobia—fear of cellars
Algophobia—fear of pain
Taphephobia—fear of being buried alive
Androphobia—fear of men
Gynephobia—fear of women
Agoraphobia—fear of open places
Aquaphobia—fear of water
Theophobia—fear of God
Heliophobia—fear of light
Nyctophobia—fear of darkness
Acrophobia—fear of high places
Thanaphobia—fear of death
Ochlophobia—fear of crowds
Anthrophobia—fear of the whole human race

Finally, one that afflicts so many of us in the spring,

Ergophobia—fear of work!

We do not know how many fears or phobias there are, nor do we see any particular advantage in making up a technical word for each one. The only advantage that we can see is that if you are ashamed to have your friends know you are afraid of the dark, you can tell them the psychologist said you were suffering from nyctophobia. And we are sure that ergophobia sounds better than laziness!

How Do We Acquire Our Fears?

Where do we get our fears? How are they ever started? What makes some of them grow more firmly fixed on us than do others? Do we inherit our fears?

These are questions that come to mind when we begin to consider how we acquire fears. Because so many people are afraid of the dark, it might be argued that fear of the dark is instinctive or hereditary.

Perhaps as good a way as any to approach the problem is to classify fears under three types and discuss each one in turn. This may not be the best way, and perhaps we shall be guilty of over-simplifying a complex problem. Nevertheless, let us at least tentatively consider three kinds of fears, classified according to the way we acquire them:

Fears that appear to be hereditary, or inborn.

Fears acquired by direct, nonverbal conditioning.

Fears acquired by verbal conditioning and mental association.

FEARS THAT ARE HEREDITARY, OR INBORN

The layman has a tendency to place too many fears in this class. The psychologists tell us that actually there are very few of these natural fears.

Some 30 years ago, Dr. John B. Watson, working in the Johns Hopkins University, made an extensive study of children's emotions. Although some of his conclusions have been questioned, and much of his experimental work has been carried out further since then, nevertheless, it will pay us to see what he found.

Watson concluded that children were not naturally afraid of darkness, snakes, dogs, rabbits, etc., but that they showed natural fear to only two things: a sudden, loud noise and a loss of balance or support. He decided that these are the only two fears we inherit; all the rest we acquire.

Other researchers have added at least one other natural fear to Watson's two: fear at the *sudden* and unexpected appearance of certain visual stimuli.

There are, then, only three, or at the most, only four or five natural fears. And we know these can be at least partially overcome.

People have learned to ignore sudden loud noises, or at least not to be frightened by them. People have also overcome the fear of falling, as witness the ease with which they dive, jump, and fly through the air. And we can grow accustomed to having strange and unexpected things pop up before us.

If our inborn fears were the only ones that harassed us, life would be relatively free from fear. The great majority of our fears are learned.

FEARS THAT ARE ACQUIRED BY NONVERBAL CONDITIONING

Conditioning is a simple form of learning. It can be best explained by describing an experiment carried out by Watson.

It was first established that a given child was afraid of a sudden, loud noise but was not afraid of a rabbit. Then the rabbit was put near the child at the same time that a sudden noise was made behind a screen. The child reacted primarily to the noise, but it was discovered that the rabbit had got caught up into the total situation. Later, when the rabbit alone (without the noise) was shown, the child exhibited signs of fear.

The fear of the rabbit, then, was a conditioned fear. No words were used in the experiment—the child was too young to talk—and so the process is called "nonverbal" conditioning.

It was found also that the child who was frightened by the rabbit, as in the experiment just described, had a tendency to be afraid of other things that resembled the rabbit in any way. Thus, an acquired fear of a rabbit may be transferred to a cat, a squirrel, a small dog, or even a fur muff.

It is suggested that many of our fears are acquired accidentally in this fashion. The child *hears* the thunder and reacts by being afraid, but at the same time he may be looking at the lightning, the rain, or the dark clouds, so that any of these stimuli may later frighten him.

If a door slams when the baby is reaching for a toy, the fear reaction may become connected with the sight of the toy. The baby later shows fear of the toy, to the mystification of his parents.

FEARS ACQUIRED BY VERBAL CONDITIONING AND MENTAL ASSOCIATION

After the child acquires some mastery of language, a new avenue is opened up for the acquisition of more fears. He begins to hear stories that frighten him. He listens to his parents discussing fearful events, like bombings, fires, explosions, murders, kidnaping, and the like. He reviews these events in his mind, enlarges on them, and in his imaginings becomes a part of them.

Older children and thoughtless adults tell him stories that have a strong fear element. He sees motion pictures and learns, through a combination of visual and verbal stimuli, to be afraid of even more things. The radio does its bit by offering dramatic sketches for children in which horror is a feature. Television also adds its horror shows.

A large number of the standard stories for children should be deleted from children's books because of the element of fear and terror in them. There are practically no movies suitable for young children. A number of children's radio programs are unfit for even adults to hear.

A child who has formerly shown absolutely no fear of spiders can, within five minutes, be verbally conditioned so that he will have a fear of spiders and spider webs for many years.

In somewhat the same way, adults acquire additional fears and reinforce their childhood fears.

The Mastery of Fear

We are not sure that "The Mastery of Fear" is just the right caption here. Perhaps we can never completely master and eliminate all our fears. Perhaps we shouldn't attempt to eliminate completely all of them. There probably are extreme instances where fear, judiciously and very cautiously used, is valuable as a means of social control. But we all would like to master the fears that hold us back from our best achievement and handicap our personalities.

There is no simple, easily applied rule that will invariably work for the cure of fears. There are, however, certain principles and techniques for overcoming fear that will be helpful to anyone who will apply them to his particular case.

THE PRINCIPLE OF NEGATIVE ADAPTATION

This means that if we are exposed to a relatively harmless stimulus or situation enough times, we may learn to ignore it. In other words, we become adapted negatively to the stimulus.

An illustration is found in the case of the person who is learning to dive. At first the falling sensation may call out the instinctive fear of loss of balance; but, as every swimmer knows, this fear may soon be overcome.

A child who has acquired a fear of dogs may be helped to overcome it if his parents will give him a small puppy. Constant association with the rapidly growing animal will frequently, though not always, result in a lessening fear of other dogs.

A six-year-old boy, afraid of the dark, was helped to overcome it by several things his father did. First, the father would take the boy for walks late in the afternoon, and they would walk until dark. The father always held the child's hand and walked close to him. Next, the father would take the child in his arms and carry him around the dark yard, exploring mysterious objects, which always turned out to be a tree, or a rose bush, or some familiar landmark. The child was allowed to carry the father's flashlight and shine it on anything that began to look too forbidding. Finally, a small electric lamp was placed on a low table near the child's bed, and he was encouraged to use it when he wanted to. Gradually darkness began to lose its terror for him.

Under no circumstances should this principle of negative adaptation be used abruptly. To throw a child into the water to make him overcome fear of water or to push him alone into a dark room in order to conquer fear of the dark is nothing short of criminal. This technique will only increase the child's fear. Negative adaptation must be used gradually and cautiously.

While the examples used here have to do with children, isn't it possible for you to utilize this same principle in overcoming some of your own fears? Just go ahead and expose yourself *gradually* to the thing that frightens you.

THE PRINCIPLE OF RECONDITIONING

This means connecting the thing feared with something that is enjoyed. This method may be used with both children and adults in overcoming conditioned fears.

After Watson had taught the child to be afraid of a rabbit by presenting the rabbit and the noise together, he cured the fear by reconditioning. The child enjoyed eating, as all normal beings do. As the child was eating his dinner, the rabbit was brought into the room a number of feet from the child, and kept there. At first the child showed some alarm, but inasmuch as the rabbit kept his distance, the child's attention soon went back to the food. The next day the rabbit was brought just a little nearer and held there, with the same results. Eventually the pleasure caused by eating so overcame the fear of the rabbit that the child would hold the rabbit's ear with one hand and eat with the other. His fear of rabbits was gone.

A teacher in a summer class told how she helped an entire rural elementary school to overcome fear of dark clouds and storms. One of the children in her school had been instantly killed by lightning at his home. Naturally, all the others heard about it, and a number of the older ones attended the funeral. It was shortly after this that the teacher observed a tenseness on the part of the children when a cloud would obscure the sun. When dark storm clouds appeared, a few children began to whimper and soon the entire one-room school would get caught up in the fear.

The situation grew worse instead of better as time went on, so the teacher decided to try the principle of reconditioning. Her problem was to find some way of associating pleasure, instead of fear, with storms.

She invented a sort of rough-and-tumble game which could be played indoors but which involved much moving about, climbing over seats, and in general, taking liberties with the somewhat prim schoolroom environment. The game proved immensely popular, but she would allow it to be played only during stormy weather. As soon as the storm clouds came up, all schoolwork stopped, papers and books were stowed away in desks, and the decks were cleared for action.

"It was pretty tough on the furniture," she said, "but before the year was over, most of the kids were looking forward to stormy weather with considerable pleasure."

Can you think of ways in which you can apply this principle to some of your own fear problems? It will work for adults as well as for children.

THE PRINCIPLE OF UNCOVERING THE HIDDEN ORIGIN OF THE FEAR

This principle is used mostly by psychologists in assisting adults to overcome fears so deep-seated that their origin is obscure. Frequently the original experience that starts the fear is so horrible that we tend to push it out of our mind. Or rather, we *try* to put it out of mind, but generally succeed only in shoving it down into what, for want of a better name, is called the "subconscious" mind.

The peculiar thing about such fears is that they frequently leave us after the psychologist has helped us dig up the original cause.

The technique of the psychologist is to probe into the subconscious, as it were, and pull out the old forgotten memory. We look it over, talk about it with the psychologist, perhaps joke a little about how much unhappiness has been caused by an incident which, in retrospect, seems rather trivial, and presto! we begin to lose our fear.

We don't know just how much of this sort of thing you can do alone. But it may help you to remember that your fear got started *somewhere;* perhaps you can recall where. Trace it back. How long have you had it? Can you remember a time when you didn't have it? Ask parents or other relatives to help you. Recall all the early childhood memories you can—perhaps the original fear-inspiring experience will be recalled. But for this sort of fear, it is best to have some expert help from a psychologist.

THE PRINCIPLE OF REASONING AWAY THE FEAR

This one is helpful in a few cases, but, in general, reason and strong emotion aren't even on speaking terms. Although this principle is of little value in helping children to overcome fears, it may be used by adults. It is especially valuable when used in conjunction with one or more of the other principles already described.

If you have an intense fear of storms and lightning, it may help you, as it has helped others, to make a scientific study of storms. Find out why lightning is more likely to strike a tall tree than a low bush. See what the meteorologists say about protecting yourself and your home against lightning. An intellectual understanding of the object of your fear may help you in overcoming it.

Overcoming Stage Fright

A speech teacher was asked what rule he gives his students for overcoming stage fright. He answered that there isn't any magic formula.

"It depends somewhat," he continued, "on what caused the fear. Not all stage fright is the same. In one person it has one origin; in another, an entirely different origin."

One college student was afraid to speak in public because of an experience he had had in the fourth grade. It was an occasion when all the children put on a program for the visiting mothers. This child's part consisted in reciting some simple poem that he had memorized—or at least he thought he had it memorized. He got

*Stage fright? There's no magic formula for over-
coming it, but a good way to start is to talk before
small groups.*

some of the words twisted around in a way that gave them an entirely different, and somewhat humorous, meaning. The audience
thoughtlessly laughed at his mistake, which only confused him
more. He stammered, tried to start again, blushed, and finally left
the platform in tears. From that day on, he feared audiences.

Some stage fright arises from feelings of inferiority and self-
consciousness about one's dress or appearance. Some is a part of the
individual's general personality pattern of shyness, submissiveness,
and lack of poise. Some may even be a disguised dislike of people
in general.

The speech teacher referred to said that if he were forced to give
one single rule for overcoming stage fright, it would be this:

*Force yourself to take advantage of every opportunity to appear
before an audience until your stage fright gradually wears off.*

Don't expect to make your first speech without feeling any fear.
But go ahead and make it anyway. You can even say to yourself,
"Oh boy, am I going to be nervous today, but here I go in spite of
it. Next time I shall be less nervous than I am now."

This is our old principle of negative adaptation—putting yourself
over and over again in a situation until the situation begins to lose
its fear-inspiring quality. The first speech didn't kill you. What if
you did get scared and forget and repeat and stammer? You are
still alive and kicking, and in all probability pretty proud of yourself for doing as well as you did. All right, then, go on back and do
it again—and again and again. This time a year from now you can

be a seasoned trouper, looking back with considerable amusement at that self of a year ago who was afraid to make a speech!

This isn't some pet theory. It works. It has worked for many of the people we know. We are sure it will work for you. Will you try it?

Here are a few more rather specific suggestions that have been useful to people suffering from stage fright.

1. Be sure that your clothing is on straight, all buttons buttoned, all zippers zipped, and then *forget about your appearance.*

2. Master your material as thoroughly as you can. Learn it so well that you know more about it than anyone else. In other words, don't go off half-cocked.

3. Practice before a small and sympathetic audience before you tackle a large and indifferent one.

4. Before you go on the platform, stand up straight and hold your head up. Avoid a weak, stoop-shouldered posture.

5. Take several deep breaths just before you go on.

6. Take it easy. Resist the inclination to speak too fast.

7. Try to be as "objective-minded" as you can. This means keeping your attention on your message, on what you are doing, or on

Hedrich-Blessing Studio

One of the most effective ways of overcoming "stage fright" is active participation in small group meetings.

the audience. It is the opposite of being "subjective-minded," in which state you continually think about yourself, your fear, etc.

8. Assume that your audience is going to be friendly and sympathetic. It may not always be so; but, at any rate, assuming that it will be gives you some added confidence at the start.

In concluding this chapter, we should point out that a number of experienced actors and actresses have never completely conquered stage fright. Many of them, after years on the stage, still have the first-night jitters. But they have mastered stage fright to the point where it doesn't hamper their performance.

You can do the same. The main thing is to keep on trying.

Suggestions for Study and Discussion

1. Are you afraid? Of what? Timid at times? Under what circumstances? We all are both afraid and timid at times if we are conscientious people. We may as well face it. Sometimes rightly so; at other times foolishly so. As a president once said in an economic crisis, "Our greatest (national) danger is fear itself." What did he mean?

2. What is a national *panic*? Why do panics take place on a national or lesser scale?

3. List your most important fears such as these: being afraid to speak up in class; being afraid to take part in a play; being afraid to sing out in church or chapel.

4. Next think about each listed fear carefully, and then write down why you feel as you do about the thing feared. No snap judgments. Only carefully considered and honest ones. Talk with your instructor about any fear that you have difficulty accounting for. With close friends and relatives, too, if you think they can help you. Ask your instructor to make your fears a subject of class discussion—impersonally, of course. Others probably have them too. So you need not *fear* that you will be identified as their only possessor.

5. Taking first the fear which seems most important from the standpoint of personality development, try to determine the steps you should take to overcome it. Write them down. Check them with your instructor and other advisers and against the suggestions for overcoming fear in this chapter. Take them at once. Stay with them until you overcome that fear. Noting these steps in your notebook, and the progress you are making with them, will help you stick to this task. Your instructor will be glad to bring up for class discussion the steps you propose to take, without identifying them as *your* steps.

6. Try to find some qualified person with whom to discuss your handicapping fears. An elderly minister once told us that he never enters the pulpit without a feeling of nervous apprehension—fear. Ask your pastor about this if you fear to speak in class or public. An actor, professional

or amateur, should be a good consultant if you can gain the ear of one. Anyone who is doing well what you fear to do will be a good consultant —an athlete, a singer, a musician, a star student, a coach, etc. Don't *fear* to consult people about your *fears.*

7. Look about you and observe fear in others—classmates, friends, relatives, and others. Try to determine the kind of fear observed and the possible reasons for it. If it looks absurd to you, list it in the notebook as such. Check the list of your own fears against the one made of others' fears. If theirs are absurd yours are too.

8. Worry is said to be at the bottom of many physical ailments. What has fear to do with worry? Would there be no worries if there were no fears?

9. Note well the listed technical names of common fears (page 185) and enter in your notebook those which you have. Be honest about this. No one will be without some of them to record. Try to classify according to this technical list the things you listed as those you are afraid of.

10. List the things of which you were afraid as a child. Check this list against your current list of fears. Are some of the old ones missing now? Why? Accounting for their disappearance may help you rid yourself of fears still felt.

11. It is customary to think of "stage fright" as being only fear of acting or speaking or singing in public. It is more than that. You may have it when you are about to confer with a new professor, or to enter a business office to get information needed, or to deliver an important message to a distinguished person, or to apply for a job. Check over the suggestions given for overcoming stage fright of the kind usually meant by this term to see how they apply to other kinds of stage fright.

12. Should you expect to overcome all your fears? Should you do so if you can? Or should you be glad to retain some of them? What good are any of them to you? Consider this carefully with a view to learning if *control* of *fear,* instead of *elimination* of it, may be the answer.

Personality Reminders

1. Have you done anything to overcome stage fright?

2. Do you know that, within reasonable limits, you can accomplish practically anything you want to accomplish?

3. Do you make a good impression on people by remembering their names?

4. Do you refrain from saying things that will cause people to be afraid and worry?

5. Are you sincerely determined to have a better personality a year from now than you have today?

Special References

Carnegie, Dale. *How to Stop Worrying and Start Living*
Emerson, William Robie Patten. *Health for the Having*
Finkelor, Dorothy C. *How to Make Your Emotions Work for You.*

CHAPTER TEN

The Last Word

THE SCIENTIFIC developments of the late nineteenth and the early twentieth centuries have brought us many blessings. There is one by-product of the scientific age, however, that is alarming to many thinking people.

Get Rid of the Defeatist's Philosophy

We refer to the widespread belief that man is nothing but a piece of mechanism, that he is a victim of his environment, that he is without power to direct his own destiny.

This philosophy of fatalism and defeatism destroys ambition and makes almost impossible on the part of its adherents any voluntary self-improvement. It robs man of the greatest endowment that distinguishes him from the lower animals: his will and capacity for purposive activity.

A more wholesome philosophy is that we are the captains of our souls, the masters of our own destiny. Within any sort of reasonable limits, we can do what we will to do and earnestly strive to do. By will and effort men *have* risen "on stepping stones of their dead selves to higher things." Under the most difficult and trying circumstances men and women have brought about improvement in temperament and personality that almost borders on the miraculous.

Get Rid of the Will to Fail

Dorothea Brande, in her splendid book, *Wake Up and Live,* says that too many of us are victims of the will to fail. We don't intend to succeed. We don't want to succeed. We are afraid to try to suc-

196

Have you rid yourself of the will to fail? One of these young men has; the other has not.

ceed. We fritter away our lives with tasks far below our powers. We can't seem to get the conviction that we should and we can strike out boldly and succeed in whatever we want to do. We spend more time and energy in making our lives a failure than it would take to make them a success.

She gives a rule for success that you can apply in your program of personality improvement. She says that one should act as though failure were an impossibility. Take it for granted that you are going to be successful in improving your personality.

Stop thinking in terms of failure and start thinking in terms of success. Keep this motto before you. Print it on a white card and pin it up where you can see it all the time: *Act as though failure were an impossibility.*

Stop building up reasons why you *can't* do what you want to do, reasons why you *can't* achieve success.

During the great demobilization of 1945–1946, colleges and universities became overcrowded. People were turned away from educational institutions. Many veterans, after two or three refusals, gave up their plans for continuing their education. One enterprising veteran, refusing to be discouraged when turned away from the college of his choice, mimeographed an application letter and mailed it to the registrars of 150 colleges. He received acceptances from 52 accredited colleges!

Here is a little item clipped from a magazine several years ago. At the top is a picture of a bumblebee and below it this legend:

THE BUMBLEBEE CANNOT FLY!

According to recognized aerotechnical tests the bumblebee cannot fly because the size, shape, and weight of his body, compared with his total wing area, makes flying absolutely impossible . . . but the bumblebee does not know this, so he goes ahead and flies anyway!

Get Going and Keep Going

"As a man thinketh in his heart, so is he." Never were truer words spoken! Let your thoughts center on improving your personality, overcoming shyness and feelings of inferiority. Think positively. Act positively. Banish all thoughts of past embarrassment, past failure, past personality defects, and *think* and *work* in terms of the future—in terms of success, happiness, a better personality.

If you have studied thoughtfully the preceding chapters and taken the tests, you should know—

1. How important personality is in your social adjustment, personal happiness, and vocational advancement.
2. The nature of personality and the kind of personality traits most admired by others, as well as the traits most disliked by others.
3. Your own personality assets and liabilities and the four essential steps in personality improvement.
4. Some definite steps you should take here and now to improve your personality.

It is assumed that you have studied this book thoughtfully and that you have already begun to do many of the things suggested for the development of a better personality. Unless you do more than study in a course like this you are not likely to benefit from it greatly—surely not nearly so much as you should.

Now as we come to the end of "our study of personality," you should take a careful inventory of your assets and liabilities in terms of the many lists of things that are the outward manifestations of your real personality with a view to answering this most important question: What do I do from here, on? Now is the time to answer that question. Not next New Year's Day. Not even next month, or next week, or tomorrow. Right now! Today! This hour!

About the best advice we can give you has already been given in the suggestion at various points in the course where you are urged to set up a record form of a suitable kind for use in checking your strong and weak personality traits or their everyday outward manifestations, as a point of departure in a long-term plan to improve your personality, and for rechecking from time to time to determine the progress you are making.

If you have followed these suggestions, you have a convenient notebook of record forms for convenient use from here on. All that should be necessary at this point is to resolve to go ahead along lines suggested, and then to follow through for as long as may be necessary to achieve the end you have in view—a well-integrated personality that can be depended on to serve you well in making the many important life adjustments you, like everyone else, will be called upon to make.

Following this chapter you will find an extensive bibliography. Among the books listed should be many of special interest to you. Get acquainted with more of such books than you have been able to read during this course.

Get one of the books included in the bibliography that pertains mostly to your particular problem; read it and do what it says. But don't hope to improve your personality simply by reading books.

Dr. Link says, "The individual who becomes absorbed in the literature of self-improvement too often acquires a whole collection of mental hazards." [1]

It is better to read *one* chapter from *one* book and do what it says than to read every book in print on personality improvement and then postpone to the indefinite future your improvement program. And remember that an attractive personality is not gained by introspection, but by practice.

By this time it should be obvious that *personality development* is an individual matter. It is something that you alone can accomplish, assisted by others of course, but essentially on your own.

In this course the fundamentals have been discussed in class, and individual needs have been considered in personal conference. We have come to the point where each problem is a purely personal one that must be individually dealt with. You should go on reviewing principles, rechecking your many ratings, and constructing your personality profile from time to time in the process of reaching the

[1] Henry C. Link, *The Rediscovery of Man,* p. 104, The Macmillan Company, New York, 1938.

Clatworthy Studios, Estes Park, Colorado

*A "hobby" is very beneficial in developing one's personality—
whether it is an outdoor sport or an indoor activity.*

goal set at the outset of the course—the development of a well-
integrated personality capable of meeting the strains and stresses of
adjustments and readjustments bound to be necessary in the lives of
all properly active people.

Consult your school or college counselors freely. Ask them to
review your reappraisals of your traits from time to time—even to
keep their own personality rating schedule on your actions, reactions, and attitudes for comparison with your own. Seek their criticisms and suggestions. Meet their requirements of you in the way
of good conduct.

Don't hesitate to ask selected close friends to make suggestions
if they note lapses of any kind in your speech, conduct, or attitudes.
This doesn't mean that you should invite or expect comments from
all and sundry, or that you are to be too much concerned with minor

slips such as are natural to all of us. Only really significant things should be noted.

Self-Criticism

You are engaged in the task of developing your personality. You therefore must have a consciousness of need for effort in that direction. You will want and welcome all the help you can get from yourself and from others. Nothing will aid you more than honest, intelligent, and persistent *self-criticism*. From time to time in this basic study of personality you are being asked to appraise tentatively your traits and attitudes and general appearance. This should be most useful as a point of departure in your efforts to eliminate defects, but it is, at best, only a start in the right direction. You must continue to watch your thoughts, words, attitudes, and actions at all times to detect mistakes before bad habits are formed. But it is not enough merely to detect wrong conduct; you must be highly *critical* of it. Others will be, and their criticisms will hurt. Be your own severest critic and thus prevent repetitions of conduct that others will note critically.

The most important job you will have through life is that of critic of your own thoughts, words, and deeds. And this is a job that may be very interesting, that pays well, and that never is lost. How well it is done depends largely on how early you begin to function on this job, how intelligently criticisms are made, and how soon good habits of doing this work are formed.

Why did I think about a certain person as I did? Why did I say what I said? Why did I do what I did? These are questions which should be asked and answered over and over again concerning important matters of daily conduct. At first you must consciously force yourself to ask these questions. In time, if this practice is persisted in, the habit of trying to account for your conduct in important situations will be formed. Then, without conscious effort you will seek reasons for what you think, say, or do.

It will surprise you to find that often your thinking is not based on facts; or that what you say is not literally true; or that some of the things you do are not the things you really should have done under the circumstances. Once you make these discoveries, you will want to make amends for wrong things said and done. But what is more important, you will be on your guard against a repetition of them. Thus, bad habits will be broken and good ones formed.

Not the least important result of self-criticism and the correction of one's own faults is the elimination, in large part, of the criticism of others. No one really likes to be criticized by his associates. The only way to avoid such criticism is to do your own criticizing, and do it first. If as a result you find you have said something you should not have said, acknowledge this fact and prevent the evil consequences of unfortunate words which may have slipped out before your better judgment could check them.

If you have done something which should not have been done, or which should have been done in a different way, do not wait for someone else to find it out and make trouble; find it out for yourself and set about the job of righting what you have done, thus avoiding trouble.

If you find yourself thinking thoughts which are prompted by jealousy, pride, envy, or any other harmful emotion, check yourself before such thoughts lead to attitudes, points of view, or conduct which may well lead to loss of friends, position, or, what is worse, self-respect.

It should be emphasized that self-criticism will be more or less futile unless something is done about wrong thoughts, words, or actions as soon as they are discovered. Don't try to cover up what your self-criticism discovers to be wrong in your thinking, talking, or acting. Don't rest content in the thought that perhaps no one else will make the discovery. It is the embarrassment incident to the admission of a wrong which may be relied on to help prevent a recurrence of the same wrong. Hence, we must not deny ourselves the assistance which the acknowledgment of our errors will give us in establishing habits of thought, word, or deed, such as will enable us to live and work with others in a way which will win their willing co-operation and enthusiastic support in our effort to advance in life.

It is a well-known fact that more people lose their jobs because of the kind of people they are than because of the faulty way in which they do their work. Others can teach you how to do your work better, but you alone must undertake the task of learning how to work successfully in association with others. Few things will contribute more surely to the achievement of this result than the habit of self-criticism and conduct consistent with what such self-criticism reveals.

But be careful not to let yourself develop such a fear of thinking, saying, or doing wrong things that you will lose self-confidence and become a hesitant, incompetent worker. Use self-criticism as a means of improving your work and conduct, but don't let it dominate your whole life even to the extent of blinding you to the faults of others. Shoulder whatever blame attaches to your own errors as they are revealed by self-criticism, but do not overlook the contributory faults of others, nor be too ready to accept responsibility for their mistakes.

If your self-criticism is sincere and is competently carried on, you need have no fear that its results will be harmful. Begin now to work at this job of being your own critic, and continue to work at it throughout your life.

In conclusion, we want to emphasize again that *you* are the person who must decide what kind of personality you are going to have in the future. In the words of Dr. Link:

Psychologists have found . . . that personality, far from being intangible, consists of definite habits and skills. These habits and skills can be acquired in the same way that people acquire the habits of writing and reading, that is, by practice and training. Almost every person, no matter what his heredity, can therefore improve or fail to improve his personality. Even people beyond middle age can create important changes in their personalities if they are willing to practice and to acquire new habits.[2]

Suggestions for Study and Discussion

1. Make a list of the things you actually have done, since you started this course, to improve your personality.

2. Check that list against the lists of things you were advised to do by your instructor or the authors of this book.

3. Make an honest *personality profile* using the Personality Rating Scale presented in Chapter Six, page 139.

4. Compare this personality profile with the first one made and note carefully your improvements, along with any failure to improve.

5. Single out for more vigorous and persistent attack defective traits that have not yet been overcome. List them separately for emphasis.

6. List the steps you plan to take individually, without benefit of class

[2] Henry C. Link, *The Rediscovery of Man*, pp. 56–57, The Macmillan Company, New York, 1938.

or instructor stimulation, for the further improvement of your personality. Check these steps with your instructor or counselor.

7. List some of the personality traits on which you should keep working for improvement all your life. Be sure to distinguish between skills, arts, knowledge, or know-how, and *personal characteristics* or *traits*. Of course you will keep on trying to learn more and to do things better, but it is equally important to improve yourself in ways which enable you to make the best possible adjustments to others in all walks of life.

8. Has your concept of *personality* changed since you began this course? Did you once think of it largely in terms of *personal appearance?* Do you still so think of it? Do you understand and subscribe to this statement: One's *personality* is but the outward evidence of one's *character?*

Personality Reminders

1. Have you read a good book in the last month?

2. Did you get eight hours' sleep last night?

3. That suit or skirt you are now wearing—when was it last cleaned or pressed?

4. Have you done anything today that would make people like you better?

5. Have you honestly tried to improve your vocabulary in the last three months?

Are you going to improve your personality, or fail to improve your personality?

It's up to you!

Special References

Mikesell, William Henry. *Mental Hygiene*
Morgan, John Jacob Brooke. *How to Keep a Sound Mind*
Reilly, William J. *How to Use Your Head to Get What You Want*
Chapman, Paul Wilber. *Your Personality and Your Job*
Peale, Norman Vincent. *Guide to Confident Living*
Lurton, Douglas. *The Power of Positive Living*

Bibliography

Alexander, James. *Through Failure to Success.* New York: Funk & Wagnalls Company, 1934.

Allers, Rudolph. *Self Improvement; the Art of Self Knowledge and Getting Along with Others.* New York: Benziger Bros., 1939.

Anderson, Camilla M. *Emotional Hygiene: the Art of Understanding,* Fourth Edition. Philadelphia: J. B. Lippincott Company, 1948.

Archer, Alma. *Encyclopedia of Beauty and Charm.* New York: Hermitage House, 1948.

Bagby, English. *Psychology of Personality; an Analysis of Common Emotional Disorders.* New York: Henry Holt and Company, Inc., 1928.

Baird, A. Craig, and Franklin H. Knower. *General Speech: an Introduction.* New York: McGraw-Hill Book Company, Inc., 1949.

Banning, Margaret Culkin. *Letters to Susan.* New York: Harper & Brothers, 1936.

————, and M. L. Culkin. *Conduct Yourself Accordingly.* New York: Harper & Brothers, 1944.

Bennett, Joan. *How to Be Attractive,* Second Revised Edition. New York: Alfred A. Knopf, Inc., 1951.

Bennett, M. E. *College and Life; Problems of Self-discovery and Self-direction.* New York: McGraw-Hill Book Company, Inc., 1952.

Bernhardt, K. S. *Practical Psychology,* Second Edition. New York: McGraw-Hill Book Company, Inc., 1953.

Bingham, Walter Van Dyke. *Aptitudes and Aptitude Testing.* New York: Harper & Brothers, 1945.

Bird, Charles, and Dorothy M. *Learning More by Effective Study.* New York: Appleton-Century-Crofts, Incorporated, 1945.

Bleecker, Katharine. *Business Etiquette; the A B C of Making Good.* New York: G. P. Putnam's Sons, 1942.

Bliss, Walton Boyd. *Personality and School: Accent on Youth.* New York: Allyn & Bacon, Inc., 1951.

Bogardus, Emory S., and R. H. Lewis. *Social Life and Personality,* Revised Edition. New York: Silver Burdett Company, 1942.

Boring, Edwin G., and others. *Introduction to Psychology.* New York: John Wiley & Sons, Inc., 1939.

Brainerd, Paul Porter. *What About Yourself? Success with People.* Los Angeles: H. H. McClure Publishing Company, 1939. (For sale by Educational Research Association, 2214 East Colorado Boulevard, Pasadena, California.)

Brande, Dorothea. *Wake Up and Live.* New York: Pocket Books, Inc.

Broadley, Charles V., and M. E. *Know Your Real Abilities; Understanding and Developing Your Aptitudes.* New York: McGraw-Hill Book Company, Inc., 1948.

Brooke, Esther Eberstadt. *You and Your Personality; a Guide to Effective Living.* New York: Harper & Brothers, 1949.

Brooks, Fowler Dell, and L. F. Shaffer. *Child Psychology.* Philadelphia: W. B. Saunders Company.

Burnham, William H. *The Wholesome Personality; a Contribution to Mental Hygiene.* New York: Appleton-Century-Crofts, Incorporated, 1932.

Calhoon, Richard Percival. *Moving Ahead on Your Job.* New York: McGraw-Hill Book Company, Inc., 1946.

Carlson, Dick. *How to Develop Personal Power.* New York: Harper & Brothers, 1937. To be used with the following book:

————, and Sylvia D. *Personal Development Manual.* New York: Harper & Brothers, 1937

Carnegie, Dale. *How to Stop Worrying and Start Living.* New York: Simon and Schuster, Inc., 1948.

————. *How to Win Friends and Influence People.* New York: Simon and Schuster, Inc., 1936.

Carney, Marie L. *Etiquette in Business.* New York: Gregg Publishing Division, McGraw-Hill Book Company, Inc., 1948.

Cattell, Raymond Bernard. *Description and Measurement of Personality.* Yonkers, New York: World Book Co.

Chapman, Paul Wilber. *Your Personality and Your Job.* Chicago: Science Research Associates.

Clarke, Harry Newton. *Life Planning and Building.* Scranton, Pennsylvania: International Textbook Company, 1940.

Coffin, Joseph Hershel. *Visual Outline of the Psychology of Personality.* New York: Longmans, Green & Company, Inc., 1940.

Cotten, Emmi. *Clothes Make Magic.* New York: E. P. Dutton & Co., 1949.

Crane, George Washington. *Psychology Applied.* Mellott, Indiana: Hopkins Syndicate, Inc., 1948.

Curti, Margaret Wooster. *Child Psychology.* New York: Longmans, Green & Company, Inc., 1938.

Davis, Howard Lee. *The Young Man in Business.* New York: John Wiley & Sons, Inc., 1931.

Dengel, Veronica. *Personality, Unlimited; the Beauty Blue Book.* Philadelphia: John C. Winston Co., 1943.

Detjen, Ervin Winfred, and Mary F. *Your Plans for the Future.* New York: McGraw-Hill Book Company, Inc., 1947.

Diehl, Harold S. *Textbook of Healthful Living,* Fourth Edition. New York: McGraw-Hill Book Company, Inc., 1950.

Donham, Wallace Brett. *Education for Responsible Living; the Oppor-*

tunity for Liberal-Arts Colleges. Cambridge, Massachusetts: Harvard University Press, 1944.

Drake, Durant, and Raymond Holdsworth Finlay. *Problems of Conduct,* Second Revised Edition. Boston: Houghton Mifflin Company, 1935.

Droke, Maxwell. *People . . . How to Get Them to Do What You Want Them To.* Indianapolis, Indiana: Maxwell Droke, 1939.

Edwards, Jill. *Personality Pointers.* Indianapolis, Indiana: Bobbs-Merrill Company, Inc., 1935.

Elliott, Harrison Sacket, and Grace L. *Solving Personal Problems; a Counseling Manual.* New York: Henry Holt and Company, Inc., 1936.

Emerson, William Robie Patten. *Health for the Having; a Handbook for Physical Fitness.* New York: Macmillan Company, 1944.

Fedder, Ruth. *A Girl Grows Up,* Second Edition. New York: McGraw-Hill Book Company, Inc., 1948.

Finkelor, Dorothy C. *How to Make Your Emotions Work for You.* Farrar, Straus, 1952.

Fenwick, Millicent. *Vogue Book of Etiquette.* New York: Simon and Schuster, Inc., 1948.

Fosdick, Harry Emerson. *On Being a Real Person.* New York: Harper & Brothers, 1943.

Fry, Clements Collard, and Howard Wilcox Haggard. *The Anatomy of Personality.* New York: Harper & Brothers, 1936.

Gaskill, Harold Vincent. *Personality.* New York: Prentice-Hall, Inc., 1936.

Goodrich, Laurence B. *Living with Others; a Book on Social Conduct.* New York: American Book Company, 1939.

Griffin, John Douglas Morecroft, S. R. Laycock, and William Line. *Mental Hygiene; a Manual for Teachers.* New York: American Book Company, 1940.

Groves, Ernest R. *The Good Housekeeping Marriage Book; Twelve Ways to a Happy Marriage.* New York: Prentice-Hall, Inc., 1938.

Hadfield, J. A. *Psychology and Morals; an Analysis of Character.* New York: Medill McBride Company, 1925.

Halsey, George D. *How to Be a Leader.* New York: Harper & Brothers, 1938.

———. *Supervising People,* Revised Edition. New York: Harper & Brothers, 1953.

Hamrin, Shirley Austin. *4 Square Planning for Your Career.* Chicago: Science Research Associates.

Harmon, Francis L. *Understanding Personality.* Milwaukee, Wisconsin: Bruce Publishing Company, 1948.

Harris, Erdman. *Twenty-one.* New York: Harper & Brothers, 1931.

Healy, William. *Personality in Formation and Action.* New York: W. W. Norton & Company, Inc., 1938.

Hepner, Harry Walker. *Finding Yourself in Your Work; A Guide for*

Career and Personality. New York: Appleton-Century-Crofts, Incorporated, 1937.

————. *It's Nice to Know People Like You.* New York: Appleton-Century-Crofts, Incorporated, 1939.

Hunter, Estelle Belle. *Personality Development; a Practical Self-Teaching Course.* Chicago: Better Speech Institute of America, 1939.

Ivey, Paul Wesley, and W. Horvath. *Successful Salesmanship,* Third Edition. New York: Prentice-Hall, Inc., 1953.

Jacobson, Edmund. *You Must Relax; a Practical Method of Reducing the Strains of Modern Living,* Third Edition. New York: McGraw-Hill Book Company, Inc., 1948.

Jonathon, Norton Hughes. *Guide Book for the Young Man About Town.* Philadelphia: John C. Winston Co., 1948.

Kettunen, Marietta. *Fundamentals of Dress.* New York: McGraw-Hill Book Company, Inc., 1941.

King, Eleanore Helen. *Glorify Yourself,* Revised Edition. New York: Prentice-Hall, Inc., 1948.

Kuder, George Frederic, and Blanche B. Paulson. *Discovering Your Real Interests* (Life Adjustment Booklet). Chicago: Science Research Associates, 1949.

Laird, Donald Anderson. *Increasing Personal Efficiency: the Psychology of Personal Progress,* Revised Edition. New York: Harper & Brothers, 1952.

————. *Technique of Building Personal Leadership.* New York: McGraw-Hill Book Company, Inc., 1944.

————. *Technique of Personal Analysis; Tested Ways of Fitting Your Personality to a Future.* New York: McGraw-Hill Book Company, Inc., 1945.

————, and Eleanor C. *Practical Business Psychology.* New York: Gregg Publishing Division, McGraw-Hill Book Company, Inc., 1951.

————. *Practical Sales Psychology.* New York: McGraw-Hill Book Company, Inc., 1952.

Lane, Janet. *Your Carriage, Madam! A Guide to Good Posture,* Second Edition. New York: John Wiley & Sons, Inc., 1947.

LaRue, Daniel Wolford. *Mental Hygiene.* New York: Macmillan Company, 1927.

Leeper, Robert. *Psychology of Personality and Social Adjustment; a Handbook for Students.* Mt. Vernon, Iowa: Cornell College Bookstore, 1937.

Liebman, Joshua Loth. *Peace of Mind.* New York: Simon and Schuster, Inc., 1949.

Ligon, Ernest Mayfield. *Their Future Is Now; the Growth and Development of Christian Personality.* New York: Macmillan Company, 1939.

Link, Henry C. *Rediscovery of Man.* New York: Macmillan Company, 1938.

————. *Return to Religion.* New York: Macmillan Company, 1936.

Lockhart, Earl Granger. *How to Improve Your Personality.* Chicago: Follett Publishing Company, 1943.

Long, Renée. *Style Your Personality; the Art of Feminine Finesse.* Garden City, New York: Doubleday & Company, Inc., 1939.

Lurton, Douglas. *The Power of Positive Living.* New York: McGraw-Hill Book Company, Inc., 1950.

MacGibbon, Elizabeth Gregg. *Fitting Yourself for Business,* Third Edition. New York: McGraw-Hill Book Company, Inc., 1954.

————. *Manners in Business.* New York: Macmillan Company, 1936.

McKinney, F. *Psychology of Personal Adjustment; Students' Introduction to Mental Hygiene,* Second Edition. New York: John Wiley & Sons, Inc., 1949.

Mangan, James Thomas. *Knack of Selling Yourself,* Revised and Enlarged Edition. Chicago: Dartnell Corporation, 1942.

Manser, R. B., and L. Finlan. *The Speaking Voice.* New York: Longmans, Green & Company, Inc., 1950.

Marsh, Hattie M. *Building Your Personality,* Second Edition. New York: Prentice-Hall, Inc., 1947.

Mason, Alpheus Thomas. *Brandeis: A Free Man's Life.* New York: Viking Press, 1946.

Maule, Frances. *Men Wanted: the New Opportunities and What They Demand,* Revised Edition. New York: Funk & Wagnalls Company, 1938.

————. *She Strives to Conquer; Business Behavior, Opportunities and Job Requirements for Women,* Revised Edition. New York: Funk & Wagnalls Company, 1937.

Melvin, Arthur Gordon. *Building Personality.* New York: John Day Company, 1934.

Messick, John D. *Personality and Character Development.* Westwood, New Jersey: Fleming H. Revell Company, 1939.

Mikesell, William Henry. *Mental Hygiene.* New York: Prentice-Hall, Inc., 1939.

Morgan, John Jacob Brooke. *How to Keep a Sound Mind,* Revised Edition of *Keeping a Sound Mind.* New York: Macmillan Company, 1946.

————, and E. T. Webb. *Making the Most of Your Life.* Garden City, New York: Garden City Books, 1934.

Morton, Grace Margaret. *Arts of Costume and Personal Appearance.* New York: John Wiley & Sons, Inc., 1943.

Murray, Elwood. *Speech Personality,* Second Revised Edition. Philadelphia: J. B. Lippincott Company, 1944.

Myers, George E., and others. *Planning Your Future,* Fourth Edition. New York: McGraw-Hill Book Company, Inc., 1953.

Osborn, Alexander Faickney. *Your Creative Power: How to Use Imagination.* New York: Charles Scribner's Sons, 1949.

Osborn, Loraine. *Your Voice Personality,* Third Edition. New York: G. P. Putnam's Sons, 1945.

Parker, Willard E., and Robert W. Kleemeier. *Human Relations in Supervision.* New York: McGraw-Hill Book Company, Inc., 1951.

Payne, Mildred M. *What Do I Do Now? A Guide to Correct Conduct and Dress for Business People.* New York: Gregg Publishing Division, McGraw-Hill Book Company, Inc., 1940.

Peale, Norman Vincent. *Guide to Confident Living.* New York: Prentice-Hall, Inc., 1948.

Pierce, Wellington G. *Youth Comes of Age.* New York: McGraw-Hill Book Company, Inc., 1948.

Post, Emily. *Etiquette; the Blue Book of Social Usage.* New York: Funk & Wagnalls Company, 1945.

Powers, David G. *Fundamentals of Speech.* New York: McGraw-Hill Book Company, Inc., 1951.

Quayle, Margaret S. *As Told by Business Girls; Problems in Personal Adjustment.* New York: The Woman's Press, 1932.

Reid, Lillian N. *Personality and Etiquette,* Revised Edition. Boston: D. C. Heath & Co., 1950.

Reilly, William J. *How to Use Your Head to Get What You Want.* New York: Harper & Brothers, 1940.

Richmond, Winifred Vanderbilt. *Personality: Its Study and Hygiene.* New York: Rinehart & Co., Inc., 1937.

Ruch, Floyd Leon, and others. *Psychology and Life; a Study of the Thinking, Feeling, and Doing of People.* Chicago: Scott, Foresman and Company, 1948.

————, and Neil Warren. *Working with Psychology; a Guidebook for Use with Psychology and Life* and other introductory texts. Chicago: Scott, Foresman and Company, 1938.

Ryan, Mildred Graves. *Cues for You; Guidance on Manners, Appearance, and Personality Growth.* New York: Appleton-Century-Crofts, Incorporated, 1940.

————. *Your Clothes and Personality,* Third Edition. New York: Appleton-Century-Crofts, Incorporated, 1949.

Sandford, William P. *Speak Well—and Win!* New York: McGraw-Hill Book Company, Inc., 1944.

Sarett, Lew, and W. T. Foster. *Basic Principles of Speech.* Boston: Houghton Mifflin Company, 1946.

Shaffer, Laurance Frederic. *Psychology of Adjustment; an Objective Approach to Mental Hygiene.* Boston: Houghton Mifflin Company, 1936.

Shellow, Sadie Myers. *How to Develop Your Personality.* New York: Harper & Brothers, 1937.

Sherman, Mandel. *Mental Conflicts and Personality.* New York: Longmans, Green & Company, Inc., 1938.

Slavson, Samuel Richard. *Recreation and the Total Personality*. New York: Association Press, 1946.

Smith, Edna Barbara. *Personality Improvement for All*. New York: Barnes & Noble, Inc., 1945.

————. *Your Personality*. Boston: Waverly House, 1940.

Sprackling, Helen. *Courtesy, a Book of Modern Manners*. New York: M. Barrows & Company, Inc., 1944.

Stagner, Ross. *Psychology of Personality*, Second Edition. New York: McGraw-Hill Book Company, Inc., 1948.

Starch, Daniel, and others. *Controlling Human Behavior; a First Book in Psychology for College Students*. New York: Macmillan Company, 1936.

Steckle, Lynde C. *Problems of Human Adjustment*. New York: Harper & Brothers, 1949.

Stephenson, Margaret Bennett, and Ruth Millett. *As Others Like You*. Bloomington, Illinois: McKnight & McKnight Publishing Co., 1950.

Stogdill, Emily Leatherman, and Audell Herndon. *Objective Personality Study: a Workbook in Applied Mental Hygiene*. New York: Longmans, Green & Company, Inc., 1939.

Stote, Dorothy. *Men Too Wear Clothes*, Revised Edition. Philadelphia: J. B. Lippincott Company, 1950.

Stratton, Dorothy Constance, and Helen B. Schleman. *Your Best Foot Forward; Social Usage for Young Moderns*. New York: McGraw-Hill Book Company, Inc., 1940.

Symonds, Percival M. *Diagnosing Personality and Conduct*. New York: Appleton-Century-Crofts, Incorporated, 1931.

Tead, Ordway. *Art of Leadership*. New York: McGraw-Hill Book Company, Inc., 1944.

Thom, Douglas A. *Normal Youth and Its Everyday Problems*. New York: Appleton-Century-Crofts, Incorporated.

Thomason, Calvin Cornelius. *Human Relations in Action; Problems and Cases in Dealing with People*. New York: Prentice-Hall, Inc., 1948.

Thornton, Francis Beauchesne. *How to Improve Your Personality by Reading*. Milwaukee, Wisconsin: Bruce Publishing Company, 1949.

Thorpe, Louis Peter. *Personality and Life; a Practical Guide to Personality Improvement*. New York: Longmans, Green & Company, Inc., 1941.

————. *Psychological Foundations of Personality; a Guide for Students and Teachers*. New York: McGraw-Hill Book Company, Inc., 1938.

Turner, Clair Elsmere, and Elizabeth McHose. *Effective Living*, Third Edition. New York: Prentice-Hall, Inc., 1950.

Valentine, Percy Friars. *The Psychology of Personality*. New York: Appleton-Century-Crofts, Incorporated, 1927.

Varnum, Walter C. *Psychology in Everyday Life*, Second Edition. New York: McGraw-Hill Book Company, Inc., 1942.

Vaughan, Wayland Farries. *General Psychology,* Revised Edition. New York: The Odyssey Press, Inc., 1939.

Vaughn, Gwenyth R., and Charles B. Roth. *Effective Personality Building.* New York: McGraw-Hill Book Company, Inc., 1947.

Wadsworth, Ruth F. *Charm by Choice.* New York: The Woman's Press, 1939.

Wallin, J. E. Wallace. *Personality Maladjustments and Mental Hygiene,* Second Edition. New York: McGraw-Hill Book Company, Inc., 1949.

Walsh, William Sebastian. *Cultivating Personality.* New York: E. P. Dutton & Co., Inc., 1930.

Watson, John Broadus, and R. A. *The Psychological Care of Infant and Child.* New York: W. W. Norton & Company, Inc., 1928.

Webb, Ewing Thruston, and John B. Morgan. *Strategy in Handling People.* Garden City, New York: Garden City Books, 1948.

Wells, George Ross. *The Art of Being a Person.* New York: Appleton-Century-Crofts, Incorporated, 1939.

Wheatley, William Alonzo, and Royce R. Mallory. *Building Character and Personality; a Discussion Text in Orientation and Guidance for High-School Students.* Boston: Ginn and Company, 1936.

Wheeler, Raymond Holder. *The Science of Psychology; an Introductory Study,* Second Edition. New York: Thomas Y. Crowell Company, 1940.

White, Wendell. *The Psychology of Dealing with People; Appealing to the Want for a Feeling of Personal Worth.* New York: Macmillan Company, 1936.

Williams, Beryl. *Fashion Is Our Business.* Philadelphia: J. B. Lippincott Company, 1945.

Wilson, Margery. *The New Etiquette; the Modern Code of Social Behavior,* Revised Edition. Philadelphia: J. B. Lippincott Company, 1947.

Woodward, Elizabeth Stockton. *Personality Preferred! How to Grow Up Gracefully.* New York: Harper & Brothers, 1935.

Wright, Milton. *Getting Along with People; a Guide to Personal Success.* New York: McGraw-Hill Book Company, Inc., 1939.

————. *The Art of Conversation and How to Apply Its Technique.* New York: McGraw-Hill Book Company, Inc., 1936.

Young, Kimball. *Personality and Problems of Adjustment,* Second Edition. New York: Appleton-Century-Crofts, Incorporated, 1952.

Research Studies

Some reports of research on personality development are listed here. Many of these reports are unpublished theses; they or information about them can be obtained only from the libraries of the institutions in which they were written.

Allyn, C. Vance. A Study of Causes for Dismissal from Office Positions. Master's thesis, Iowa, 1946.

Anderson, Agnes E. An Analysis of the Literature Dealing with Personality Development on the Secondary-School Level. Master's thesis, Tennessee, 1942.

Bilger, Aubrey Ellsworth. Personality Traits of Business and Other Professional Men and Women. Master's thesis, Colorado, 1941.

Bowman, Gladys S. Personality Qualities Necessary for Business Success. Ed.D. thesis, Colorado State College of Education, Greeley, 1947.

Gordon, William C. Personality Adjustments in Relation to Business Behavior. M.Ed. thesis, Buffalo, 1945.

Hastings, Jessie P. The Improvement of the Personality of Students of High-School Age During a Course in Salesmanship. Master's thesis, Chicago, 1942.

Kelly, Cherry. The Development of Personality in Secretarial Classes. Master's thesis, Iowa, 1941.

Loomis, Stuart D. A Survey of Current Definitions of the Personality Concept. Master's thesis, Chicago, 1946.

Martin, Alfreda Bernetta. Desirable Skills and Traits of Office Workers as Determined by Corvallis Businessmen. M.S. thesis, Oregon State College, 1948.

Michelman, Clarence Alva. A Technique for Classifying Occupations According to the Demands Made on Certain Personal Characteristics of Workers. Doctor's thesis, Northwestern, 1942.

Mullen, Sister Florentine. An Evaluation of Personality Traits in Stenographers. Master's thesis, Colorado State College of Education, 1944.

Paul, John Walker. The Modifiability of Attitudes with Special Reference to School Situations. M.A. paper, Chicago, 1947.

Russell, Robert. An Analysis of the Traits and Abilities Needed by Clerical Workers in Salina, Kansas. Master's thesis, Kansas State Teachers College, Pittsburg, 1945.

Sears, Herman T. A Study of Some Personal Traits of Employees in Certain Retail Establishments. Master's thesis, Ohio State, 1941.

Skilling, Marie P. A Study of the Personal Relations Problems of Secretaries. Master's thesis, Southern California, 1947.

Personality Tests and Scales

Tests and scales are widely used in the field of personality training. Usually, they are not for sale to the general public but will be sent to qualified persons—such as college professors, personnel directors, counselors, and certain school officials—to administer and interpret them.

For the benefit of those interested, some of the publishers of such tests and of organizations offering a testing service are listed below.

Science Research Associates, 228 South Wabash Ave., Chicago 4, Ill.
California Test Bureau, 5916 Hollywood Blvd., Hollywood 28, Calif.
Bureau of Educational Measurements, Kansas State College, Emporia.
Psychological Corporation (The), 522 Fifth Ave., New York 18, N. Y.
Rutgers University Press, New Brunswick, New Jersey
Public School Publishing Co., Bloomington, Illinois
Stanford University Press, Palo Alto, California
Minnesota University Press, Minneapolis, Minnesota
Gregg Publishing Division, McGraw-Hill Book Company, Inc., 330 West 42nd Street, New York 18, New York
World Book Company, 313 Park Hill Avenue, Yonkers, New York
Houghton Mifflin Company, 2 Park Street, Boston 7, Massachusetts

Famous Persons Test (Page 130)

(3) Joe Louis	(12) Lily Pons
(14) Grantland Rice	(7) Edward L. Thorndike
(20) Walter P. Chrysler	(18) Alexis Carrel
(16) Lawrence Tibbett	(19) William Mauldin
(1) Lowell Thomas	(10) Arthur H. Compton
(17) Fred Astaire	(8) Maude Slye
(2) John Steinbeck	(13) Walter White
(15) Margaret Mitchell	(9) Joseph Stalin
(11) Edward Steichen	(5) Fritz Kreisler
(6) Diego Rivera	(4) Jack Benny

Test of English Usage (Page 131)

1. *a*	5. *a*	9. *b*	13. *b*	17. *a*	21. *a*	25. *b*	29. *b*	33. *b*
2. *b*	6. *b*	10. *a*	14. *a*	18. *a*	22. *b*	26. *a*	30. *a*	34. *b*
3. *b*	7. *b*	11. *a*	15. *b*	19. *a*	23. *b*	27. *a*	31. *a*	35. *a*
4. *a*	8. *a*	12. *b*	16. *b*	20. *b*	24. *b*	28. *b*	32. *b*	36. *b*

214

Index